The Songman
A Journey in Irish Music

The Songman

A Journey in Irish Music

Tommy Sands

The Lilliput Press
Dublin

First published 2005 by

THE LILLIPUT PRESS

62–63 Sitric Road, Arbour Hill,
Dublin 7, Ireland
www.lilliputpress.ie

A CIP record for this title is available from
The British Library.

1 3 5 7 9 10 8 6 4 2

ISBN 1 84351 063 4

The Lilliput Press receives financial assistance from
An Chomhairle Ealaíon / The Arts Council of Ireland.

Set in 10.5 on 13 pt Garamond
Printed by MPG Books, Bodmin, Cornwall

For my parents and Dino

Contents

List of Illustrations

Acknowledgments

Thanks to my parents and family, Catherine and children and a multitude of friends and relations whose story and stories knowingly or unknowingly touched and moved my own. Thanks to Jack L. Bacon, Sadbh Baxter, Hilary Bell, Barney and Marge Brady, Kerstin Caffo, Fil Campbell, Steve Cooney, Dominic Cunningham, Peter Emerson, Roy Garland, Bobbie Hanvey, Seamus Heaney, Phylis Jackson, all at Lilliput, Paul Lyle, Colum McCarthy, Frank McCourt, George MacDonald Fraser, Tom McFarland, Mark McLoughlin, Siegfried Maeker, Peter Makem, Mick Moloney, Tom Newman, Gearóid Ó hAllmhuráin, Annie Prince, Mary Rowley, Pete Seeger, Vedran Smailovic, Daragh Smyth, Marsha Swan, Robin Troup, Mike Wolke, and Itka Zygmuntowicz.

The Songman
A Journey in Irish Music

I

The Songman

'Are you the son of the man that pulled my granny out of the coffin?' The Royal Ulster Constable lowered his voice, and his Heckler and Koch automatic, for the question and then bent his ear round the car's turned down window for an answer.

This was all I needed. I was already late. All the other questions had been easy. A child could have answered them.

'What's your name, sir?'

'Tommy Sands,' I'd replied.

My father used to say that any time he was called 'sir' he would cover his pockets for fear of being robbed. He had a deep suspicion of such niceties.

I reached for one of my passports. The British one.

'That's me,' I said. 'I'm coming from Rostrevor. And I'm going to Stormont,' I added quickly, hoping to pre-empt the next two questions. It would save time, I thought, and police breath. And they were fairly safe answers too. Neither place would send the shivers up a lawman's back.

'And where are you coming from sir?' he continued dutifully. The Law would take its own course and not be rushed.

'Rostrevor,' I said again resignedly, waiting for the next question with wearily rehearsed respect.

Satisfied that I had learned my lesson for the moment at least, he went on calmly. 'And what takes you up to Stormont, sir?'

'To sing,' said I.

'To sing?' said he.

'To sing,' said I. 'At the Talks. The Peace Talks.'

'And have you permission?' He asked, with a recharged interest.

'I do,' I said, trying to hurry things along. 'From George Mitchell, the American man, the chairman of the Talks.'

He looked at me silently for several seconds before unleashing the final question, the answer to which he was now patiently waiting for. It was close to eleven o'clock on the morning of Holy Thursday 1998. I had to be at Stormont by twelve.

It wasn't the first time, of course, that a roadblock had stood in the way of a performance. Back in the civil-rights days in the sixties it wasn't unusual to be held up for hours, or for as long as it took for the concert or rally to be well and truly over by the time you got there. A sense of urgency, however, told me that today's performance would be more important than most.

I had grown up singing at enough wakes, weddings and gatherings in my home townland of Ryan in County Down to realize that music is too valuable to be confined solely to concert stages. After the first lust for public recognition is sated, the musician feels ready to seek out the 'real gig'. It can be in a prison or a school or an old folks' home, or in the house of a neighbour when things are low and where the magic of music passes through performer and listener, easing the mind and the soul in a strange sacramental harmony.

The politicians of Northern Ireland were badly in need of some harmony. The negotiations taking place at Castle Buildings in Belfast had faltered, and this had been the toughest week of all. Some looked back to see where their followers were leading them; others looked ahead and pressed forward. We had condemned them in the past for not talking and it was no less important to applaud them now that the talking had begun. For years it had been like watching two buses meeting on a narrow bridge with neither driver wanting to give way for fear of letting his passengers down. It would only be when those passengers would slowly begin to rise and say, 'Look, it's all right, you can reverse a little, because we all want to go forward,' that the scenery would ever change.

Outside, in the surrounding stillness, spring was silently intensifying the greenness of the grass and the orange of the dandelion and spreading blossoms on the Mourne hawthorn like Easter snow. Decaying smells of winter were yielding to the subtle spell of speedwell and robin-run-the-hedge, and the small birds of Ulster were tuning up for a song yet to be sung.

A bracing north breeze, laced with bitter memories, browsed the scattered remains of one of yesterday's newspapers before brushing it gustfully round the black boots of the policeman. With a graceful kick, he sent the latest helping of media opinion up in the air. Headlines of hope and despair alternated in the tumbling wind. It was touch-and-go and the journalists were saying that anything could happen. Time was running out. There would be an agreement by Good Friday or there wouldn't be an agreement at all.

When the Talks began in 1996, they had been met with a cautious optimism. Every news space seemed to be filled with hope and relief. But in no time the newshounds were sniffing around for fresh stories to report. That's their job. Peace meant less action, and less action meant less entertainment for the punters. How long can you hold a shot of calm sea and blue sky before your audience wants the thrill of a storm and your advertiser a new channel? On television it wasn't long before it seemed that no one wanted the Talks to be happening at all. Everyone was up in arms about compromise, trickery and treachery. The viewing figures would be on the increase, sure enough, but just as surely the viewers' hearts would be sinking.

The people I knew from both sides of the hedge in the hills and valleys around me and in the towns and villages before me were crying out for the politicians to carry on, but their voices were not being heard. People in search of peace seldom shout loudly. It was time now to gather their voices together and sing, to give a song to the six o'clock news, and to give the media its storm – a storm of peace for a change.

> Carry on, carry on, you can hear the people singing,
> Carry on, carry on, till peace will come again.

I had rehearsed the song the night before with Vedran Smailovic, a cellist from Sarajevo. He would be waiting for me now in Burren, just a few miles away in the home of my mother's people, with a borrowed cello in a blue case. His own was lost in the rubble of his native city. Protestant and Catholic children from two schools in Dundrum would be travelling to Stormont as well, and my good friend Roy Arbuckle would be on the road from Derry, sporting the ultimate loyalist instrument, the Lambeg drum. The chorus was simple. Hopefully the television crews would pick it up, so that the people at home would hear their own message being broadcast and the politicians would be reassured that the passengers on the bus were behind them.

> In the Bogside and the Waterside, in the Shankill and the Falls,
> All around the hills of Ulster, you can hear them sing this song.
> Carry on, carry on, you can hear the people singing,
> Carry on, carry on, till peace will come again.

It had been a long struggle to reach this day. There had been much soul-searching and risk-taking. What would happen to the political life of Ulster Unionist Party leader David Trimble if he dared to sell short the unionist cause? We all remembered Brian Faulkner's political collapse in 1974 after he reached an agreement at Sunningdale on behalf of unionism, with shades of compromise. And what would happen to Sinn Féin leader Gerry Adams if he betrayed the ideals of Irish republicanism? The fate of Michael Collins was well known. He had been shot in 1922 during the Irish Civil War. Our song would have another view of betrayal.

> Don't betray your children's birthright, that's the right to stay alive,
> For there is no greater treachery than to let your children die ...

In the streets and schoolyards, at crossroads and village squares, at fairs and football matches, everyone was talking about the Talks. In churches, chapels, and meeting houses people were praying, and in mixed public houses drinkers who would usually avoid contentious issues were now openly discussing the negotiations at Castle

Buildings. At last there was something everyone could agree on – the need to talk. The world's media were gathering for the showdown of the century. The patience of people like Social Democratic and Labour Party leader John Hume, who had been attacked from all quarters for entering into a dialogue with Adams, was beginning to bear fruit. American President Bill Clinton was on the phone to Stormont every day. Bertie Ahern, the Irish Taoiseach, would be there, and British Prime Minister Tony Blair had arrived in Belfast to say that he felt the hand of history on his shoulder. I wanted to be there too, but there was a policeman's ear in my car, still waiting for an answer, and I couldn't move.

I don't think I had ever been so close to a policeman before. I could see the harp and crown on his cap, emblems that weren't traditionally the easiest of allies. 'Hang all the harpers' had been the order from Elizabeth I during her struggles to defeat the old Gaelic Order. What did this officer think of 'peace-loving' musicians kicking up trouble and change? Regardless of what permission I had from the top, right now this was the man who would make the decisions on the ground. How did he feel about all this talk about talk? What would happen if peace did suddenly break out? There were republican calls to disband the RUC as part of any new settlement. Why would a man in his position have any more enthusiasm for that than a turkey would have for Christmas? What about the overtime pay that would disappear? What about the mortgage for the new house?

His trained hearing seemed to suck all the sound from within the car, leaving an awkward silence. All I could hear was that high ringing tone that the souls in Purgatory send out to Catholics when they want prayed for. Since 95 per cent of the RUC was Protestant I assumed that this policeman wouldn't hear or if he did, he wasn't impressed – he was only interested in finding out whether my father had pulled his granny out of her coffin. He turned his head and looked into my eyes. Did he see the bitter eyes of a Catholic looking back, a man who hadn't much faith in the police force? A force that upheld the laws of a state, whose 'Protestant parliament for a Protestant people' had discriminated against 40 per cent of the population because they were Catholic. A force that was used to put down a civil rights movement that had attempted to right those wrongs, thus igniting the violence that had held the North in its grip for thirty years. A force whose members colluded with loyalist paramilitaries to kill innocent Catholics. And did he see an incurable rebel whose people had been opposed to his country from its inception in 1921; whose tribe had silently supported the IRA, with its list of legitimate targets, which included policemen like himself? We may have been standing on the same ground, but in our heads did we live our lives in two different countries?

There was something familiar about this man. I tried to see him without his policeman's cap. It was his eyes. Without warning his lips began to move. Suddenly he began to whisper the words of a song in a childlike voice:

It's eleven by the clock and I've only on one sock

The bike's punctured so you understand my rush
I'm for the town today, stand back and clear the way,
For I've got to catch that half-eleven bus.

I was taken by surprise, not only by a policeman uncharacteristically breaking into verse but by the song itself, which began to unravel half-forgotten memories. It was the first song I had ever written.

'What comes after that?' he said with a grin.

The traffic was piling up behind us.

My memory searched for the next verse.

Well, away I go at last and I'm moving pretty fast,
I've just passed Davy Wilson riding Flo,
Nora tells me from the gate, 'Hurry up or you'll be late,
For Tommy's gone at least an hour ago.'

'How do you know that song?' I stared out at him, flabbergasted.

'Because you sang it for me forty years ago,' he said, 'while we tied bands on corn stooks on the back hills of Turnavall. The Nora in the song was an old friend of my mother's, and she still is, for she's as alive and well today as ever she was.'

'Yes, yes,' I said, 'for goodness' sake, Nora Wilson. Many's a time she lent me her green bike with the three speeds on it. Your name's Ross. Ivan Ross,' I stammered, with growing certainty. 'We worked together as children during the harvest all those years ago. My God, how the time and times scatter people. You used to come out from Newry to visit your granny and your Uncle Jim. We must have been nine or ten.'

'Remember tying the corn?' He took up the story. 'My fingers were full of thistles but you daren't have stopped to pull them out or you were called an oul' woman. You country people were a tough crowd. And you and your family were always singing and your da always playing tunes. I've followed your music ever since, on the television and the radio and all the rest. Do you mind the last time we met? Your da playing the fiddle at my granny's wake?'

It was all coming back to me now – my father, his granny, the coffin ... every toe-curling detail. We had gone to the house to play, but not before my father had paid a visit to the pub, 'just for the one, to rosin the bow and graize the throat'. Then we headed for the wake, for they were waiting for him and for the fiddle too.

In Ireland music has always celebrated the happy times, but even more importantly it marked the sad times. Traditionally, at a wake or at a wedding (because sometimes that was sad as well, with a young bride leaving the family to set up a new home) crying women would be sent for. Their job was to keen (from Irish *caoineadh*, 'lament') and to get everyone in the house crying too. Musicians would have the same effect. They would play a lament to help people cry. These slow airs were not intended to make the listener sad but to draw the sadness out, so that the people could get back to the living and the dance of life. I suppose nowadays it's the psychologists and counsellors, rather than keeners and musicians, who make a living drawing the sadness out of people.

I remembered now, right enough, when Elizabeth Maharg died, and my father landed at the wake, together with my brother Colum, my cousin Petesy on the Hill, and I. My father played a lament called 'Dinnis O'Reilly', and followed up with 'William's march'. Then he went over to the coffin and looked at the corpse.

'You were one of the other sort, Bessie,' he said, 'but you were always a good neighbour to me. I'll say a mouthful of prayers for your soul and if they do you no good, sure they'll do you no harm.'

Down he went on one knee and in that position there certainly was no evidence of harm being done to anybody, living or dead. It was when he was getting up that the trouble started. With the bottles in him and the years on him, my poor father wasn't the steadiest, and reaching out for support, didn't he grab on to the side of the coffin.

'Is that the time you're talking about, Ivan?'

'The very same,' he said, 'and if it wasn't for the quick reflexes of your cousin with the big hands, she'd have been a goner.'

He was right. Petesy on the Hill, the goalkeeper for the local Saval football team, had jumped forward to save the day that night.

The constable's face had slackened into a broad familiar smile. 'But sure everyone understood and no remarks were passed, for we all appreciated the music and your da was a good man. They were the good times. That was before the Troubles,' he added quietly.

'Will this be the end of them, do you think?' I gave him a direct look.

'I hope so,' he answered. 'Good luck with the music today. I'm all behind you.'

'I hope we meet again before another forty years have passed,' I said. 'I'd like to hear how you've got on.'

He reached out a hand and I couldn't help noticing his fingernails, chewed to the quick. I tried to remember the last time I had shook hands with a policeman, and couldn't. 'I'd like to hear more about your life too and what makes you keep singing,' he said, 'Please write!' He made no attempt to reveal his address and I made no attempt to ask for one. I thought I felt a strange reawakened pulse pass through our handshake, like a long-lost dance, shaking out sadness.

Then he moved away from the window, straightened up his gun and shouted to the policemen ahead. 'It's all right, boys, let him through. It's the songman.'

2

Between Sleeping and Waking

The Golden Eye of God peeped over Slieve Donard and slowly, in its own good time, lit the small farms and fields of south Down in light green, soft yellow, bright orange, dark brown and a deep mysterious transparent grey. The sun didn't rise too early in December, nor indeed did anyone else, for that matter, in that particular part of the country.

Auntie Maggie got up earlier than most that day. She had visitors. She opened the curtains and eyed the *Irish Weekly* the breadman had brought. It was lying stretched out and bedraggled on the sofa. She looked at the picture of the man standing on his head on the front page. It was Benito Mussolini hanging upside down in Italy. She turned it around to see how he looked standing up. He reminded her of old Doctor Taylor.

With a shiver, she separated the front and back pages from the rest of the paper, folded them twice, and began to twist them into a rope, like she was wringing out one of her brothers' shirts. Then she worked the paper ringlet into a circle and set it down upon the cold grey ashes in the hearth. She noted how the ring of newspaper began to slowly unravel into a horseshoe when she let it go, and the man's face seemed to slacken into a strange smile. She smiled back sourly. Auntie Maggie didn't read, there was never anything in papers she needed to know, but that face reignited a spark of forgotten apprehension inside her. She had watched her own mother die in childbirth due to the neglect of old Doctor Taylor. She quickly moved on to the next two pages.

There was a photograph of a new group of people who were going to stop wars. They were called the United Nations. She thought they looked like the Burren Gaelic Athletic Association committee. The GAA was set up in 1884 to promote Irish sport and to stop faction fights between parishes. In the front row sat a man, arms folded, the spit of her brother James. James was chairman of the local committee. She smiled a different smile, and began twisting the pages again.

The Connolly Clan, Burren, 1932
(standing) *Patrick, James, Peter, Katie, Bridie (my mother), Fr Tom, Maggie*
(sitting) *my grandfather Eoghain Connolly, the poet*

When all the paper was in the hearth, she placed small twigs on top, and then larger ones, and took a flame from the Sacred Heart lamp hanging on the wall above her head and set them alight. It was the first smoke to curl up a Burren chimney on the morning of 19 December 1945.

Then Auntie Maggie let out the hens.

'Come on out now, like good hens, and I'll know by your cackle if you've laid an egg.'

The two children of her youngest sister Bridie were at her heels. They loved boiled eggs.

After breakfast, Auntie Maggie made a startling announcement.

'You'll have a wee brother before the night,' she whispered.

'How do you know that?' they asked in wonder.

'It's clear as day in those tea leaves,' she said. 'And his name will be Thomas.'

No one ever doubted Auntie Maggie. She had a way of knowing things long before they happened. She would even predict the day and date of her own death. But that would be many years later. Now was a time for celebrating life. The war was over. Hitler was dead. Mussolini too. And a lot of other people were dead as well, but the darkest nights would soon be gone, Christmas and New Year were just around the corner, and today a child would be born.

It was still too early for Bridie to celebrate. She was the youngest of the Connolly family and the life and soul of every
party. She had played camogie with Burren and acted in all the plays. She had
inherited her talents on accordion and
concertina from her grand-uncle Eoghain
Smith and her love of words from her
own father, Eoghain Connolly, the poet.
Now she was waiting to go into the theatre in Rathfriland Hill Hospital in
Newry. This would be her third Caesarean and the operation was scheduled
for eleven. She had no way of knowing if
it would be a boy or a girl. She only
prayed that all would be well.

If the baby was a boy, she had
decided to call it Michael Thomas –
Michael, because Mick Sands was the
name of her husband, and Thomas after
her uncle, Whistling Tom Connolly,

*Eoghain Smith, my mother's grand-uncle on
concertina, c. 1900*

and her brother, Father Tom Connolly. Father Tom was coming home from the
Philippines to do the christening. She had decided to ask her sister Maggie to be the
baby's godmother.

Mick Sands wasn't celebrating either, at least not yet. He was six miles away,
picking blue spuds at a brown pit in the townland of Ryan, where he had lived all
his life. When he sold the spuds, the money would come in handy with the addi-
tion of a new baby in the family. Later in the day, he intended to celebrate in the
usual way with Big Harry McManus and Wee Harry McManus, not for a day or two
days but for the week his wife would be in Burren with the children and her own
people. She would be well looked after there.

That evening in Tim Collins' pub in Newry Big Harry shouted, 'Turn that
"Cruisin' down the river" song down, Tim. I'm sick listening to it.'

'You have to keep up with the times,' Tim called from the bar. The song was the
number one hit of the year.

'I'll sing you a song,' said my father. 'One that'll be around when "Cruisin'
down the river" is as dry as a blind man's buff.'

'Is it a boy or a child?' asked Wee Harry.

'It's neither,' said the father of whatever it was, for that's what he had just become.

'What in the name of God is it then?' said Big Harry.

'It's a jaynius,' said my father, launching into a ballad about the birth of some
genius or other called Daniel O'Nayle and a wet-nurse called Judy Callaghan. It was

My father's family, 1924, musicians all
(back) *James, John, Kath, Patrick (senior), Pat, Hugh and Mick (my father)*
(front) *Peter, Mary Alice, Vera, Mary Ann, Benny, Annie and Clare*

a song that gave itself liberally to numerous asides, shaking of hands and humorous toasts and could last anything up to an hour in the hands of Mick Sands.

Next he took out the fiddle. 'On your feet,' he shouted. Tunes learned from his father's four brothers, who were fiddlers, and his father's four sisters, who were diddlers, danced around the rafters. He was the carrier of a clan tradition and later would become known to all and sundry as the 'Chief'. He could handle any gathering with ease and there were few entertainers in the whole of Ireland like him whenever he got into his stride. By the end of the week, however, there would be little left of the pit of blue spuds.

When my mother came home, she and my father seemed to recuperate at a more or less equal pace and things slowly returned to normal.

The events of that day I can only assume to be true. It's what I was told. I wasn't exactly there myself – I was too busy being born in Rathfriland Hill Hospital – but it is certainly in keeping with a family ritual, with which I would later become familiar.

All seven of us were Caesarean born. Mary Philomena came first, called after our two grandmothers, Mary Ann and Mary, and a saint called Philomena. Hugh James was next, called after Uncle Hugh, who was in prison in China, and our two Uncle Jameses. I came after Hugh and Patrick Benedict came after me. He was named after our two Uncle Patricks and Uncle Benny, who was soon to die in Africa. Then it was Peter Colum, so named because we had two Uncle Peters and an Aunt Columbanus, who was a nun in Dublin. After that, John Eugene came along and although he was named after the only Uncle John we had, as well as the bishop of the time, Eugene, the Pope of the time and our maternal grandfather, Eoghain Connolly, he ended up just being called Dino. Last came Brigid Anne. She was called after our mother, our great Aunt Brigid, St Brigid, and three Irish goddesses, all called Brigid. Later she was simply called Anne. According to my mother, Anne was the name of God's granny, the mother of Mary, the mother of God. A child's name, the old people would say, is more than a word to call it by. It's a history of its own past and an assurance that the souls of the ancestors and the sacred spirit of creation will continue into another generation.

Without doubt, both sides of my family had a strong sense of belonging and felt a close link to the distant past. The Sands side had a Norman connection, but according to my Uncle Hugh, we were here long before the Norman Conquest, being descendants of Seanán, who founded a monastery in the sixth century on Inis Cathaigh (Scattery Island) at the mouth of the river Shannon. Uncle Hugh always signed his name Aodh Ó Seanán. The Connollys were descendants of the local chieftain, Mac Chineallaí, who is buried with earlier chieftains under the ancient cromlech in Burren.

My grandparents were dead and gone before I arrived in Rathfriland Hill, all, that is, except my father's mother, Mary Ann. She wore a long black shawl and came from the Cooley Mountains, where songs were sung in Irish (Gaelic). Looking back, I see her faintly, like the Old Woman of Beara, bearing the joys and the pains, the questions and the answers of a thousand lifetimes. She was going and I was coming when we met, and I sometimes feel that in that short time she had an effect on me I can't explain. When a person is too old to talk and another too young to understand, it is time to go beyond all that and sing:

> I remember
> When I was two,
> At least,
> I think I do.
> Or maybe, then again
> It was because
> What happened then
> Has been so often spoken of
> Again
> And now again.

> It was the day that we rushed
> To the banks of the Rushy Bottom,
> Mary and Hugh and I.
> The moily cow
> Had fallen into the flax dam,
> She had no horns that you could catch her by.

'Catch a hoult of her there,'
Said neighbouring men
On the brink of the bog.
'Has nobody a rope?'
The dog barked out the clear confusing
Darkening hope ...

My granny wept at the haw-lit hedge
With blackened shawl and whitened head.
'If I was at myself,' she said,
'I wouldn't let that happen.'
She sang a song of Ireland's tears,
Her present, past and future fears
In lyrics of her younger years
And music without ending.

A dhruimfhionn donn dílis
Is fhíor-sgoth na mbó
Cá ngabhann tú san oíche
'S cá mbíonn tú sa ló?
Ó! bím-se ar na coilltibh
'S mo bhuachaill im chomhair
Agus d'fhág sé siúd mise
A sile na ndeor.

Oh beloved little cow
Oh silk of the kine
Where do you sleep at night
What pastures are thine?

In the woods with my herdsman
I always must keep
And it's that now that leaves me
Forsaken to weep.

'Please wee God, bring Mammy home' was the first song I ever sang and the first prayer I ever said. We were kneeling on the windowsill, facing nightwards, Mary, Hugh and I, and I was four years of age. Later we changed it to, 'Please wee God, *send* Mammy home,' for, as Mary pointed out, you would hardly expect God to bring her home on his back, and him so small.

The wee God in question, the Infant of Prague, sat vague and motionless on the mantelpiece between two sad dogs. There was another picture of God hanging in the bedroom with the blood coming out of his heart, who had enough troubles of his own without taking on heavy lifts over hedges and ditches. We knew, though, that the power was there if only we got the singing right. Ben, the new baby, cried in the cot without care.

The only one who seemed to be taking notice of our prayers was a cautious spider parked in a cobweb at the top corner of the small eight-paned window. He reversed a few legs backwards and listened. A cobweb or two wasn't out of place in those days, for as the old people used to say, 'Why would you get that oul' dirty fly paper when there's a good clean spider about?' Our good clean spider still waited and watched, and so did we, and somehow his witness helped to relieve the strain of it all.

We were used to waiting, of course. My mother was often out working in the fields, tying summer sheaves behind my father's scythe, stooking sheaves and shigging stooks. Then it was butting stacks with bushes and thatching them with rushes to keep them dry till McConville's threshing mill would come around. It was only when wee God sent a sudden spit on the windowpane that we knew she'd be home soon with corn for the hens and chaff for the tick. Or maybe she'd be gathering autumn spuds behind our father's spade, hopping at a pit or skipping at a skip. Then wee God would send the hat of darkness and that would bring them both home, trudging with a half-hundred of spuds for the dinner. But tonight it was different.

There had been no work done today. The darkness already had settled over the small empty fields. A bodiless coffin lay in my granny's house. Her youngest son and my father's favourite brother, Father Ben, lay dead in Jos, Nigeria. Forty years later his ant-eaten diaries would be found, telling the story of his life and death, but for now there was nothing, save an empty wooden box in the corner of the parlour to remember his once full-of-life presence, and to have something for people to gather round. My mother had been at the wake making sandwiches and meeting mourners but she should be home by now. There was something wrong. It was only three or four fields of a journey she had to make and she had crossed that path a thousand times.

There were things out there in the dark that we didn't understand, especially at times when souls were making their way between worlds. There was hardly a field or loanin in the townland where someone hadn't seen or heard something strange or unearthly. There were stories of ghosts galore and even occasional sightings of the boyo with the horns and the tail. And then of course there were the fairies. I was already vaguely aware of their powers and inclinations. According to my father there were many tribes of fairies, all with their own sense of place and space and each expecting the respect of humankind. Our Uncle Hugh had once heard their music in those fields and we knew they had their way of enchanting the most sensitive souls into their world.

During that night I must have fallen asleep in my sister's arms, for the clacking of the latch startled me awake. It was almost day. My mother stood there strange and frightened. My father's arm was around her.

'Kneel down,' he said quietly. 'We're going to say the rosary. Your mother stepped on a stray sod tonight.'

He had found her on his way home from the wake, wandering around lost in

Mother, 1939

the Field above the Dams, close to the Rushy Bottom, searching in vain for the stile she had crossed a thousand times. The fairies had planted the stray sod there and the only way to escape their spell was to take off your coat, turn it inside out and then put it back on again.

She smiled as she bent over and gently kissed me. 'Everything will be all right,' she whispered.

The Infant of Prague still sat on the mantelpiece, looking vague and mysterious, but we knew our song had done its job. My mother sang another now and soon we were asleep.

I remember her as she was that night, young, strong and beautiful. A lifetime later as she slipped into another world, unable to walk or talk with the plague of Alzheimer's disease, she still had that same gentle smile. When people would say, 'Look at her soft skin; she must have been very beautiful!' I would nod my head and think of those times. That same smile brought us through many a troubled hour.

The lilt of my father's fiddle leaking under the bedroom door, accompanied by the faithful flicker of the kitchen's double-burner oil lamp, was my first sense of awakening in the world of music. I should have been asleep, of course, but when the neighbours came, with black bottles squeaking in their inside pockets and magic stories swilling from wicks of well-oiled lips, it seemed, even for an innocent child, more sinful to sleep than to wake. Besides, there was still some blue left in the late summer evening, taking one last look, through the small sashed bedroom window, at my half-opened eyes.

They had been gently closed earlier on by the soft sound of my mother's singing. 'Daily daily sing to Mary', she sang. At first the words puzzled me. 'Why do you always sing to Mary instead of me?' I asked, and now that I had raised the subject, 'Why does everyone thank Hugh all the time and never thank me?'

My sister and brother shook hilariously at my sincerity but my mother smiled seriously.

The Mary in the song is God's mother, not your sister,' she explained quietly. 'And it's "thank you", not "thank Hugh",' she added with a chuckle.

That song would often fill me with both relief and frustration. It would ease me into a heavenly sleep, but I didn't always want a heavenly sleep, especially so early on an earthly summer's evening with the house filling with voices and fiddles.

It was almost dreamlike; I was somewhere between waking and sleeping. The four small panes in the top half of the sash window vibrated slightly. Perhaps it was their shivering dance that prompted a new awakening in me. Its tune was being called by a more distant voice, effortlessly now, searching for a listener. It was louder, thundering, and it came tumbling over the hedges and ditches of Ryan from Desert Orange Hall, one full mile away. It was the sound of the Slashers. Sometimes my father's bow arm would slacken or speed up, willingly or unwittingly, to the pace of the rumbling drum and, in time, the hum of the Lambeg seemed to drone in perfect beat with the fiddle. The sounds were coming from different places, a mile apart, into the same room, my room, under the door and through the window.

When I was older, I would be told how these sounds represented cultures that were light years apart, but then, innocent and unladen by such learning, I knew no better and sailed deeper into a sleep-filled, peaceful ocean, with a Fenian fiddle in one ear and an Orange drum in the other. The tunes being served in my mother's Irish Catholic kitchen were to be played by us the world over and had as much of a Scottish snap as an Irish lilt, and no wonder. Among the fiddlers who played were Glennys, O'Haras, Reids and Cowans, neighbours good and Protestants all. Tunes drawn from the same well cemented our friendships and strengthened the traditions of both. The Slashers' loud drumming, like shots over the head of such quiet alliances, beat out an unease my innocence could not hear.

Later I would learn that the Lambeg drum had come on horseback with King Billy and boomed out the triumphs and failures of his battles. Was its sound, which owed half to the way it was played and half to the way it was made, playing out the fear of a planter culture being integrated into and disappearing within a strong native tradition? In coming years, as many Protestants would retreat into their own communities and militant loyalists would threaten to bomb pubs and clubs where traditional music was played, I would wonder and ponder upon these sad, strange ironies. You can be sure, however, that such complexities were far from my consciousness that night, or I would not have slept at all.

Outside, the moon peeped over the hedge that shielded our small rented farmhouse from the canaptious moods of the north wind. It was made of boxwood, trained especially to keep Wee Willy Wilson's three cows from eating my mother's primroses and daffodils, and to keep his sow from eating our rooster and four hens. The hens were useful, for they laid eggs, some of which would be eaten by Wee Willy's half brother, Big Davy, who was our landlord and who came faithfully each week on Flo, his mare, to collect the rent of sixpence.

I would always know when Davy Wilson was in the house, for my mother would change her pronunciation slightly when he came. She would try to sound the *g* at the end of words like *sowing* and *mowing*. Some Protestants tried to talk 'proper' English, like the royal family, and my mother would lapse into that language out of respect for them. She wouldn't go so far as pronouncing the letter *h* (*haich*) as *aich*,

I stood as a marker for the 'corn fiddler'

or *lough* as *lock* or call Derry Londonderry, but that was because her tongue had no experience of shaping itself that way. My father would speak the way he always spoke no matter who was about, for he didn't give a 'dang' about the Queen, and besides, 'Protestants would respect you all the more for being yourself,' he maintained. 'When I'm sowin', I'm sowin',' he would say, 'and when I'm mowin', I'm mowin'.'

From the minute I was on my feet, I'd stand as a marker in the field when he sowed grass seed or corn out of a brown bag apron or a red box fiddle, and he'd walk straight towards me, taking in one breadth at a time. And when he mowed with the scythe, I would hold back the heavy corn with a long stick to make the cutting easier, reversing down the field in front of him, keeping bare legs well away from the swishing blade. I also held back for Wee Willy, who, for his size, took a very wide span with the scythe and called it a 'swathe' rather than a 'sward'.

Wee Willy and my father owned a billhook between them and anyone who wanted to borrow it needed permission from them both. The shaft and blade had been replaced several times over, but it was still the same billhook nevertheless.

In many ways my father was as Catholic as Willy was Protestant, as Irish as Willy was British, as green as Willy was Orange, as republican as Willy was loyalist. They had their differences but making war was not for them, they made hay instead. In later years their relationship inspired a poem.

> I see him now half hidden by the hedge,
> Briarding.
> Hacking away with the billhook, that
> He had joined in
> With Wee Willy Wilson. Half
> Cutting them through, then

Bending them over.
Crossing the march with thorns
To make good the divide,
And keep the peace,
To save bother.
Fresh new blood drops
Fell from his fingers
Like ripe cherries.
'This work has me crucified,'
He said.

As a young child growing into a troubled Northern Ireland, those first five years were formative and unforgettable. We were soon to move just a few fields away to Elm Grove, the home house willed to my father, an inheritance he found more often a burden than a bonus. His visions and ambitions lay far beyond the Ryan Road, but he was tied to the small farm and it would have been nothing short of treachery to have forsaken it. Besides, there was little else to make ends meet.

We lived there happily beside the Protestant neighbours, but during the 'Davy days' it was something special, like one big family. We were in their houses, drinking their tea, pooching for goodies in their drawers, eating their buns before they were baked, following kittens under their beds and singing their songs. The kindness and friendship of the Wilsons, Davy and Margaret, Wee Willy and Martha, Tom and Nora, and Iris and Willie McMullan, would be forever reassuring and would endure deep into the tense years that lay ahead. It wouldn't mean that convictions would change or differences would be denied but it would ensure that we would begin the long journey not as enemies in search of a conflict but as friends in search of a solution.

'Martha's going to heaven, Protestant or no Protestant,' said my mother. It was the first time I heard that a Protestant might have a problem getting into heaven.

Many years later, on some far-off Good Friday, the Lambeg and reel would be heard once more, as weary politicians agonized over new answers to old questions. Their music would represent different sides of the same coin, the only currency available. They would somehow sound strangely harmonious, like a cushioning twilight, between waking and sleeping, between sleeping and waking.

3
Before Books

Summers were hot then, with colour-coated butterflies floating above the primroses and cowslips of the front garden, which was really a field like the others except it was smaller. In the centre stood a long lone stone like a last stump of a tooth in the gums of history. It had been there nibbling at, and being nibbled at, by time, according to my father, for maybe 4000 years. It stood at ease now without the need to do much. We chased around it trying to catch butterflies with cages made from rushes and if we managed to catch one, we would bring it into the house and keep it as a pet on the windowsill, in the hope it might live longer when the cold weather came. Sometimes we would make a train out of a plank of wood placed on top of empty treacle and syrup tins and roll down the mossy hill for hours and hours until the stone cast a long shadow and our mother would shout, 'Childer, childer, are you not going to come in the night at all at all?'

When the dark nights came, we would take turns at the bellows wheel, and the blue flame from the slack would lick the bottom of the big three-legged pot that hung from the crook that hung from the crane that reached across the hearth from hob to hob. The seasons went round too, wheeled by another hand, each with a special sign to tell the tale of its turning.

Above the fireplace hung the Cailleach, the old woman who hid in the cornfield like the spirit of the harvest. She would stay there during the winter for good luck. All that was left of her were the neatly plaited corn stalks of hair. She had arrived on the back of the north wind, with a besom in her hand to sweep away the old year in preparation for the new. I couldn't wait for a new harvest to come when I might catch a glimpse of this mysterious Cailleach in her prime, all of her. The old people said that at present the rest of her was in the earth for it was in darkness that the story of life was born.

'Whenever you go to school,' my father said, 'you'll learn about things written in books, but first of all you'll have to learn about things that happened before books were written. Did you know that there were no books in Ireland before St Patrick came with his monks and their goose-feather pens? History was memorized and handed down in song and story by the poets and the bards from generation to generation, from when Adam was a child until the present time. It was a holy thing to recite the paths of the past, because it led back to heaven and will lead there again, if you're all good childer,' he went on, warming to his task and poking the slack with a stick that he used for coaxing cattle. The bellows wheel would have stopped when the story started.

'How could they remember everything?' asked Mary, who had already started school and was trying to learn her catechism for First Communion.

'Well, right enough,' says my father, 'there were a couple of Ice Ages and a

Father and Mother, 1959

flood or two, so they might have lost concentration now and then, but the gist of what the old people told the monks and what the monks wrote down in the seventh and eighth centuries would be as true as any ancient history. Although,' he continued with a wink of an eye that wrinkled his nose and a half of his mouth, 'you can be sure that the monks gave it a twist to suit themselves and fit it into the new religion they had brought with them. Just like the Sumerians or the Hebrews, though, stories were told and pictures were painted to explain mysterious happenings, because our wee brains can't grasp it any other way.'

My father had little formal schooling but, as he said, he met the scholars coming home and listened to old people who had learned to school themselves.

The stories lasted for weeks on end and would be continued the next night or the next day as we followed behind his spade, gathering spuds into a bucket. 'Gather up now, yiz boys yiz,' he'd said. 'The rain's coming on.'

'If we do then,' bargained Hugh, 'will you tell us the one about the first people that came to Ireland? Not the one about Noah's granddaughter who was thrown out of the ark and arrived on a raft, for that's too sad. The other one about the fairy people.'

'At the head-rig maybe,' he'd answer, and with a contented grunt, his left knee would prise out a spadeful of heavy dark brown clay, laced with dead stalks, redshanks and gil-gowans. From somewhere within, there'd suddenly float a flood of bouncing, bright, newly born spuds. Another flick from the spade's shiny point, like that of a master hurler, would fire them individually into our field of play.

Under the hedge in the Low Field, with the silver drops of rain tapping on the hessian sacks about our shoulders, we'd learn how Michael the archangel, with his gang of good angels, lined up in heaven against Lucifer and his gang of bad ones, and how that affected Ireland to this very day.

'When the word got out that the battle was going to take place, there was a lot of recruiting, as you can imagine,' said my father. '"All good angels this way," shouted Michael, "and we'll soon drive these bad angels out to hell."

'"All bad angels line up behind me," said Lucifer, wagging his tail in all directions. "Come to my side of the fence and you won't be far wrong. We'll teach these good angels a lesson or two."

'There was one group of angels, though, who didn't want to go to either side of the fence. "We'll sit where we are," they said. They didn't want any fighting and they even went as far as to suggest that God and the Devil should shake hands, if you don't mind.

'"I'll remember you crowd," said Michael under his breath.

'"I won't forget you either," hissed Lucifer.

'Well as you know, the fighting started and the Bible can tell that part far better than me, but at the heels of the hunt Michael won the battle and proceeded to throw Lucifer and the bad angels out of heaven. As he was heaving out the last of them, though, he saw out of the corner of his eye the ones who had not taken part, all trying to look very small and giving wee innocent smiles as if to say, Did you hear us cheering for you?

'"Out you go as well," roared Michael, for the vengeance of war was still inside him and out he pushed them, twisting and turning, begging and pleading over the hedges of heaven and into the general direction of hell.

'Well as it happened, God, whom they say is very merciful, was walking past at that very moment and he saw what Michael was doing.

'"Are you not a bit hard on those wee angels?" he asked. "They might not be good enough for heaven but they're hardly bad enough for hell." And he pulled an almighty lever, which put a brake to their fall, and they landed exactly halfway inbetween, which was, of course, the earth. Now, whatever way the earth was turning at the time, Ireland was pointing upwards and that's where they landed and here they remain to this very day. And that's how the fairies, or the *sí*, as they're called, arrived in Ireland. They must be respected,' said my father finally. 'They have a lot of power and they're full of tricks.'

I thought about the stray sod. It seemed believable enough. I looked up to the top of our lane and saw the fairy thorn bush that no one would ever cut a twig from. I had watched our cousin Johnny Brennan give his fairy thorn a wide berth as he awkwardly arched his ploughing horses well clear of its whitethorn fingers. Another cousin, less wise, had cut down a fairy bush and was well rewarded with a slobber and a stammer which he would carry to his grave.

'Have they white blood?' I asked, knowing that they had, but trying to prolong the story, for the rain was beginning to ease.

'But it wasn't the fall from heaven that crashed them under the ground. Isn't that so?' said Mary, who was the eldest and knew more.

'How they got under the ground is another story altogether,' said my father, rising. The rain had stopped.

'But that's the story I wanted to hear,' Hugh complained.

'Bobby Graham, the potato man, will be wanting to hear another story,' said my father. 'We have to have a ton dug, gathered, skipped, bagged, weighed and sown with a packin' needle before this day week. There's a lot of bills to be paid, you know. Gorman's grocery shop at the Bridge can't wait forever and there's new brogues to be bought.'

I looked down at my boots. They had been handed down from Mary to Hugh to me. Ben would be next in line but my toes were already looking out and the boots were letting in. I slowly followed the others back to the digging.

It would be a long time before we would hear the end of that story. We had hoped to get Geordie O'Hara or Pat Brennan to come with the wee Ferguson tractor and drag digger to finish the digging but the weather turned for the worse and it rained for weeks. My father dug on with the spade, his back 'broke', and we gathered around him until it was well into frosty December. Our fingers were bitter with the cold but wearing gloves would have been out of the question. 'What sort of an oul' woman are you?' he'd say, if you even mentioned the word.

When the job was done and the sacks of potatoes sat in the shed, we prayed we had not put any bad ones in, for we had heard that Mr Guy, the inspector with the moustache, was very particular. Buster Lennon came for the spuds and we hoisted them up on Graham's lorry. Soon they would go to Newry and the cheque would arrive. Gorman would be paid. We would get new boots and proudly head off to the pictures in the town and get chips afterwards in Pegni's, for that was the treat when the spuds were sold. We watched the lorry slowly drive away up the loanin, tired out but with a great hope inside us.

It was not to be. Mr Guy had found rust on the spuds because of the wet season and had turned them down. It would mean we would have to pick and sort them all again. We didn't have much time for men with moustaches for a long time after that.

My poor father took to the drink for a week with Big Harry and Wee Harry, while the condemned spuds remained in custody in a corner of Bobby Graham's yard in Newry.

It would be many weeks before those spuds were sold and many more again before the story of how fairies got under the ground would be told. In the meantime, we would have heard of other wondrous happenings and learned how to cut new seed spuds through the eye for dropping in drills and to prepare a ground for the fiddling of corn and grass seed.

The first flower I remember seeing was a snowdrop. It appeared on the ground as silently as a snowflake. There were as many secrets in the earth as there were in the sky. No one remembered planting it. Perhaps it always was there, just awaiting a wink from the eye of heaven. Slowly the days were becoming brighter and birds were singing. The first bird I remember was the lisinaree. Its real name was 'finch' but at the end of every verse it sang *lisinaree!*

When the first of February came, the Cailleach was replaced with a brand new St Brigid's cross that Mary had made from rushes in the Rushy Bottom. That was St Brigid's feast day and Auntie Maggie would arrive on foot to take us to St Brigid's Well in Faughart. We walked the two miles up the Ryan Road and got a bus to Newry, took another bus across the border, and then walked the last three miles to Faughart.

Auntie Maggie had great faith in the water from that well and she always took children with her. My father used to say that all Burren children had one arm longer than the other from being dragged all over the country by our well-loved Auntie Maggie. She sprinkled the holy water on us, on the animals and on the ground too, for the earth was full of growing and needed to be looked after. She whispered to us that Brigid was a saint even before Jesus was born. We peered down the well, hoping to catch a glimpse of her, but Auntie Maggie warned about the wee girl who wanted to know too much and the well swallowed her. Her name was Shannon and that's how the river Shannon began, and it was a very knowledgeable river.

When I was young our faithful horse, the dolly mare, died of old age. We were left with no horse to pull the harrow to cover the seed in the School Field. The harrow was too heavy for us, so my father sent to Wee Willy's for the billhook and cut a blackthorn bush out of the hedge. We tied a rope around the jagged trunk and harnessed ourselves for the pull. Up and down the field we went, taking generous breadths, our heels digging into the soil like a horse's hooves.

'Does a horse pull a cart or push it?' grunted my father.

We knew the answer wouldn't be obvious but we grunted back anyway, 'It pulls it!'

'It doesn't.' said my father. 'It pushes it.'

We had expected that.

'How's that?' we asked.

'Well, isn't the cart shafts attached to the horse's collar and doesn't the horse push the collar with its shoulders? Now get in behind the shaft of the bush and push.'

Straining hard, we dragged and pushed the heavy blackthorn bush onwards, turning over a light covering of soil to hide the young seeds from the eagle-eyed elements. Caught between the death of the horse and the arrival of the tractor, it was easy to imagine the struggles of earlier people, who had hoked and scraped this land so many years before us. We found white flint stones in the soil and rubbed them together under our half-coats. As we watched them crack and sparkle in the darkness, we prided ourselves in how modern we had become with our fires and matches and hurricane lamps without realizing that there was so much about our own life that hadn't changed for centuries. The crows and vermin that competed for our food were as much enemies today as yesterday, just as the rabbit that gave us broth for the table was still a friend to be thanked.

> I checked the snares we had set the night before
> And found a rabbit there.
> I should have cried at the sight of his bunny bulging eyes
> But with pride and appetite instead
> I thanked him for the soup that was to come
> And the precious pat ordained for my growing lad's head.

Mowing was just as strenuous as sowing and later in the year my father called to us, 'Gather up those heads, yiz boys yiz, for the Cailleach can't be far away now.'

Talk of the Cailleach revived morale in the field. We were coming near the end, only the hollow left, and my father, with strickle singing, was putting a final edge on the scythe's rounded blade. 'If you sharpen it too much,' he said, 'you take the edge off it. The art is in knowing when to stop.'

He had a handkerchief on his head, tied with four knots, one at each corner. It was too hot for a hat. Mary was holding back the corn in a slant, away from the blade, with a long stick of hazel to make the cutting easier.

'You told us we might find the Cailleach yesterday,' said Hugh, 'and the day before yesterday and there's still no sign of her.'

'We'll find her soon,' insisted my father, wading into the final few swards. With renewed enthusiasm, Hugh and I warmed to our task; with backs bending and fingers raking at the ungathered stray stalks left by the tiers. What we scraped up from the stubble would be used as bands for the stooks, which were the sheaves standing together in fours. My mother was tying behind the mower and humming a song she had penned as a teenager. It was about Broxtown hall, on the mountain road between Mayobridge and Burren, where she had first met my father.

> Oh it's down the Carrick Road you go, and up by Charlie Grants.
> If you're coming with us for a good night's dance.
> Round the mountain road and then it's just beyond the bend.
> In four and twenty minutes, sure, you're at your journey's end.
> It's there you'll find the Valley hall and it's certain you'll enjoy
> A cheerful greeting at the door, by a Broxtown Boy.

> The Old Tyme dance is still in vogue and the music it is grand
> Especially when it's flavoured by the Benagh Pipers band
> Set dances and square dances, jigs and reels also,
> And of course we're not forgetting the old polka heel and toe
> The foreign dance is not allowed, yet you couldn't but enjoy
> An Old Tyme dance out on the floor with a Broxtown Boy.

The dancing is controlled you know by a man they call 'Big John'
A better MC won't be found, should you travel to the dawn.
A few songs will be sung too, and there's nothing wrong with that.
When John Sands from Benagh sings 'The Old Skiddera Hat',
You're sad when it is over but it's certain you'll enjoy
To leave the hall, accompanied by a Broxtown boy.

There was a great sense of satisfaction and peace coming towards the end of the harvest and even though the next day would bring another job to be done, the finding of the Cailleach was a triumph in itself.

'I've found her,' said my father suddenly, leaning the scythe against the hedge and raising a cheer for all to hear. She was hiding in the very last corner of standing corn. We ran excitedly towards him.

'She has disappeared into the ground like a rabbit, but at least we have her hair,' he said.

We stared at the last strands of golden straw mysteriously plaited and sticking up from the earth.

'Who wants to cut her hair?'

We all lent a hand to the shaft of the scythe and let free the Cailleach back into the stubbled earth, where she would rest for the winter. That was the nearest we would ever get to laying an eye upon the Cailleach for, as my father said, she wasn't a real woman at all but a spirit instead and such creatures were even harder to fathom than women. With the return of the dark days there came more stories of magic and wonder, and if they were true then, they are just as true today.

Winters were cold then and the hills from Benagh to Edentrumley, from the Mournes to Slieve Gullion, were clad in white and silver icicles hung from the eaves of every house. It was a good time to sit beside the fire and watch the large snowflakes swooping against the window, like seagulls trying to get in to the heat. It was also a good time to learn how we got ourselves into the state of the world and how the world got itself into the state that it was in. I was allowed to stay up late to hear more if I kept the bellows blowing to keep the room warm.

It was on one such night, while we were preparing to hear the story of the Ice Age and how mankind came to Ireland for the first time, that a knock came to the door and the latch lifted. It was Tom Wilson and Liam Daly (or Ó Dálaigh, as he preferred to be known). They looked like snowmen. They often came to our house to swap books, and good books didn't last long in weather like this.

My father read everything from Dickens to Dumas, from Buffalo Bill to William Shakespeare. Tom, being a good Protestant, read the Bible every day and cowboy books at night. Liam read science and the *National Geographic* and was sceptical about all religions.

'Don't let us disrupt your craic,' they said, as they stood with their backs to the fire, the steam from their topcoats curling up the chimney and into the night air.

'Not at all,' said my father. 'I was just about to tell these youngsters how the first people came to Ireland. Get up and give these boys a seat, like good childer.'

Hugh and myself jumped up on the stone hobs. Ben sat on my mother's knee, and Colum, the new baby, sat looking out of the pram with a curious frown on his face. We were all waiting patiently to hear how the world began. Mary, who already knew, was over at the home house, sleeping with our sick granny, keeping her back warm and stopping her from falling out of the bed.

'Didn't God make the world and everybody in it in seven days?' said Tom slowly, 'and if you Roman Catholics were allowed to read the Bible, you would know that.' He looked serious but there was never any way of knowing how serious any of these neighbours were when they began talking, nor was there any way of knowing whether they meant what they said or the opposite of what they said.

Liam always cleared his throat noisily before he began talking, and the louder the clearance, the more profound would be the pronouncement.

'Scientific research and the reading of rock structures tell us that the earth was formed 4500 million years ago or so,' he declared. 'A hundred million years later the first signs of life, like bacteria and algae, appeared. It was not until 570 million years ago that there were vertebrates – animals with back bones, like fish – and only 120 million years ago have we evidence of mammals. That's a long week, Tom Wilson, and still no sign of humans,' concluded Liam.

'He didn't say it was a week,' said my father, jumping to Tom's defence. 'It might have been seven different days during that 4500 million year period, might it not?'

Liam wasn't taking questions. He cleared his throat again, this time louder than before. 'As a matter of fact, it was only 55 million years ago that our crowd arrived,' he said.

'Whose crowd was that,' I asked innocently. 'Protestants or Catholics?'

A question from a child who should be seen and not heard was often ignored. On this occasion, however, whether it was in the cause of education or the effect of the cold snow still falling outside, Liam stopped talking in the middle of my query and took a long sip from the hot cup of tea my mother had silently handed to him. Then a serious throat-reddin' action developed into a helpless spluttering guffaw and a half mouthful of tea landed in the fire with a loud sizzle. The other half came down his nose, over his Adam's apple and dripped onto his tie. Liam always wore a tie.

'By our crowd, I mean,' he said, composing himself and drying himself off with his hands, 'the general group that human beings belong to, like rodents, insectivores, horses and primates. We evolved in Africa from a common primate ancestor shared with African apes only six or seven million years ago.'

There was silence. The Infant of Prague looked sheepishly down from the mantelpiece, but the two sad dogs on either side seemed to be more at ease than usual.

'Don't take my word for it,' said Liam, interpreting the silence as some form of scepticism. 'Read the *National Geographic*.'

'You might be better off reading your Bible,' said Tom solemnly. 'Try Genesis for a start. Chapter One.'

'Is that the bit about the talking snake?' said Liam with disbelief. 'I've never come across a snake yet that can talk and, mind you, they have progressed quite a bit.'

'Can I get a word in edgeways?' said my father, pouring a helpful of whiskey into his tea and handing me the bottle to pass to the neighbour men. It smelt like the paraffin I had poured into the oil lamp earlier that evening, but its colour was shimmering gold in the glimmer of the fire, which was sulkily beginning to recover from Liam's liquid expulsions.

'Go ahead,' said Liam, pouring the water of life into what was left of his tea. 'You're the man of the house, you're the *fear an tí*.'

'Any word of the spirit people or the *sí* in your *National Geographic*?' asked my father.

'Good man, Mick,' supported Tom, 'put him to the pin of his collar. What do your rock formations tell you about the Holy Spirit, Liam Daly?'

'Would anyone like another drop of tea?' asked my mother.

'Now you're talking,' said my father, ignoring her attempt to sidetrack the conversation, which was getting a bit heated. 'That's the truest question that has been asked all night. Man wasn't too long up on his hind legs, anyway, until he decided to head for Ireland.'

'About six or seven million years, actually,' cut in Liam. 'After the last Ice Age, when there were still land bridges between Britain and Ireland.'

'That was a good time,' said Tom, 'when Ireland and Britain were united. We were better off then.'

'Did you not know,' said Liam, returning to his geological delving with a loud cough, 'that Ireland north and south was separated by the Iapetus Ocean, the father of the Atlantic, at one time?'

'Do you see,' said Tom, 'isn't that what I'm trying to tell you all the time? The north and south were two different places up until lately.'

'Four hundred million years ago or so, actually,' said Liam. 'That's when this unification took place.'

'What's a few hundred million years between friends?' smiled my mother, offering Tom more tea. 'Do you want another drop to warm it up?'

'Did it cause trouble?' asked Tom, nodding his head.

'Maybe between rocks,' said Liam, 'but not between politicians, for at that time they were all at the bottom of the ocean with scales on their backs and the land was the last place they wanted to be.'

'That's where they should still be,' said my father, and whiskey was poured into tea on the strength of that.

'This land was connected to Europe also,' said Liam, 'and to America as well at one time, and, before that, we were even connected to Africa.'

'I'm talking about other connections,' said my father mysteriously, 'and the beginnings of our dealings with the otherworld.'

That silenced Liam for a while, since there was no specific scientific evidence for or against such an alliance. And Tom also decided to hold back his comments until he could couple them with some biblical irregularities that were likely to emerge in any history espoused by a Northern Irish Catholic.

We realized that my father was at last picking up the story he had begun in the potato field many weeks earlier, from the part where the angels fell from heaven. Tom and Liam sensed it too and soon eased themselves into a state of listening.

'We don't know exactly what time these events occurred,' went on my father. 'There was no clock then, and even if there was, a clock's the last place I would look for telling the time.'

That made sense all right. Around home, people rarely had their clocks set to the right time. 'What way's your clock?' might be the question asked on arrival. 'She's ten minutes fast or so,' might be the answer.

'How long it took the angels to fall from heaven to earth cannot be measured any more than you can measure how many of them would fit on the point of a pin,' my father continued. 'Whether they arrived today, yesterday or tomorrow, or all three, I don't know, but I do know that they are here now.'

'Can you prove it?' laughed Liam. 'Now, wouldn't that be an interesting study?'

My mother smiled and said nothing; she saw little need in studying something she already knew. She handed out egg sandwiches.

'I don't see a spirit,' said Liam, searching the kitchen with his eyes.

'Nor do you see intelligence or common sense,' said my father, 'but you can see signs of it if you open your eyes and the sound of it if you stopped to listen for a while.'

The snow was still slapping against the window with great white swoops.

Liam straightened himself in the chair. He liked a challenge. 'Go ahead!' he said.

My father motioned for another drop of Powers. He wouldn't be rushed by anyone. Then slowly, as the firelight set shadows dancing on the white wooden ceiling, we listened, believers and unbelievers alike, to how we all came to be the way we were.

'The spirits who had been too good for hell but not good enough for heaven,' he began, 'were soon making good use of the new world in which they had landed. With the magic powers they had inherited from heaven and the lessons they were learning from their new earth queen, Dana, they were succeeding in sourcing rivers, carving valleys and raising mountains, and in time their new home had become so beautiful that it was the envy of the entire universe, both human and divine.

'At this time the sons of a man called Míl, who had been wandering the earth in search of a suitable place to settle, heard rumours of this magical land. Their leader, who had been blessed with the power of far-sightedness, and a good head for heights as well, climbed a high tower in a place that is now called Spain and declared to all the Milesians who had gathered below that, sure enough, in the far distance he could vaguely see the outline of a green and misty island, and it could well be the answer to all their wildest hopes and dreams.

'Boats were built and sails were hoisted and soon they were braving the storms and ploughing the waves and sailing the seas towards the Promised Land that lay before them.

'As it happened, three of the most beautiful daughters of the tribe of Danu were out sunning themselves along the banks of the ocean on the very morning the boats were approaching the island. They were the goddesses Fódla, Banba and Eriu, and the Milesians, impressed by their presence and intoxicated by their beauty, asked if it would be all right for them to land and settle down in such a lovely place.

'"You may," said Eriu, "providing you call the island after me."

'"That would be no problem at all," they replied. "In fact, it would be a great pleasure. Besides Erin, the land of Eriu, seems a very suitable name for a place like this."

'In truth, perhaps, they would have called it Fódla or Banba, or anything else, just to get permission to land, but Erin it had been agreed and Erin it would remain. The Milesians were still patting themselves on the back at their apparent ability to charm the ladies when another sight and another sound confronted them.

'"Not so fast," said the followers of Danu, the Tuatha Dé Danann. "You haven't got our permission. Go back beyond the ninth wave and begin it all again."

'With that, the Tuatha Dé Danann blew up a storm and the boats of the Milesians were tossed in the air like wisps of straw. Terrified, they looked towards their magic minstrel Amhairghin for inspiration and protection. Amhairghin retaliated in the only way he knew how. He threw back his head and let out a song that could be heard throughout the length and breadth of the land. It was the first song ever to be sung in Ireland.

> I am the wind on the wave
> I am the wave on the ocean
> I am a rock on the land
> I am the hawk on the cliff
> I am the cry of a bird
> I am the salmon in the pool
> I am the lake in the plain
> I am the art of the strong
> I am a dewdrop in the sun.

'The battle that followed raged from days to weeks, from weeks to months and from months to years. Where they fought, hard ground was made soft and soft ground was made hard. It was no surprise that in such a battle many would lie dead at the end of each day but what was surprising was that the following morning they got up again and continued to fight.

'It took a long time for both sides to realize that they could not defeat each other, so they stopped fighting and divided the land of Erin in two. The spirit people would own everything below the ground and the Milesians would own everything above it. Furthermore, the Milesians were given ownership of the day and the Tuatha Dé Danann were given ownership of the night. The Tuatha made their homes in the mounds and became known as the *sí*, for the word for "mound" in Irish is *sí*.

'By the time the agreement was finally thrashed out, however, many mixed marriages had taken place and children had been born with a human body and a spirit soul, both here and in the otherworld. We are the descendants of these people,' concluded my father, 'and we have both a body and a soul to keep together and to keep us together.'

'What about the banshee?' I asked.

'Well, I suppose,' said my father, 'that would be a woman fairy from the otherworld who would come to warn of a death in the family of her relatives in this world, for there are people in the other place who would be like ourselves and it was just the luck of the draw that they ended up on the other side.'

'Are fairies bad?' asked Hugh.

'I suppose, like many's another,' said my father, 'they can be good at times and bad at times, and like ourselves, they have their own jobs to do to make ends meet. The leprechaun, or lenanshee, would be a shoe-mender by trade and would have gathered up a lot of money with a job like that, but you'll learn more about these things as you grow older.'

'What about Fionn Mac Cumhaill?' Hugh put in quickly, knowing that we had to keep the ball rolling or our mother would remember to send us to bed.

'Aye, now there was a man and a half,' said Liam.

Stories of Fionn Mac Cumhaill filled my head night and day, and racing through the fields, I dreamed of being a member of the Fianna, jumping over branches higher than my head, running under branches lower than my knee, and all the while disturbing no leaf or making no sound. It wasn't easy being part of the Fianna but it had to be done, for who else was there to defend Ireland against the wiles of the world?

I was learning many things about Ireland before books. I learned about the curse of Macha, and Cú Chulainn and the warring Queen Medb. And Oisín, the son of Fionn Mac Cumhaill, who returned from Tír na nÓg and met St Patrick.

With so much information, my head was already full and could see little reason for having to walk six miles each day to go to a schoolhouse in search of more learning, but I had to go anyway. Hadn't St Patrick said to Oisín, 'It would be a good idea if you would learn to read and write,' and who was I to be any different?

4

Bad Boys and Good Uncles

My mother left me to the end of the lane, the verge of a strange new land for both of us. She took my hand and looked into my eyes. I was already lonely and a little tearful, and I think she was too. In the brightness of the morning light she spotted the relics of a breakfast egg perched below my lower lip. Such outward manifestations of healthy nourishment on children's chins were sometimes proudly left intact in those days, but not by my mother. She neatly spat on the corner of her handkerchief and washed my face all over again. Then, feeling the love and care of a well-licked calf, I parted with a hug and a kiss, both of us waving until we disappeared from each other's sight. So I took a hand of Hugh and a hand of Mary and footed up Kate Daly's lane on the first leg of the long three-mile walk to St Patrick's Primary Elementary School in Mayobridge, and the world of bells, books, canes and crayons.

The first leg was a short cut through the fields, over mossy stiles, through guttery gaps, past the curious gaze of unfamiliar cattle, grazing for breakfast, and finally over a wooden gate on to the rain-washed Crossan Road. At the top of Billy's Hill we met the 'Hill ones': our cousins, Pat, Nan, Kathleen, Josie and Petesy, and as we crossed Billy's river, to be joined by John and Mary O'Hare.

There were dandelions and daisies growing in the middle of the Crossan Road, which was where I was walking now, the centre of attention, and all the other scholars who were joining us from side-roads and winding loanins were asking me what my name was. I was learning theirs too and the names of all the hills and bends along the way. At Mooney's Corner, where Padge O'Callaghan fixed old clocks, I met the Fegans and Finnegans from Croan. They were nearly finished school and ready to go to America. Bull Ha Hill was next and the Murphys, who would be in England or Scotland soon, and then the Master's Hill, where more Fegans, who would shortly be on their way to the Yukon in north-west Canada, joined the growing band.

Paddy Gribben, the postman, met us here on his bicycle with the news that it was ten past nine; and Paddy Moore, the roadman, was up to his oxters in a *sheugh*, with a billycan in one hand and a spade in the other, declaring that 'Schooldays are the best days of your life.'

Next, Big Bill Fegan, who had just come home from Chicago with a Yankee hat on his head, looked out over Liam and Sandy Daly's half-door and flung a big shiny half-crown and three sixpences up in the air. There was a stampede and a scuffle, and as hands clapped on grounded coins and feet grounded monied hands, my companions stopped asking me what my name was, at least for a while. When everyone got back to their feet again, we marched past Livelys and Lindens to be joined by McGeowns, Higginses and Meaghers, and Parky Twamley, who said he would be going to Australia when he left school. And so he did.

The girls had formed their own group now, and were playing tig and singing songs.

> I'll tell me ma when I go home
> The boys won't leave the girls alone,
> They pull my hair and they stole my comb
> But that's all right till I get home.

The boys were kicking stones up in the air, pulling skullcaps off each other and singing a song about a man called Big Paddy Dan.

> Big Paddy Dan's a big fat man,
> He washes his face with the frying pan,
> He combs his hair with the leg of a chair,
> And scratches his belly with his big toenail.

I would soon learn that Big Paddy Dan was the schoolmaster.

We could now see the school just half a mile away in the distance and my heart began to race.

'We take to the fields again now,' said Mary. She and Hugh were still holding my hands.

Opposite Mick O'Hare's gate, we turned left, filed down a stone stile, took a short cut across a bog, through a field of nervous sheep and a suspect buck goat, with no langle and no fixed abode. Then out onto the Broad Road, which had no grass in the middle, for it was the main route between Newry and Hilltown and the grass had no time to grow.

'It's not too far now,' whispered Mary, feeling my feet dragging. 'Look, sure there's Bendy's Loanin.'

There seemed to be a gathering of hundreds at the lane, talking and laughing, fidgeting and fighting, doing deals with marbles and chestnuts, and slowly meandering their way to the house of learning at the Bridge of Mayo. I had arrived at school at last.

Suddenly a nun was looming over me. In her starched white headdress and long black robe, she was easily the biggest woman I had ever seen. Softly softly at first and

Tommy and Hugh, aged 8 and 9
(photo Mavis O'Connor)

then less softly, she separated me from my brother and sister, for what I suspected might well be forever. I was scared to death but too afraid to object.

'What's your name?' asked the nun in a deep voice, even though Mary and Hugh and everyone else had already passed on this information several times over within the first few seconds of our meeting. 'My name is Mother Mary Evangelista. What's yours?' She bent low and looked into my terrified eyes.

'Thomas–ss–Sands,' I lisped, and a small spit from my effort landed on her glasses.

'Will we call you Tommy instead, for short?' she said, wiping her lens with her wee finger and straightening up to her full height of 5'11".

'All right,' I answered obediently, although I thought it odd that someone with such a long name should want to shorten mine. But I didn't mind, for it got rid of all those s's, which were hard to pronounce anyway.

Slowly I was led away through corridors that smelt of paint and chalk, and skirting a small puddle (my personal contribution), I was introduced to another nun.

'You are a big boy now, Tommy Sands, aren't you?' Mother Angelina had a kind smile. 'Welcome to Baby Infants.'

My suspicions that one and one were two were officially confirmed on the first day. And the alphabet was sung to the tunes of 'Twinkle twinkle little star' and 'Ba ba black sheep', so no surprises there either. In less than a week I knew the air of the two times table, although the words would take a little longer. I also learned the names of the children all around me – O'Hare, Magee, Rooney, Spence, Coulter, Small, and Mary Morgan.

I thought Mary Morgan had no tongue at first, a possibility the nun had suggested on hearing her silent responses, but later I knew that was wrong, for she stuck it out at me when I made the same suggestion. I liked Mary, though, and soon we were friends.

I found it easier to draw than to write and I was happier singing spellings, like 'H–A–T' and 'P–A–T', than simply saying them. I learned that 'Humpty Dumpty sat on a wall, Humpty Dumpty had a great fall,' and that 'All the king's horses and all the king's men couldn't put Humpty together again.' I also learned that Protestants hadn't much chance of going to heaven, which saddened me a bit when I thought of Martha Wilson, but when I later learned that Protestants believed

Catholics wouldn't be going to heaven either, I concluded that we'd probably all end up in the same place, wherever it was, for we were all Christians after all.

'Which reminds me,' said Mother Fides (a far-out relation of ours) one day, 'St Patrick's Night concert will be landing in on top of us in no time. We'll have to get you to sing a song, for I never heard a Sands yet that couldn't sing a song.'

I dreaded the prospect, but as the day got closer and I heard more about St Patrick my excitement began to overcome my nervousness. I learned much about him from Mother Fides, and more again on the way home from school from Liam Daly.

Liam was always reading books and 'knew more than his prayers', people used to say. According to him, Patrick came to Ireland with one God to replace the many gods of our country. The Irish accepted the one God, but they took back their own gods whenever Patrick left and called them saints instead, to fit in with Christianity. Danu, or Anu, the pagan goddess of fertility became St Anne, the mother of Mary. The sun god Grian became St Grania; and Bridget, the goddess of art, became St Brigit. The Christian Church later accepted the holy well of Brigit for Christian use and it was now called St Brigit's Well.

Liam laughed when I told him that Patrick had used the three leaves of the shamrock to explain the fact that there were three persons in one God. 'That's like teaching your granny to suck eggs,' he said. 'Didn't the Celts already have triple goddesses all over the place, when Patrick was still trailing sand in a tin.'

'Liam's a wee bit of a pagan, you know,' said his Uncle Sandy, smiling over the half-door. 'Any slaps the day?' he asked, trying to change the subject.

'No,' I shouted. 'No slaps.'

'What sort of a school is it becoming at all?' said Sandy. 'Old Fegan was the Master in my day and he would have driven you through the window with a single blow. He used to send us out to the hedge to pick our own stick to beat us with, and it never done us a button of harm.'

'I'm not big enough for the Master's room yet,' I said

'Ah well,' Sandy said with a sly smile, 'there's hope yet.'

I think it started in the toilets. I can't remember why. I don't think even then I knew of any reason good enough to spark off the fight. Dan Barr called me some name or other, 'oul' sand man' or something, and maybe I called him 'oul' bar man' in return. Then before we knew it, we were yelling at each other, 'Who do you think you're calling names at?'

That would probably have been the end of it if our verbal tussle hadn't scattered into the schoolyard and attracted our contemporaries, who were never ones to turn a blind eye to diversion and devilment. Tig and hide-and-go-seek were quickly abandoned. One potato two potato, and even cowboys and Indians, were dull stuff compared to the real thing. 'Big fight, big fight,' they shouted breathlessly, and the word spread like an Easter fire in a dry whin hedge.

Deep inside, neither of us had had the slightest intention of fighting but now it was too late: our inner thoughts were of little concern to a growing mob baying for bleeding noses.

'The best man shouts buff, hit the other man a cuff,' someone shouted.

I had seen big fights before and had been charged with the excitement of it all but now I was the one who had to fight and I had no stomach for it. The first man to draw blood would be the winner – that was the unwritten rule. I looked at Dan. He was as terrified as I was.

'The best man spits over my fist,' someone said, holding his fist between us.

My mouth felt dry. I wanted to grow wings and fly to the Rushy Bottom. Dan was pushed against me and when he tried to get away, he was pushed into me again. Meanwhile, my 'supporters', not to be outdone, were using me as a sort of battering ram against Dan. We felt ourselves being gradually shunted and spirited away from the gaze of the Master's room down Bendy's Loanin, a meeting place that was usually engaged in peaceful pursuits, like marbles or hopscotch. For me, Bendy's Loanin would never be the same again.

I had often wondered what it would be like to die. Sometimes in nightmares, when I found myself in the middle of a war, I would pretend I was dead and hoped the other combatants would leave me alone. No chance of that happening here. I was now being more violently pushed and shoved against Dan. Then, more for defence than attack, he pushed me off. Now it was his supporters' turn to fling him against me, and I pushed him off.

The plan was working perfectly for the promoters of pandemonium. Their work was nearly done. The roar of the crowd was frightening. They were all boys too. The girls didn't care. They had baby dolls to dress and talk to and they felt nothing but disdain for their brawling classmates. 'You're never at peace,' scolded Mary Morgan, 'unless you are fighting.'

I didn't want to fight. I wanted to run away but I was hemmed in by boys determined not to be denied an entertainment they considered to be rightfully theirs. A circle of wild faces was swirling in a ring.

'Stick into him. Don't let him away with that,' they shouted.

Soon the palms of defence tightened into the fists of attack and the blood began to quicken. There was no going back. There was no going anywhere. Like two helpless windmills, we just stood there, flailing.

At first we were both more anxious not to be hit than to be the one to land the first punch, but when the scent of a thump whistled past your nose, you knew that this was for real. Body blows meant very little, it was all face – nose, eyes and teeth stuff. There was no pain any more, just the odd star floating about. The battle raged on, eye to eye, toe to toe, and knuckle to skin. I could no longer hear the crowd and lost all track of time. I remember the second last blow of the contest. I connected with Dan's left ear. It must have been sore, for he abandoned the rules, raw and all as they were, and let me have it on the ankle with his wellington boot.

My brother Hugh quickly jumped in and stood between us. 'The fight's over. Tom won. Dan kicked,' he announced. It wouldn't be the first or last time I'd be rescued by Hugh. Petesy on the Hill who would later become the official goal-keeper for the parish and the unofficial hardy knuckle champion of the county backed the verdict.

Despite howls of protest, the decision held. And with tears and slabbers of relief, Dan and I walked away.

As regards who won, I had no doubt. I had two black eyes for a week and could see no victory. The two shiners did elevate me, perhaps, to a kind of war veteran sta-tus in the eyes of smaller boys, but for Mother Evangelista it was state of great shame.

'What would your uncles think,' she said, 'if they saw you now?'

When I did anything wrong, she would always say that. I had many uncles, of course, and most of them would hardly be traumatized by a black eye or two. Like the one who had been railroaded into the British army in England, for example, only to come home and discover that two of his brothers had already taken the path of the IRA. His uniform was burned and its brass buttons ploughed into the soil of the Field above the Dams. He had to leave and could never live in the North again. A neighbouring fiddler and local lawman had sadly shaken his hand, bade him farewell and informed him that if he ever came home again he would be forced to arrest him as a deserter. But he did come home occasionally, though only late at night, and sang beautiful songs for us.

The uncles that the Big Nun was referring to were three different men. They were the missionary priests, and wouldn't be seeing me for a while. One was in the Philippines, another was in a Chinese prison, and the third was in a grave in Africa. Mother Evangelista would ask the question on behalf of each of them, starting off with, 'What would your Uncle Ben think of you?' I would look at the ground in shame, trying desperately to think of an answer, but never could.

Uncle Ben was the youngest and everyone's favourite. He was a wonderful musi-cian by all accounts and his feats on the sports field were legendary. He was picked to play Gaelic football for Down, which in itself would have ensured a local immor-tality, but his dreams and ambitions lay in the furrowing of further fields. He would die at thirty-three in Jos, Nigeria, from an obscure and little understood tropical ill-ness that we heard was not unlike malaria. During his short life, however, he made a great impression and his grave would become a solemn place of pilgrimage for those touched by tales of his life. A little boy called Gonsum, whom he had befriended and baptized, would later acknowledge his influence when he became Archbishop Gabrial Gonsum Gadaka of Nigeria. Back home we would know little of his life or death in Africa until his journals were sent to us many years later. Evi-dence of his severe sacrifice and self-punishment was then all too apparent. There was talk of his name being put forward for canonization because of various cures worked through his intercession, but with or without Vatican recognition, his saint-hood in the eyes of Ryan people was well beyond doubt.

Mother Evangelista reminded me of that, of course, and my skinned knuckles seemed bloodier, my black eyes blacker, and my blushes became redder.

'And what would your Uncle Hugh think of you?'

Uncle Hugh was my father's eldest brother. Money was scarce, so he left Mayo school at the age of twelve to work on Jem Glenny's Protestant farm in the autumn of 1908. He could handle a plough by day and bow a fiddle at night and this pleased Glenny no end, for within his family tradition there had long been a soft spot for hard work as well as hard play. Jem was a fiddler himself and his memories of old tunes and old musicians shortened many a winter's evening.

The skull of the seventeenth-century blind harper Turlough O'Carolan had rested in the Glenny family collection of artefacts for many years, and stories of special powers bestowed upon those who drank milk from it were legendary. Whether those gifts included a love of a fellow human and a respect for another's beliefs is hard to say, but Jem would soon prove that he was endowed with both.

One spring morning Hugh mentioned that he would like to be a Catholic priest.

'I don't believe in your Church,' said Jem Glenny, 'but I believe in you.' And immediately he offered to pay whatever school fees were necessary to launch him on the long road. And a long road it was. It ended up in China. That's where he was now. Father Hugh was the only Irishman to meet Mao Tse-tung for it was Mao who was the leader of the band of guerrillas that had captured him. News of his trials and torture was being serialized in the newspapers and neighbours would come into our kitchen at night to ask about him.

One Christmas Mao's little son brought Father Hugh a present, a white rabbit.

'Thank you,' said Hugh, 'but I don't have enough food for myself, so how could I feed that little rabbit?'

The next morning Mao himself arrived and soon the two men were discussing religion and politics.

'Are you British?' asked Mao.

'No,' said my uncle. 'I'm Irish. Ireland is a separate independent country.'

Mao threw back his head and laughed. 'Ireland will never be an independent country as long as Britain is an empire,' he said.

At the time I didn't know what these things meant, but we prayed for Father Hugh and for Ireland in Mother Fides' classroom.

'Please God, may the Reds soon release Father Hugh Sands from that awful prison in Shanghai and return him to his family in Ryan, Mayobridge, Newry, County Down, where he belongs, which is in the parish of Saval and in the diocese of Dromore. Amen.'

We would later learn that his ransom money had been paid but he refused to leave the cell because an old monk, who had no one to pay for him, was being left there to die.

'Take him instead,' said Father Hugh.

His subsequent suffering and torture at other locations would affect him for the rest of his life. The latest news, however, said he might be coming home soon. We weren't sure what to expect. 'You'll have to smarten yourself up when he comes,' said the big nun, threateningly. 'He'll take no nonsense from anybody.'

My only fear now, however, was the Big Nun, for I still had no answer for her. She had a ring on her wedding finger indicating her relationship with God in heaven but it was known to have also been used as a kind of knuckleduster for bad boys on earth.

'Use your loaf, you nincompoop you,' she scolded. *Nincompoop* was a new word that Mother Evangelista had brought to Mayobridge from England, along with her knuckleduster, and no one knew exactly what it meant. 'Well then, what would your Uncle Tom think?'

My mother's older brother, Father Tom, was my favourite far-off uncle, the one I was named after and the priest who had christened me. He often sent home parcels of 'candy' and photographs of himself, youthful, laughing and happy, with pretty Filipina girls smiling under banana trees. He lived in a place called Singalong, which looked impossibly sun-washed and beautiful. Yet when he came home to Ryan in the winter of 1955, the lines of a hard life would be seen clearly despite his gentle smile. Long after his death, I would visit his old parish church in Malate and hear firsthand some of the strange events behind those lines.

When the war broke out and the Japanese invaded, a fellow priest in the lake town of Cardano was killed and a great terror filled the community of Columbanus. Father Tom was in Malate with some Irish companions, Joe Monaghan from Banbridge and three others. Life was relatively safe there but when a volunteer was needed to take the dead priest's place in Cardano, Father Tom stepped forward. It was a move fraught with danger. Ironically, however, it was a decision that would save his life. A short time later, the church he had left in Malate was viciously attacked and burned and his four comrades were dragged away. Their bodies were never found. When Father Tom had come home for the christening, he visited Joe Monaghan's family in Banbridge. He gave them a shoe. It was the only item recovered after the attack in Malate.

'Are you not ashamed of yourself for fighting in Bendy's Loanin,' said the nun finally, 'and causing further pain to your three uncles, as if they didn't have enough of that already?'

'I didn't want to fight,' I blurted out. 'Honestly. I was pushed into it.'

'Isn't that what they all say?' she answered, punching her right palm with her ringed finger menacingly. Then her face changed and a great tenderness came over her. She decommissioned her big fist and put her hand on my small head. 'What are you going to be when you grow up?' she asked softly.

What a day for hard questions. I had already turned enough hay in the wind and rain and gathered enough spuds in the frost and cold to make the natural choice of farming somewhat less obvious. It was a job with no money and no ending and the danger of eventually being killed by a bull calf about to be dressed, or a sow pig about to be wrung, seemed as likely as being mauled by a lion or tiger in the mission fields.

I had thought once about being a musician when I grew up but my mother had remarked with a half smile that I couldn't be both a grown up and a musician. The other half of her smile was on my father's face as he shaved a home-made tuning peg for a fiddle with the best bread knife in the house.

I could always fight for Ireland, of course, but with nothing but a pair of black eyes to show from my battles so far, I decided to drop that one too. Besides, Mother Evangelista was English and I was still within striking distance.

'I want to be a priest,' I said. 'I want to go to Singalong in the Philippine Islands.' At least the weather would be warm, I thought, there'd be bananas and Mother Mary Evangelista might stop asking me questions.

The Big Nun was right about one thing. Father Hugh wasn't one to take nonsense from anyone. We soon found that one out. His arrival resembled the return of Moses with a new set of austere tablets under his auxter, heralding a new order for the entire townland. Shoes were shone, hair was combed, clocks were wound and bottles were hidden.

He usually got up at six every morning and turned on the wireless. Our house was awake before Raidió Éireann was awake. All we heard for the first fifteen minutes was the sound of a continuous high ringing tone coming from their studio, like an unstoppable alarm clock. If that didn't make their newsreader jump out of bed there was a further half hour of O'Donnell Abú on the harp to make sure neither he nor we would sleep any longer.

'Here is the news!' growled the announcer eventually. I knew how he felt. It was usually about Eamon de Valera or some of those boys. After the news Father Hugh read his breviary walking up and down the loanin and then said mass in our hallway with a chest of drawers for an altar. We boys answered in Latin. His sermons were in English with smatterings of Irish and if he smelt alcohol in the air there would be clear references to the evils of drink. My father sat suffering, head bowed, unable to raise a word in his own defence for it wasn't the time or place. Sometimes his old cronies, regardless of their denomination, who had dozed overnight and weren't up early enough to miss mass the next morning bore their share of the brunt. Religion didn't matter; there was no discrimination in our house. If you stayed in the house you went to mass.

While he was around home people accepted his ways and if he had shortcomings people said he had been through a hard time enough and had suffered much for us all.

Uncle Hugh seldom spoke to us about those hard times. In fact, he hardly spoke to us children at all. When he came home in 1953, he seemed strict and scary. He was based then in Magheramore, the home house of the Columbans, but loved to spend as much time as possible in the house where he was born, which was now our home. The problem was, sometimes no one knew when he was coming. Because of a shake in his hand no one could read his writing properly except my mother and even for her it was sometimes impossible. He usually wrote on old *Irish Press* newspapers and the vital date details sometimes fell on the photo of a priest in black or a politician's eye that was often the same colour as Father Hugh's ink. Confusion regarding his date of arrival often posed problems.

One day my father came home from the town with a fair few drinks on him and a fine parcel of fresh herrings under his arm. Isaac Scott left him to the head of the lane. When he got to the door, though, he sensed that 'his Reverence', although not in the house, was not far away from it. He saw his umbrella in the hallway. No locals carried umbrellas for that would be an admission that the rain had beaten us and that would never do. Fr Hugh was enjoying the good weather walking up and down the Ryan Road, visiting every resident on it and reading the *Irish Press* in-between. Neighbours of all persuasions had already been alerted into a state of fresh aprons, well-brushed floors and sudden sobriety. My father, being far from the latter state of mind, quickly got offside and went to bed. He was fully aware of his subordinate position in the circumstances and wanted no verbal tangles with the older brother who had been ordained. He said he was very tired and that maybe it was because he had taken too much out of himself. 'Maybe you put too much into yourself,' smiled my mother barely under her breath. Soon Father Hugh was seen coming down the lane, holding a herring by the tail with a finger and thumb, at arm's length. It was among several that had effortlessly slid a little earlier from my father's less-than-certain grasp.

'I see Mick's home,' he concluded. The verdict had been pronounced. There was no more to be said.

Much would be sung, however, when the brothers would sit down at night and their friendship and obvious fondness for each other would be clearly demonstrated with boyhood banter and the taking out of fiddles. The Communists had destroyed everything my uncle owned except his fiddle. When he was expelled from China as 'an enemy of the people' he took it home with him. Lizzie O'Hagan, who cycled fifteen miles on her black bike from Lissummon, often joined the two on piano and their music of reels, jigs, marches and laments recalled memories that words had long forgotten.

Sometimes Uncle Hugh had nightmares, waking in the middle of the night and shouting in Chinese, and we would shake in our beds as though a sudden cold wind had just blown through the window. 'I wonder where he is tonight,' my mother would whisper. He dreaded going to bed.

'I'm afraid the old man has to go on a long journey,' he would say, as he retired for the night. '*Oíche mhaith.*'

Fr Hugh and Fr Tom
(photo Bobbie Hanvey)

Sometimes when we were having our own late music sessions, a scream from his room would stun us into silence until my father would whisper, 'Keep playing!' We would and we knew why.

When he first came back from China, his mental state was very fragile. He lay in a Dublin hospital, delirious, and believing he was still in prison. Among the many people who went to visit him were two brothers, Frank and Brian O'Higgins. Both had fought in the 1916 Easter Rising and Brian was one of the main driving forces behind the Gaelic League. A poet and a writer, he wrote under the name Brian na Banban, taking inspiration from the goddess Banba. He also edited the *Wolfe Tone Annual,* which ran at the behest of Hugh Sands from 1940 to 1950. Brian O'Higgins wrote of him that he had never met a man who had loved his country so much. His song 'A stór mo chroí', sung and played by Brian and Frank by Hugh's bedside, brought Hugh some peace.

> *A stór mo chroí,* when you're far away
> From the home you will soon be leaving
> There's many's a time by night and by day
> That your heart will be surely grieving.
> The stranger's land may be bright and fair
> And rich in its treasures golden
> *A rún, a rún,* won't you come home soon
> To the love that is never olden.

Father Hugh would speak about how that song slowly brought him back home, away from the pain, the suffering and the terror. That's why he liked to hear music being played at home. When he woke up from a nightmare and heard music he knew he was all right. He was at home. Later I would get to know him much better and grow to love and admire him very much.

Everybody loved home. Even people who never saw beyond their own parish would say, 'This is the nicest place in the whole world, there's no place like it.' Even Protestants who weren't supposed to be Irish at all loved this place.

5
Religious Persuasion

There were no Protestants at Mayobridge school except Harry McGarry. We knew he was different, for he didn't come into the catechism class when the rest of us were learning about who made the world and who God is. 'God is our father in heaven, creator and Lord of all things.' Instead, Harry kicked a ball about the schoolyard on his own. While we were becoming good Christians, he was becoming a good footballer.

But he told me that he also believed in God, and that he even believed that it was God who made the world. I said I liked football and we became good friends.

I noticed that he never touched the ball with his hands when he played.

'We're not allowed to,' he said.

'Is it a sin?' I asked.

'I suppose so,' he said.

What a strict religion, I thought.

Later that evening my father explained that it wasn't really football he was playing, it was a game called soccer and it came from England. Our football game was called Gaelic and it was Irish.

'Is it a sin for a Catholic to play soccer?' I asked.

'If you play for a Gaelic team, then you're not allowed to play for a soccer team,' he said. 'That's rule 32 in the official GAA guide.'

'Would you go to hell if you did?' I asked.

'Not necessarily.' He smiled. 'But you might be told to.'

He explained that all down the years England wanted Ireland to become English, but by playing their own games and singing their own songs, the people here were saying, 'We're Irish.' England didn't want Protestant people here playing Irish games either, in case they would become Irish, for then Ireland would not become English after all.

It all sounded very complicated to me, but I passed it on to Harry as best I could. And we played a mixture of Gaelic and soccer in the schoolyard.

The next day, Harry told me that his da had told him to tell me to tell my da that even if good Protestant policemen wanted to play Gaelic, which they didn't anyway, but even if they did, the narrow Gaelic rules would not allow it, and to 'put that in his pipe and smoke it'.

That night my father told me to tell Harry to tell his da that the rule only came about because the police force had made an earlier rule banning their own policemen from playing Gaelic games, and to put that in *his* pipe and do what he liked with it.

I don't think either of them even smoked pipes, but I knew they liked whiskey and I wondered why they didn't tell each other all those complicated things while they were drinking together in Hale's pub in Newry on a Saturday night.

Still, some of the messages rubbed off on the messengers and we learned a lot, Harry and me, in that playground of knowledge at the Bridge of Mayo. I imagine Davy McGarry sent his son to a Catholic school because he felt two and a half miles was long enough for a child to walk on a winter's morning. The state school, geared for Protestants and rarely attended by Catholics, was almost five miles away.

Sometimes Harry and I wondered why Catholics and Protestants didn't go to the same school in the first place.

'Tell young Sands to tell his da that Catholics won't go to state schools because the Church of Rome wants to keep control over them, and while he's at it, would he ask him if he could lend me the loan of the stirrup pump for a few days' whitewashing.'

'Tell young McGarry to tell Big Davy that for years England made it illegal for Catholics to receive any education at all and hounded and hanged their teachers and holy priests during the Penal days and was it any wonder Catholics built their own schools, and what the hell stirrup pump is he talking about?'

'Tell that wee skitter's get to tell his oul' Fenian da that the Penal days were years ago and there are now lovely schools and dinners and warm fires in every room for everybody to learn in, and there would be one in Mayobridge too, but the Catholics wouldn't go to it, and the stirrup pump is the one he said was great for whitewashing with last Saturday night in Hale's pub.'

'Tell that black-mouthed son of a Presbyterian Orangeman that they can stick their soup, their pot-bellied stoves and their state schools where the monkey stuck the bananas, for those schools tell only an English view of Irish history and well he knows it, and that I can't lend him the stirrup pump because I lent it to him last summer and he never gave it back, but if I had it, he would get it, for he's a decent man, and if he isn't doing anything next Monday, would he give me a day at the threshing.'

And so it went on until the seemingly insoluble conflicts would be shelved for the time being, for friendships were just as deep as differences and life went on from sowing to mowing and from mowing to threshing.

'He says, he would go to the thresher surely but the blue cow's due to calf at the weekend and if she's still hanging on by Monday, he'll have to hang on as well, and are you dead sure he didn't give you back that stirrup pump?'

The Thresher: (back) *Jim McConville, Tom Wilson, Nora Wilson, unknown, Pat Brennan, Mary Ann Brennan, Davy Wilson*
(front) *Jasper Cowan, Wee Willie Wilson, Willy McMullan, my father, Joey Sands, unknown*

The arrival of a threshing machine in the townland was an occasion of epic proportions, but when it landed at your very own farm door it produced an excitement something akin to the arrival of a flying saucer. Pulled by a snorting, smoking Ford Ferguson and piloted by a cursing, coughing Jim McConville, accompanied by his easygoing son, Big Joe, its mountainous frame brushed the top branches of the high elm trees arching over our laneway and seemed to darken the very light out of the sky. Dogs barked, hens fled, ducks squawked and cows crowded round the gate, blowing breaths of inquisitive wonder down their flared-up nostrils. School was out of the question, for everyone had a job to do on a threshing day.

'Stand well back there, youse youngsters,' somebody shouted unnecessarily, like a linesman at a football match.

In its wake marched a gather-up of neighbour men, shirt-sleeved, waistcoated and armed with pitchforks and graips, like a regiment in search of a great battle. There were strangers and stragglers too, some in need of a good feed and a bottle of stout, and others who just followed threshers around the countryside.

'Keep well clear,' somebody shouted.

Then the wheels began to move, the belts began to turn, the beaters began to beat, the shakers began to shake, the mill began to grind and the very ground beneath our feet began to tremble. The army of men began to move in cautiously, strategically taking up pre-arranged positions above and below, behind and before the quivering machine.

Pat Brennan and Willie McMullan were two strong strapping fellows, who would pitch the sheaves from the stack on to the mill with long-handled forks. The 'loosers', Tom Wilson and Davy McGarry, if his cow calved in time, would 'loose' the sheaves and pass them on to Big Joe. He was the feeder, who carefully fed the sheaves down into the savaging hole of the thresher. Many a good man, both feeder and looser, had lost an arm or a finger at that work. Charlie Fegan, the one-armed singer of 'The maid of Ballydoo' was one unfortunate that came to mind, and the previous year Joey Sands had lost his good half-coat, twenty Woodbine and a box of matches to those same treacherous teeth.

Down below was my father, tending to the bags of grain at one end, and Wee Willy Wilson tirelessly 'bottling' the freshly threshed straw at the other. There were others too, carting bags of corn, clearing out the shed, building bottled straw and 'spelling' the pitchers and loosers when they began to weary. We children were responsible for clearing the chaff and participating in the thresher's main entertainment sideshow – 'good dogging' dogs, as they chased rats that had been surprised out of their winter quarters in the butt of the stack.

My father motioned to Hugh and I. 'You'll have to loose today,' he said. 'Davy hasn't turned up, the blue cow mustn't have calved. You'll have to go up on the mill, but be very careful.'

Hugh gave a victorious, 'Yihoh!' He always wanted to get on top and so did I.

'Go with Tom Wilson,' said my father, 'and do whatever he says.'

With hearts beating, we climbed the ladder behind Tom. He had big black hob-nailed boots that nearly stepped on Hugh's grasping climbing fingers as we clambered up behind. Hugh was eleven and I was ten. We were men at last. Ben, six threshers of age, proudly moved up to the chaff area with a three-pronged graip.

That first ascension into manhood was a rare baptism of fire. Showers of stubbled sheaves sprayed and stabbed from all directions. When I was loosening the band of one, the next came in a diving somersault, butt first, slapping my face and scrabbing my cheek, like a cross cat. Sometimes dried thistles in the corn pricked your finger but you daren't stop to dethorn yourself, for the hungry thresher was always roaring for more and the next sheaf was already looping the loop towards your burning cheek with a new trick up its sleeve. One highly strung mouse suddenly landed on the side of my neck, glanced into my equally surprised eyes, and then, without so much as a squeak, leaped past Big Joe into the gurgling gulf of eternity.

I ducked and dodged for hours, loosening some, feeding some and cursing the curses of a child on a man's errand, but the mill was still whining and grinding like a seething monster and no one heard a thing.

The hay, 1958: My father, Geordie O'Hara, Hugh, Tommy, Colum, Talbot O'Connor, Ben, Dino, Anne and Frank O'Connor (photo Mavis O'Connor)

The great thing about pain I learned that day is, it's so good when it stops, and like all things, good, bad and both, there is usually an end to everything. At least for a while. Gradually I became conscious of not being hit on the cheek any more, nor in the eye, nor indeed anywhere, by butts, thistles or flying mice. It was a beautiful feeling, almost too beautiful to comprehend. I looked over the side of the mill and discovered one of the pitchers had disappeared. The fork was standing up in the ground but its owner was gone. Big Joe nodded towards the road. A car had stopped and the driver was looking over the hedge. 'It could be the Sick man,' he said quietly. Everyone knew what that meant.

There was a certain time of the year when many local farmers would take a bad back. Usually it would happen when the crops were nearly all gathered up and there wasn't much to be done. Then they would have to go on the Sick. It would mean they would get paid some money every week, which in turn would mean that they would not be allowed to work. This arrangement was a bit awkward at times, for usually there were some things to be done, like helping out at a thresher.

My father often took a bad back. He would go to the doctor and explain his problem and get a line. That would keep him safe for a certain period, but if his back didn't get any better, there would come a time when he would have to go before a kind of super doctor who had completed the full circle of medical training and had become a Mister again. He was known as the referee.

On the night before the examination the neighbour men would often trade their experiences and expertise in dealing with this smart man. There was a saying that anyone who could find a cure for a bad back or a smoking chimney would be a millionaire. The back was a complicated piece of machinery that even a Mister had difficulty in gauging. There was no shortage of anxiety as stories floated around the fireside about the tricks referees would get up to in order to catch out the unfortunate farmer. Sometimes they rehearsed the possible scenarios, like the loosening of a decent man's gallowses. When the trousers would drop to the ground, a person would be inclined to bend down and lift them, especially if there was a female nurse in the room. If he stooped too quickly, the referee would stroke him off the Sick.

If you passed that test, there were others in store, and finally the most worrying one of all – the Sick man on his rounds, hassling and harassing the entire countryside, peeking through hedges and over ditches.

My father wrote a play about the hard times farmers had to endure at the hands of this character and we put it on in Sheeptown Hall one winter's night. It was a big success, for many in the audience could identify with every line of it. One man, who could identify better than anyone else, had just dived into the pile of chaff beside the thresher. Nothing could be seen but his boots.

'The less them boys know, the better,' whispered the man at the bags, and he kicked a spray of chaff over the pitcher's boots.

But it was a false alarm. Whoever it was climbed back into his car and drove away.

Soon the pitcher was back spitting out chaff and throwing up sheaves until the thresher's hungry howling eventually ground to a halt. It was now our turn to eat.

There was a silence the like of which I had never heard before. It seemed sacred, almost eerie. I could hear the heavenly sound of birds singing, dogs barking and people talking. It seemed now there was a world more peaceful, more beautiful than the one before the thresher came up our lane.

Mary, Colum and the new baby, Eugene, had arrived with my mother and a feast fit for a thresher was being laid out on a white winnie-cloth.

As we sat down to eat, Davy McGarry walked over to my father.

'All's well Mick,' he said, holding up a thumb. 'The cow calved. They're both doing well. Those two lads of yours seemed to be happy at the loosing, so I lent a hand at clearing out that shed of yours for the straw. There was an awful lot of stuff piled up in there – including this!' He stepped to one side and revealed the long-lost stirrup pump.

Both men cursed and laughed and sat down on two bottles of straw and began to drink their bottles of stout.

Children around home were never called kids; that name was reserved for young goats and we had one. It was a billy goat and we called him Billy the Kid. Most of the time, though, we just called him the Kid.

'Where's the Kid now?' my mother said.

'He's away with Mary to get the loan of the new pair of pliers from Pat on the Hill,' said Hugh.

'Thank God for that,' she said. 'As long as he's not eating lettuce or roses again or the new privet hedge, for if he's not going into trouble, he's coming out of it. What does your da want with the new pliers?' she added.

'He's got the toothache,' said Ben.

'He's only got one tooth, sure,' she laughed.

'That's the one he wants to pull out,' said Hugh.

My father was never in good form for two days prior to pulling a tooth, or for two days after.

'Thank God I won't be here for that,' said Mother.

I didn't know why my mother was going away, but I knew she was going to the hospital and I was worried about her. Willie McMullan was coming soon to take her into Daisy Hill in Newry. 'So be good to each other now,' she said, giving us a kiss and a little wink, 'and keep an eye on the Kid.'

It was really Mary's goat but she shared him with us all and he followed us everywhere like a pup. He was generally accepted as trouble incarnate by the wider farmyard community, and although hens and ducks would cast their eyes to the heavens at the very sight of him, he was somehow just about tolerated.

My father wasn't too fond of him. He had been left with nothing to wear to the pub one Saturday when the Kid had eaten his Sunday shirt off the line, leaving only two sleeves hanging from the clothes-pegs. 'You'll just have to go in your shirt sleeves, I suppose,' joked my mother, but my father didn't laugh much.

And there was no knowing the Kid's ambitions when he would grow up. The last free-ranging adult gentleman goat to visit our townland had caused mayhem and terror. Before his execution, he had even butted my father up against our barn door for daring to break the curfew, which explains the grudge he harboured against buck goats in general from that day forth.

'But isn't the Kid lovely?' said Mary, trying to coax my father round.

He had a white body with a black and brown waistcoat of furry hair, brown eyes and two tiny horns that were beginning to sprout from his mischievous brain. He came to mass with us in Sheeptown sometimes, down by Desert and out over Crow Hill, until the priest booted him out of the sanctuary one morning for trying to eat flowers ordained for Benediction. We'd actually left the Kid at home that day, but he found his way to the chapel on his lonesome. He walked through the door and into the vestibule, as pleased as punch with himself.

The place was packed, for Father Slowey was saying mass. Father Slowey was badly named. He was on release or on open-ended loan from some frantic parish in America and he said the fastest mass and gave the shortest sermon in parish history. 'If you don't strike oil in five minutes,' he used to say, 'stop boring.' That's what attracted the crowd.

It was the fresh flowers, presumably, that attracted the Kid. He stepped daintily up the central aisle, like he owned the place, amidst surprised tuts and suppressed titters from the congregated people of God. The altar rail gates were lying open, so, more cautious now, he took an interested look up at the sanctuary lamp. Then he marched boldly and unceremoniously through the rails and occupied the sacredness of the sanctuary, where the flowers were. No one knew what to do. It was before Vatican Two and Father Slowey had his back to the people.

'*Introibo ad altare Dei,*' he said.

'*Ad Deum qui laetificat juventutem meum,*' answered the altar boys.

Father Slowey was so engrossed in prayer, he noticed nothing for a long time. It was difficult for the faithful to notice anything else. The altar boys had bravely retreated to a safe distance behind the pulpit. Everyone wanted to shout, 'There's a goat behind you, Father!' but no one had the courage to break the reverential silence.

I once heard Alfred Hitchcock distinguishing between fear and suspense. 'Fear', he said, 'is created from a situation where the hero is about to be attacked, the audience knows he is about to be attacked, and the hero knows it too. Suspense, on the other hand, is the situation where the audience knows that the hero is about to be attacked, but the hero does not know.'

This was a suspense situation.

The first opportunity for facing the congregation came at 'Dominus Vobiscum'. The agile padre swiftly swivelled a 360° turn on his left toe. 'Dom'isum,' he said and in a flash had his back to the world again. But a most unusual feeling began to dawn on him, and distract him. Not only was there no 'Et cum spiritu tuo' from the altar boys ... there were no altar boys ... not one clean-faced boy kneeling with hands joined in surplus and soutane. There was somebody though, he was sure of that ... or there was something.

The next 'Dominus Vobiscum' came earlier than the liturgy demanded. It was spoken in a less spiritual tone this time, more deliberate like, and he saw what the thing was. It was a feckin' goat, that's what it was, and it was right behind him, chewing the carpet like it was the sweetest whin bush in Ireland.

Father Slowey had a good mental picture of the Kid's location even though his back was now turned once more. He could think of no provision in canon law for dealing with such situations, but he had already decided what would be done. He would take discreet but firm action. He would get in his retaliation first. He drew forward the heel of his black boot, and with a circular upward kick in the goat's general direction, he struck backwards. It connected all right, more firmly than discreetly, a direct hit with the goat's vulnerabilia and sent Billy the Kid guldering and gathering speed over and back from one side of the altar to the other.

'Remove that beast,' hissed the Master through the altar rails to the three boys, still hiding behind the pulpit.

They were good altar boys, not good goat-catchers, but their fear of the Master surpassed their fear of the goat. They chased the Kid gallantly, making sure to genuflect carefully as they ran across the middle of the altar, and kept a safe distance in case they would catch up with the animal too quickly.

Eventually it was the Digger McKinley, a man with no education at all, who made a grab for the Kid and carried him out, under his arm, through the door and across the fields.

That was the last time the Kid went to mass, but he came with us everywhere else. He came to school with us, to football matches in Glenvale, when Saval played Ballela, to gather Gael Linn money for the promotion of the Irish language, and even up to the bull in Edenmore, when we took the white heifer for her visit.

The day after my father pulled his tooth, Hugh, Ben, the Kid and I were coming from Mrs Linden's shop with a sliced loaf, some cheddar cheese and twenty Woodbine, all on one bike, when Liam Daly looked over the half-door. 'How's your da and how's that stab of a tooth of his?'

Liam had had all of his teeth removed before any toothaches could start, like most people around home at the time.

'That's why we're here,' I said. 'He pulled it out last night in front of the mirror with Pat on the Hill's new pliers. It took him an hour and a half, for it broke a few times, and he cursed a lot but he got it out in the end. He wants to know, have you any whiskey to put in the hole it came out of?'

'Is it his last one?' asked Liam.

'It is,' I said.

'Thanks be to God for that,' said Liam. 'Will he be getting in the government mouth?'

Liam had no false teeth, because he didn't recognize the government.

'I think he talked about getting the upper row,' I said truthfully.

'More than enough,' said Liam, pouring out whiskey like Lourdes water into a baby Powers bottle. 'Look after the Kid,' he said, giving the goat a liquorice all sort and waving after us as we headed home with my father's cure.

My mother being in hospital for an illness that no one had told me about was bad enough, but my father's lack of patience and finesse in the art of cuisine left us hungry as well. He would mix raw eggs and milk in a glass and make us take it. 'That's better than any grub,' he said. 'There's eating and drinking in that.'

Sometimes we got strange concoctions and combinations of the unknown mixed with spuds, buttermilk and nettle soup, which he maintained was 'better for you than being bled', but after a week or so, there was so much disenchantment in the ranks that we were considering being bled, whatever that meant, as a good option. It was the surprisingly original colours and strange, unfamiliar smells coming from his cooking that was most disconcerting, I think. Dishes that he'd proudly introduce as being 'out of this world' were so far out, we couldn't go near them. We also noted, with interest, that he didn't eat them either, and when he pointed at his tooth, or its absence, as a reason for not partaking, we were not entirely convinced. Noses were turned up and the grumbling became vociferous and unanimous. We wanted something we had seen before, or even something that somebody had seen before. We wanted meat.

'I'm starving,' said Ben.

'Me too,' said Colum.

Eugene couldn't talk much but he could cry better than any grown-up.

'Here's the whiskey for the hole where the tooth was,' said Hugh, handing over the baby Powers bottle.

Mary got a glass and put it on the table.

The Kid was there too, deeply interested in the proceedings.

'What in the name of God kept you?' said my father. 'This pain is driving me mad.'

'The Kid knocked us off the bike and the groceries fell in a puddle and it took us a brave while gathering up the cigarettes too.'

He blew through his nose and we knew he was in bad form. He didn't like it when his cigarettes got wet. He didn't like white sliced pan bread either, dry or wet. It gave him bad heartburn and a good reason to send one of us scurrying to the hedge for sorrels. This had not been a good day. He looked like he wanted to say something but he held back, and hungrily poured the golden liquid into the glass and licked his toothless gums, as best as he could in the circumstances.

Suddenly the Kid jumped up on the kitchen table and scattered the whiskey in all directions. It was the empty glass, rather than its sacred contents, that connected with my father's jaw, somewhere in the vicinity of the hole where the tooth had been.

I thought at first he was going to cry. But he just sat there and stared with disbelief at the Kid standing on the table. The Kid looked down at him as if to say, Isn't life one big hooley?

Then my father's face turned into a strange smile I had never seen before and a kind of glaze came over his eyes. I thought his unusual expression was caused by the soreness of his mouth, but I wasn't sure. He was saying things like, 'You're such a great kid altogether,' and 'Aren't you so polite and well-mannered too?' I thought I detected a hint of sarcasm in his voice, but I wasn't sure about that either. His lip seemed to curl a little at one side. Then his voice lowered into a kind of hiss.

'Kid,' he said almost inaudibly, 'you won't be going to school tomorrow.'

We went to bed that night and we were very hungry. My father went to bed, too, and he was very thirsty.

Coming home from school the next day, as soon as we turned down the lane, tired and ravenous, we were assailed by the most fabulous culinary aroma imaginable. It smelt like some wonderful manna cooked in the highest kitchens of heaven. We couldn't believe our luck. It seemed almost too good to be true. Breathless, with saliva running down the wicks of our jaws, we rushed through the kitchen door.

'What is it?' we cried. 'Where is it?'

My father stood defiant and proud, with a bag apron around his waist. 'It's meat!' he said, setting down a plate of steaming roast on the table. 'Now go ahead and get on the outside of that and never let me hear you talking about hunger again.'

'It's beautiful,' we said, full of awe. And then we attacked it like wolves at a birthday party.

Suddenly Mary stopped eating, knife and fork suspended in mid-air. 'Where's the Kid?' she asked urgently.

The reluctance of my father's response and his sheepish turning away began to fuel our suspicions.

'I'm sure it's about somewhere,' he said eventually.

We ran outside. 'Hi Kid. Here Billy. Here kiddy, kiddy kiddy. Kiddy, kiddy, ki–'

We found him all right, or the bit that was left of him, hanging up in the pantry.

'It had to be done,' stammered my father, slowly now, realizing the devastating effect of his semi-well-intentioned actions. 'But life is like that you know,' he said quietly. 'It always has been. If you want meat, something must die.'

'But why the Kid?' we wailed. 'The Kid was different.'

We looked at him hanging there. He had a peaceful, almost heroic, look on his face, as if to say, Isn't that what friends are for? We couldn't believe we'd eaten him. And it turned out that my father even had plans for the tender skin on his back. It would be used to make a bodhrán.

A general hunger strike and period of mourning continued in the house until my mother came home from hospital. Then the tears of sorrow quickly turned to tears of joy. I learned the reason why she had been in hospital too. They had been afraid to tell us beforehand that she was having a serious operation. Doctors thought she might die.

It was her seventh Caesarean and she didn't die. Instead we had a beautiful baby sister. Her name was Anne and she would become a great singer and play the bodhrán in Carnegie Hall.

Master McEvoy didn't believe in teaching us things that we would learn in other ways. For example, he never taught us how to count money. 'You'll learn that yourselves,' he said, and we did. He never taught us about politics either. 'You'll learn more about that than you need to,' he said. But he did show us a history book with no cover on it and a lot of dates inside it, and told us how lucky we were to have an education at all. He spoke of the Penal times in Ireland when education was denied to Irish Catholics and when land, which was life itself, could not be owned by one of our kind.

I understood how important land was. Local farmers would still fight over a few rudes and fall out over right-a-ways and bogs and who owned what. Every inch was precious and I often heard my father curse tractors with their big wheels for only ploughing 'a little bit in the middle of a field' whereas the horse could plough a neat head rig and foot rig and make use of the land right into the ditch. Once I saw him taste the soil in the Wee Field with his tongue and say, 'Isn't that great stuff and well worth fighting for?'

Sometimes people heading for America brought a handful of their own earth just to have it near them and Tarry 'the Tra' McComiskey, it was said, carried a spread of it in the bottom of his own boots just to be standing on home ground if a row broke out.

The Master told us that the Irish had a long tradition for respecting justice but, 'Bad laws turn good people against all laws.' He liked the old Brehon laws. The Brehons were ancient Irish judges and if one of them made an unfair ruling his face would break out in blotches because his heart was connected with the truth. Nowadays the judges wouldn't even blush, he said. He began to read out dates relating to the losing and gaining of land.

In 1170 the Anglo Normans arrived in Ireland and eventually accepted the native customs but in 1366 England introduced the Statutes of Kilkenny to stop the English born in Ireland from accepting the Irish way of life.

In 1603 the Irish earls and chieftains were forced to flee and their lands were given to Scottish and English planters.

By 1641 only half of Ireland's land was held by Irish Catholics and they rose up in rebellion. England's Oliver Cromwell put down the rebellion and banished Irish Catholics 'to hell or to Connaught' and now less than a quarter of Irish land was held by Catholics.

In 1690 King William of Orange defeated the Catholic King James at the Battle of the Boyne and the Penal Laws were introduced. By 1714 only 7 per cent of all Irish land was held by Catholics. In 1795 the Orange Order was formed in Armagh to defend Protestant land against rebel Irish Catholics who wanted it back again. It was still the Orange Order that held power in Northern Ireland today.

One local story was told about an Irish Catholic labourer who went to his boss, a wealthy Protestant landowner, and asked, 'Where did you get all that good land from?'

'It was willed to me by my father,' answered the farmer.

'And where did your father get it?' asked the labourer.

'He inherited from our ancestors.'

'And how did your ancestors get it?'

'Oh, I suppose they fought for it.'

'Well,' says the labourer, whipping off his coat, 'I suppose you won't mind if I now fight you for it.'

It was a joke with a jag, good for a laugh but too serious to be laughed at. For many, the fact that the land was taken by force at one time or other in the past justified its retrieval by force at some time or other in the future. For 800 years there had been uprisings against the English. Litanies of martyrs had fought and died for the cause.

On the stile that led from the short cut through the fields to the Broad Road and Bendy's Loanin there were three letters chiselled out on the last stone step. It read I–R–A. Coming home it was written on the first stone step.

'That comes from the bad times,' said my mother when I asked her about it. 'It means Irish Republican Army.' She didn't like to talk about those days but we learned about them anyway.

The IRA first came into being under that name in 1866, when a group of Fenians attacked a British army unit in Canada. They had decided they would attack the British army anywhere they could find them and there were plenty of places where they could be found. The Fenian Brotherhood remained prominent in the years that followed and young men, ready to fight for the cause, often suffered the consequences.

One way or the other, many families around our part of the country had been connected to one side or the other in the not too distant past. It was all too recent and too raw to talk about. My father and mother with their brothers and sisters had been taken out of their beds as children and stood up against the wall. Black and Tans' guns pointing at them. That's why my mother rarely spoke of such things. Her own family's hay barn had been burned down by the Black and Tans when she was a little girl. That was the time her Uncle Tom had to flee to County Louth. Every day, from the other side of Carlingford Lough, he could see his own townland but he could never go back to live there. She may not have talked much about those days, but there were many memories that wouldn't go away, and terrible tales of local people being taken out and shot or dragged behind lorries until they were dead were still remembered at gatherings.

'People on all sides suffered,' she said. 'God protect us from the Troubles ever coming again.'

It was 1956 now and things were different. Apart from the letters cut out on the stone step near Bendy's Loanin, the IRA was nowhere to be seen. There was no British army either, and the Troubles seemed confined to the odd row over Twelfth of July Orange parades.

Admittedly we heard troubled news from Belfast like whispers and rumours of a fifteen-year-old Catholic girl called Maura Lyons being abducted by some strange Presbyterian preacher called Ian Paisley, who wanted her to become a Protestant. This worried us children at the time, for fear that we could be kidnapped too, but it was all very vague and our worries were soon diverted by the many other things going on in the world. The Russians had invented a 'satellite' and people called scientists were speaking about it on the radio. Ronnie Delaney had just won a gold medal for Ireland in the Melbourne Olympic Games and we raced each other home from school, the winner shouting, 'I'm Ronnie Delaney!'

One night that year, however, we were awakened by a loud noise. We thought the wall had fallen down beside the house. The next morning we discovered it wasn't the wall coming down at all, but the Mayobridge police station going up. The IRA was back.

Police roadblocks were set up and reserve police, called B men, were driving around in grey tenders and practising shooting just a mile from our house. Many local Protestants were in the B Specials, but when they stopped you at a roadblock, they would ask your name as if they didn't already know it.

In early 1957 a new song about the IRA was being sung. It was written by Seán Costello and called 'Seán South from Garryowen' after a man who had been shot with his friend Fergal O'Hanlon as they attacked a police station in County Fermanagh.

> No more will he hear the seagull cry o'er the murmuring Shannon tide,
> For he fell beneath a Northern sky, brave O'Hanlon by his side
> He has gone to join that gallant band of Plunkett, Pearse and Tone,
> Another martyr for old Ireland, Seán South from Garryowen.

Dominic Behan would later write a song about Fergal O'Hanlon called 'The patriot game'. We were learning more from these songs than listening to the radio or reading history books. There were now new jokes going around at school at breaktime.

'Did you hear that the IRA have a new satellite?'

'How is that?'

'Sure, don't they set-a-light to everything?'

Some thought the IRA was a good idea and even the youngest had quotations to back up their argument. 'Ireland unfree shall never be at peace,' they said. And, 'The only way you can talk to England is down the barrel of a gun.'

Others disagreed, and argued that there was free schooling now and poor people would be able to get an education. 'That will change everything for Catholics,' they said. A good education would bring a good job. Hoking and scraping in bad land wasn't so vital now, there were new opportunities and brain was better than brawn.

Adults were also talking about some newfangled thing called the eleven-plus.

One day I put up my hand in the Master's class. 'What about the eleven-plus?' I asked daringly.

'You're too young to be talking about that,' he replied.

I was ten at the time and thought by his answer that it had something to do with sex or how children were born, so I kept my mouth shut.

About a year and a half later I thought I'd chance it once more.

He looked at me over his glasses. 'You're too old now,' he replied.

He told us that the eleven-plus was an examination that some people did to get into a grammar school, but he had got fed up with it. 'If the child passes,' he said, 'all the neighbours say, "Isn't that a very smart child?" but if they fail, they say, "Isn't that a very stupid oul' master?"'

He taught us how to make a cart for a horse instead.

And so it was, at the age of twelve and with no eleven-plus under my belt, I headed for the new Catholic boys' school in Newry. It was called St Joseph's Voluntary Intermediate School, although there was little I could see that was voluntary about it for me.

There was a smell of new paint and voices echoed around the corridors. On the first day a row broke out in the schoolyard. Seanie Ruddy, a Newry boy, made a swing at a muscular schoolmaster's jaw. I heard someone remark that he had problems with authority. Many years later we would walk behind his coffin, after he had been shot in the town with two others by British soldiers from Woolworth's roof in Hill Street. In the riot that followed, I would get my first whiff of cs gas and feel the whish of a rubber bullet flying past my nose. But those frightening and tragic days were a far cry from all our young dreams on that first day at St Joseph's.

Outside the school gates older boys with long side locks kicked their heels with pointed toes. They were the Teddy boys and some said they liked to fight with chains and knuckledusters in their spare time. Perhaps they'd had no Big Nun to sort them out. Town people had lots of free time, for they didn't have to gather spuds or pull weeds or briard hedges every hour God sent.

The Teddy boys listened to music called rockabilly and Master McGill, our geography teacher, said he liked that music too and in particular a singer called Tommy Sands. I blushed hotly – so there was another Tommy Sands in the world besides myself. Many years later the ex-wife of the 'American' Tommy Sands would mistakenly invite me to Hawaii, but such places were now only on a map in a geography class.

Mr Kearns was the headmaster. 'Just because you haven't some silly little examination doesn't mean you have no future,' he boomed.

Pat Jennings, in the back row, smiled quietly to himself. Later he would become a famous goalkeeper and a great ambassador for Newry, and we would ride two bicycles together from Belfast to Dublin to raise money for Co-operation North and economic development.

I spent an enjoyable year there before sitting an exam and being spirited off to St Colman's College further up the road. It was a minor seminary for the diocese of Dromore, where it was thought I could make something out of myself. For five years I would share a new class there with clean-fingered colleagues attempting to turn ploughs into pens.

6

Changing Times

My father was not by any stretch of the imagination a violent man. With one rare lapse, however, in 1960, he managed to cut off all relations between our house and the rest of the world.

Admittedly, when he was younger, he had pulled a pushy politician from a podium outside Mayobridge chapel one Sunday morning; and then there was that Saturday night he put some big man out through the window of Hale's pub in Newry, but such behaviour was very uncharacteristic. I remember once when a row started in a pub, he whispered to me that he was feeling a bit frightened. Not of anyone in the pub, mind you, but of 'this fellow here', he said, pointing to himself. Yes, he had a bit of a temper in him but he very seldom let it out. Someone invited him to fight at Rathfriland fair, but he said he'd rather sing a song, which drove the other man mad entirely. Eventually they agreed to a wrestling match instead. My father won and then sang the song.

In August 1960, however, he coolly picked up the biggest knife in the kitchen and stabbed our old wet battery wireless in the speaker. He followed this up by throwing a cup of tea in its face, soaking such far-flung stations as Stockholm, Oslo, Frankfurt and London with hot, wet tea leaves. His general target on that occasion was Athlone, the headquarters of Ireland's national radio station, and Mícheál Ó Hehir, the brilliant sports commentator, in particular.

'Take that, ye karn ye,' he roared.

'What in the name of God are you at, Mick!' said my mother, who was only half listening to the match and half doing the *Irish Weekly* crossword.

'And that, you knob-faced knur,' he shouted, delivering a bare-knuckled blow to its hitherto smiling dial.

It was all because of a Gaelic football match. Down were trailing by two points against Offaly. It had been a bruising All-Ireland Senior Championship semi-final.

There were just a few minutes left in the game and James McCartan, the dynamic Down centre half forward, had been downed in the square. Paddy Doherty was getting ready to take the penalty kick. All around Croke Park, you could cut the tension with a knife. Around our table, things were no less fraught and a bread knife that usually cut simple soda farls for quiet country people was lying relaxed and innocent nearby.

Ó Hehir was almost hoarse with excitement. 'Paddy Doherty is now standing back to take the penalty. His socks are down around his ankles. The crowd is hushed ...'

At that moment the whole population of County Down, it seemed, was either in Croke Park or gathered around a wireless like ours, teething prayers and threats alike to saints and other holy people who might have influence on Providence in such times as these.

'Can Doherty score this and save the day for Down and put them into their first ever All-Ireland final in history?' Ó Hehir went on breathlessly. 'He's placing the ball on the fourteen-yard line ... this could be the most important kick of his life ... the most important kick in the life of the County Down ... he's stepping back now ... the crowd are holding their breath ... Here he comes ...' Ó Hehir lowered his voice to a whisper. 'He puts his head to one side in that familiar style ... a hush has fallen over the crowd ... here he comes ...'

There was deathly silence. We stopped breathing, waiting for the kick. We waited and waited ... and waited.

But Paddy Doherty never got the ball kicked in our house. Our wireless had stopped breathing too. The wet battery had run out. It needed to be charged again but not in the manner that it was being charged, battered, butted and knifed by my father.

'Bad scrant to you for a dirty, rotten treacherous two-faced son of a bitch's ghost of an excuse for a wireless,' he roared, with lefts and rights to AFN Frankfurt and the BBC Home Service. 'If you were playing that pop rubbitch on Radio Luxembourg, you wouldn't break down, I houl ye, wouldn't ye not!'

Perhaps we had the volume turned up too loud. Liam Daly told us later that high volume could drain the power out of a battery. Others said that even a wireless could suffer the effects of tension, which in turn could have drained the battery. And then there was the weak signal from Raidió Éireann. If the game had been broadcast on BBC Northern Ireland, it would have been clearer and less work for the old wireless, but the BBC never broadcast Gaelic games.

As it happened, Paddy Doherty scored that penalty and Down had qualified for its first ever All-Ireland final, but we wouldn't know that until the next morning when Jack Grant would come with the *Irish Press* and the groceries in Gorman's lorry.

We decided that we would go to Dublin for the final, just to be sure, and hopefully we'd see for the first time a team from the Six Counties win the All-Ireland Senior Championship.

It would be an unforgettable expedition. Josie Shevlin from Armagh said she would take us in her car. We would all go, even my mother. With egg sandwiches, flasks of tea and a red and black flag we had sown together from a dress belonging to my mother and an old soutane belonging to Father Hugh, we headed for the border. All along the way, through the counties of Armagh, Louth, Meath and Dublin, Down flags hung from every tree, in support of the Wee North against the mighty Kingdom of Kerry. We went to the red church in Drumcondra, near Dublin airport, for eight o'clock mass. There were Kerry people in the congregation too, who would be expecting a different result from God. He had already delivered them nineteen All-Irelands. Down had been given none. 'Maybe', I respectfully suggested to God, 'it is time for a change.'

We were waiting outside the gates of Croke Park from nine-thirty in the morning, along with thousands of others, singing and swapping sandwiches. At one-thirty we crushed in and got carried away with the crowd to a heavenly spot, right down beside the wire under the Cusack Stand, and there in a kind of euphoric trance we witnessed one of the most memorable spectacles in the history of Irish sport.

Through the two-inch mesh, twelve-foot-high wire fence, we roared, wailed, wept and cheered as these modern day Cú Chullains leaped in the air like the very grass was on fire and swept up and down the field like waves of myth and magic. At the end, unable to hold back any longer, we scaled that fence like spiders and sped out onto the Croke Park grassland just to touch the hem of a red and black garment.

Down had beaten Kerry and amid unimaginable celebrations, Kevin Mussen, the captain, carried the Sam Maguire Cup across the border. For a long time there was no work done on the farms around Ryan, and that victory united Catholic and Protestant for many weeks and the whole of the County Down walked on air.

My father's attack on the wireless that year cut us off from the outside world for many weeks, until Hugh and myself walked the battery two miles up the Crossan Road to Mrs Linden's shop to get it charged. More than thirty years later her grandson Mickey Linden would lead Down to further All-Ireland victories and I would write a song with my son Fionán as we watched a new generation train in Kilbroney Park, Rostrevor, under the watchful eye of Pete McGrath. Every evening they ran up and down the side of Slieve Martin to Cloch Mór, the big stone thrown there by Fionn Mac Cumhaill to dislodge Benandonner, the icy giant from the wintry north. They seemed to be suffering sweatfully for the very hills that were rising around them, to bring a sparkle of light to a loved homeland in a year of hate and a time of darkness.

> The cheering like thunder rolled
> The flags they flew from every pole
> And we sang and danced the whole way home
> On the day we won the All-Ireland.

When the wireless returned, however, it was never the same again. The newsreader, Charles Mitchell, seemed to be talking through his nose, or like a man who had been shocked by a sudden 'dig in the bake'. But he talked on regardless, and we heard news of John Fitzgerald Kennedy being elected president of the United States and scientists talking about exploring the moon. The whole world was changing. Changes were coming to Ryan too.

There was word that we were to get the 'running water' in. We couldn't wait. The only running water we had had before that was running to the well for it, with a bucket, or better still, as my mother would say, 'Take two buckets. It'll balance ye.'

Not everyone agreed, however, with this so-called progress. Rumours were rife of complications and dangers that were liable to accompany the wooing of such modern moves. Some said the running water tasted terrible, especially for tea, and others warned of sinks overflowing and houses being flooded out.

Jamie O'Hara was sceptical of bathrooms. 'They say the most dangerous thing you could have is a bath, for it opens your pores and God knows what might come in.'

Ned Callaghan shuddered at the thought of an inside toilet, when a complete stranger could come into your house and 'dirt' in the corner of your room.

John Grant from Glenn was more enthusiastic, for he was a bit of a handyman at pipes and plumbing. He waxed wisely on the anatomy of toilets and spoke of the advantage of a good lively sewer rat in the system and assured us all that the planting of a dead hen in the septic tank was a godsend for speeding up the transformation process.

John Campbell, the storyteller from Mullaghbawn, told of how a woman got a shower-bath installed. All newfangled, she couldn't wait to get the children out to school and the husband off to work till she could go upstairs and try it out. She took off her clothes first, got soaped all over and was just about to turn on the shower when there was a knock on the door.

'Who's that? Blast ye,' she shouted through the window.

'It's only the blind man,' came the reply.

'Well,' says she, 'there's no need to be getting all dressed up for a blind man,' and down the stairs, she went, the way she was, and pulled open the door.

'You're looking very well, Missus,' said the man, with a long parcel under his arm, 'but where do you want me to put these blinds?'

There were all sorts of tales being told between songs at the big nights in our house and we often wondered if we were doing the right thing at all, getting this running water in, and pushing the boat out even further by getting a bath. But the wheels of progress were scrunching their way slowly down the Ryan Road and on the first day of May, in the year of Our Lord nineteen hundred and sixty-two, my father sent for sand and cement.

'We're going to build a bathroom,' he said. 'It'll be a lean-to built on to the back of the house.'

Thatching the stack: Johnny, Pat and Mary Ann Brennan with my father
(photo Mavis O'Connor)

The decision was final. We couldn't believe it. Our faces struggled to suppress the signs of inward excitement. Outward celebration was a little inappropriate, we thought. This was serious stuff and we didn't want our father to think that in pandering to our whims he was bowing to modern decadence or lowering his credibility in any way.

While we were at it, we would build on an extra bedroom as well, which would later become known as the Postman's Room. We welcomed a spare room as it would mean we could offer refuge to the occasional benighted music-maker or late-night rambler who might chance to stray our way.

But change, we were told, would not come without a price. The old Modern Mistress stove would have to go. For years it had sat like an old faithful granny in the corner keeping the house from the cold. She was fed mainly on sticks that we gathered or logs that we cut, as well as the odd bag of turf or coal for a special glow. There were two little black doors at each side leading into an oven that was meant for baking bread but seldom was it used for that purpose. Most bread was baked on a griddle on the top. The oven was used instead for toasting our freezing toes on cold nights and there was always a great dash to get our feet into the oven when stories were being told in the wintertime. A cold-blooded cat called Mitsy had ended her days in there. Roasted alive, she was. On the morning she was discovered, stiff as a poker – there was a certain amount of family grief but on Mitsy's face there seemed the remnants of a strange triumphant, sentimental smile. She hated the cold and no goalkeeper could keep her out of the house winter or summer. Her whole nine lives had been sacrificed in one last great gamble.

Now the old stove was being pulled out and there would be no more toasted toes or roasted cats. A cold-looking Doric cooker was going in instead with pipes coming out of the side of it and running under the floor. For weeks it was like living in a quarry with men hammering, banging and cursing and when water would squirt from somewhere suddenly they would shout things like, 'Jaysis Kryste I'm drownded.' They shouted other things too, but not if Father Hugh was around for he didn't like that sort of talk.

My mother welcomed the running water. 'It will be handy,' she said, but my father refused to be impressed: 'A damn good bucket of clean water flung round you is a far healthier job,' he maintained, and as for toilets, 'What's wrong with them seven fields out there?'

When it came to the light, however, it was a different story. His eyes were beginning to fail a little and he was fed up blinking and squinting at the small print of Charles Dickens in the one hand and a flickering candle in the other. The Tilly lamp was a big improvement, admittedly, but when John McClory from Burren arrived to put in the gas the first reluctant signs of enthusiasm for modern contraptions began to spread across my father's face.

'You'll have to repaint the house you know,' said John knowingly, pulling the little chain with his finger and thumb and lighting the new white mantle with a match. 'Everybody has to do that.'

He was right. Instantly the light leapt in all directions, filling the kitchen's every crack and crevasse. Soon it was mocking every mark, blotch, scrape and stain that were emerging now shamefacedly out of the shadows. We looked up and around the tops of the walls and ceiling and suddenly there were spiders forsaking webs and scurrying hopelessly in search of dark corners. The dark corners had gone forever. The oil lamp looked sad. Its once cheerful glow that lit the smiles of a generation was now a pale reddish orange.

Around this time Hugh brought a guitar home from London, where he was studying. My father eyed it suspiciously. 'Where's the bow?' he asked. The fiddle had always reigned supreme in the Sands household. In his youth, he had made a fiddle out of tin, and according to neighbours, it was better for the dancing than a wooden one.

At first we tuned the guitar like a fiddle and picked out notes on it. Most of those who sang traditional songs would not be nudged or bullied into the 'oul' cowboy' rhythms of a guitar. They liked to take the song at their own pace and leisure, like they were telling a story or going for a stroll. Sometimes they would pause midsong for a sup of stout or to give subtle space for neighbourly comments, like 'Well done,' 'Keep her going out,' or 'God bless us,' and 'Clare to Christ,' if a death or a near miss occurred near the end of a verse. A guitar rattling behind like a terrier yapping at the heels would not be tolerated and would promptly and politely be eyebrowed into silence. The guitar was guilty by association with the 'rubbitch' coming out of Radio Luxembourg and our youthful attempts to place the sacred fiddle in historical perspective as an instrument that only came out of Italy a few hundred years ago made Irish traditional blood boil.

'We were playing fiddles in Ireland when Stradivari still had spit on his bib,' growled my father.

But the guitar was here to stay and providing it 'didn't get into the road' of things, it was slowly becoming part of the musical furniture. Our cousins from England, the O'Connors, who came to stay with us in the summertime, also had a guitar and they were introducing us to songs that were popular in England and America. They mentioned names like Joan Baez and Tom Paxton.

Soon there were visitors from America dropping in whom we had never seen before, new types of Americans. Not loud speakers with white hats, jingling coins in the deep pockets of checked trousers saying 'Gee Whiz,' and 'Gaddammit,' but younger ones with torn shirts and long unruly hair saying things like 'neat'. They wore jeans with ragged patches that they seemed not to need. We wore ragged jeans without the patches that we did need. They felt no shame being dressed like that. They talked about Woody Guthrie, who was the best singer in America, and he dressed like that all the time. It was cool to be dressed like a worker. We were sweating after taking in a load of bales. We wanted to clean up a bit. 'No,' they said. 'Stay like that, man, and sing your folksongs.'

When we said we couldn't think of any, they laughed. 'That's folksongs you bin singing, man. Songs of the ordinary folks.'

> Oh come all ye gallant heroes, no matter where you be
> And don't hire with any farmer till you know what your work will be,
> For you must rise up early, from the clear daylight till the dawn
> And you never will be able to plough the rocks of Bawn.

One day Father Hugh came home with a parcel under his arm. It was a record player. We already had a gramophone in the house that played records but this was not a gramophone, it was a 'record player'. It was made of plastic, not wood, it had no wind-up handle either but batteries instead, and the sound came out of its opened lid. It had a special needle too, which did not need to be constantly changed nor replaced by a black-thorn in times of necessity. We gathered round it but we were not allowed to touch it. The records were bigger than the old ones and we couldn't touch them either or they would be ruined. Suddenly John McCormack began to sing as if he was in the room itself. He sang eight songs without stopping as we sat attentive as altar boys reverently watching the record going round and round. Next came The Gallowglass Céilí Band with reels, jigs and hornpipes and

The Sands, 1960: (back) *Tommy, Mary, Hugh*
(front) *Ben, Mick, Anne, Eugene (Dino), Bridie and Colum* (photo Duffners Newry)

then, 'Now then,' said Father Hugh, 'who could this be?'

He showed us the cover and our eyes lit up. We had heard one or two of their songs before on Raidió Éireann. It was The Clancy Brothers and Tommy Makem. A whole record full of them, all the way from America. They were different to anything we had heard before. With Hoohs, hoots and whistles, they pulled old songs out of the grave and danced them all around our kitchen. We willed them on excitedly through 'The foggy dew', round by 'Brannigan's corner' and as far as 'The holy ground' and 'Fine girl you are'. I could see that my mother loved them and my father licked his lips when it came to the 'Jug of punch'. Father Hugh seemed to be reserving judgment but I noticed his toe kept tapping. Then, disaster. Liam Clancy made a bad decision. He began to sing a song about a jolly tinker going into some woman's bedroom. I didn't understand half of what was going on in the woman's bedroom but I did notice that Father Hugh's toe had stopped tapping in our kitchen.

'That'll be enough of that!' He snapped and made a grab at the needle. It skidded across the record tracks and scratched a lump out of 'Dick Darby the Cobbler' before screaming to a halt in the centre circle. That was the last we heard of 'The jolly tinker'. The record was returned to Carlin's record shop in Newry on the double, accompanied by a good dressing down for Mr Carlin. It wasn't the end of the Clancys though. It was just the beginning. Songs that had been sung for generations in the quiet kitchens of Ireland were now being served in plush restaurants and spacious theatres all over America. Many years later I would be honoured to share a wide stage and a long friendship with this great band of troubadours. One night I recalled the fate of 'The jolly tinker's' first arrival in our house. Liam Clancy looked at his brother Paddy and laughed.

'Would you believe it,' he said, '"The jolly tinker" never even got in the door of *our* parent's house. We actually had a one off copy of that LP specially made for them, which excluded "The jolly tinker". And so we never got the scolding that was coming to us for they never heard the song.'

The Clancy Brothers and Tommy Makem gradually introduced many Irish songs into the American folk music scene. Bob Dylan hung out with the boys and reinterpreted many of their songs with his own prolific pen. Behan's 'The patriot game' had become 'With God on our side'; 'Brennan on the moor' had become 'Rambling gambling Willie'; 'The leaving of Liverpool' had become 'The leaving'; and 'The croppy boy' had become 'Bob Dylan's dream'.

Many young Americans dreamed of digging up some more old songs in the highways and byways of Ireland. There were plenty to be heard at the big nights at home from neighbours all around. Songs that were embedded in the poverty of the past had now a reason to be sung again proudly in this new world of folk music. Irish folksongs were fashionable all of a sudden. Even Raidió Éireann, which had been so anxious to foster the 'modern' Ireland, was realizing that the future was empty without the riches of the past. If America liked these songs, perhaps they were good after all.

Tommy Makem, who came home to Keady with money jangling in his pockets, was the envy of the countryside.

'How much does it take to get to America?' asked a neighbour.

'I suppose ninety pounds would buy a ticket,' said Tommy.

'Ah for God's sake,' said the neighbour, 'sure if I had ninety pounds, I wouldn't have to go to America.'

Even Father Hugh would gradually come round to the Clancys. They revived old songs that he knew as a child. The more things change, he said, the more they remain the same. We would soon learn that changes in Ryan other than lighting the darkness would reveal what was beyond the dark. Like that night in the Postman's Room.

A ghost or two here or there never did anybody much harm. Supernatural beings seemed to be all around us anyway – at the fairy thorn at the head of the lane; at the ruins of the old crossroads shebeen; at the Ryan Hill five-acre gate; at the bog field gap round by Crossan; at Brown's old house down by Desert. And that was all within a hundred yards of home. There was a ghost, however, that was often spoken of, but seldom seen. According to the talk around the fire, there had been sightings years ago of a dark figure on the path between the well and the back of our house. The story went that a postman had come to the house many years ago to deliver mail. It was coming up to Christmas and being that time of year, he was offered a small whiskey in every house. By the time he reached us, all he wanted to drink was water. There was plenty of good clean water in a big brown crock in the pantry but nothing would do that postman but to have a fresh sup drawn directly from the well with his own hand. It seems he had asked for water at the other houses but had been given *poitín* instead, since it was regarded as unlucky to give water to a postman around Christmas time. Off he went to the well with a tin can in his hand, which he borrowed from the house.

After a while, when he hadn't returned the can, they wondered what had happened to him. They would soon find out. Whether he fell in, jumped in or was pushed in, the postman was found the next day, as dead as any man would be after lying at the bottom of a ten-foot well for a night in December.

Time passed and then there were rumours that a dark figure like the cut of the postman was seen at the back of our house. The new bedroom, which had come with the new bathroom, had been built over that path.

I was telling this story to two visitors late one Christmas Eve. The two Miss McKeowns from Belfast often came to stay with us over Christmas. Maureen, extrovert, blonde and babbly, was a schoolteacher. She and her two dogs, Pepi and Peter, had arrived in the first and last bubble car that ever came into our yard.

Phil, her sister, was quite different. Artistic, sensitive and intense, she had a thin pale face and raven black hair that fell to her waist. She seldom spoke, but when she did, it was in low, confidential whispers.

They both took the ghost world in their stride. Their own house in Salisbury Avenue was said to have its fair share of them. My story, however, drew from Phil a sudden gasp of recognition that filled the parlour with a strange chill.

'My God,' she said.

'What's wrong, Phil?' we asked.

But she said it was nothing and sat quietly watching the fire. This reluctance to volunteer information was characteristic of her. She was always very secretive.

'I'll tell you later,' she whispered to me, when I pressed her to say more.

When the others had gone to bed, she reminded me that she had stayed in the new room during the previous Christmas. Something had woken her. She didn't know what. It was pitch black. She listened intently. The only sound she heard was the occasional moan from Father Hugh, who slept in the next room. She knew about his experiences in China and how they affected his sleep. Then the handle of the door creaked and the door slowly opened.

Phil sat up in the bed. 'Yes?' she whispered. She thought that perhaps Father Hugh had forgotten she was in the room, or else he was sleepwalking.

A figure walked to the bottom of her bed and stopped. She still thought it was Father Hugh, for the moaning sound was now much closer. But when a loud shout came from Father Hugh's room, she realized that this was someone else.

'So it wasn't Father Hugh,' Phil concluded quietly. 'I'm glad I didn't ask him about it. It must have been the poor postman.'

The room has been known as the Postman's Room ever since. One night I slept there. No one had used it for a long time, at least no one else who knew the story.

Fergal McAuliffe, a fiddle player from Dublin who used to visit us occasionally, once saw someone going through with a candle, and later candle grease was found on his bed. Nevertheless, I wasn't worried about ghosts or the likes. I lay down and must have been sleeping, for I had the sensation of being awakened by a light tugging on the sheets. I smiled. Pure imagination, I told myself. A moment later there was another tug. I smiled with less conviction now, but still reminded myself of the tricks the imagination can play. I did feel uneasy, I must admit, but I tried to forget about it and turned round to sleep. Whereupon a third tug left me almost naked in the bed. I didn't wait for a fourth. I ran from the room, through the kitchen, and jumped into bed beside Colum and Dino.

Colum still talks about never seeing me so scared. Without the changes the postman would have been happily outside on his path. Then again, maybe he was lonely out there. Whoever was in the room that night, I'll never know, but be it the postman or some other poor soul wandering about trying to find a way out of the dark world, may they find peace and may perpetual light shine upon them.

7

A Feast between Politics

The boarders were always hungry. 'What have you got in your sandwiches?' they would ask us day boys.

'A turnip,' I said. It was beetroot actually.

'That'll do rightly,' said Gene Fitzpatrick. 'You can get another one when you go home, and you can count yourself lucky that you can go home at all and eat as much as you like too and watch *Top of the Pops* on TV.'

We had no television, but we heard all the pop songs on Radio Luxembourg and listened to everything from Burl Ives to the Beatles. There were indeed advantages to being a day boy. One evening after school we waited for hours with hundreds of others to see the Beatles leave the Boulevard Hotel in Newry. But we saw neither hide nor hair of them.

'I'll *beetle* youse!' said my father when we arrived home too late for gathering spuds. He hadn't much time for the Fab Four and their likes with their yeah, yeah, yeahs.

Other day-boy attractions included a visit to Newry courthouse to watch the arrival of Robert McGladdery, who was accused of murdering a local girl by the name of Pearl Gamble. The whole country was shocked by the crime, and people outside the building were shouting abuse at him as police led him past in handcuffs. He had blond wavy hair and he seemed to look straight into my eyes as he walked by. He had done a terrible thing, but I couldn't help feeling sorry for him, for I knew he would soon be hanged.

'Hanging's too good for him,' said one bystander, without a hint of humour. 'It's a bloody good kick up the backside he needs.'

Robert McGladdery was the last man to be hanged in Britain or Ireland.

It was a great shame in Ireland to be hanged for a crime that was not political. Many had suffered that fate fighting for Ireland's freedom, every one a martyr to the cause, and great songs had been written in their memory. We all knew of Kevin Barry and Tom Williams.

A particularly quiet and rather mysterious schoolmate of mine came to me one day. 'Could we have a chat?' he said.

I knew he didn't want sandwiches, for he had his own.

'What about?' I asked, as we walked up past the statue of Our Lady, under which students placed their pennies in the wake of examinations.

'Would you be interested in joining the Fianna?' he said in a low voice.

I had been reared on stories of the Fianna, the heroic band of warriors who had been carefully chosen by the legendary Fionn Mac Cumhaill to defend the land of Erin. But this Fianna was of more recent origin.

'Why me?' I asked cautiously.

'I've been observing you of late,' he said, 'and I'm aware of your interest in the language and music, and things that are Irish. We are looking for an OC in the Newry area and you might be the man.'

'Tell me more,' I said.

He explained how Fianna Éireann, inspired by the legends of the old Fianna, had been formed in 1909 by Bulmer Hobson, a nineteen-year-old Quaker. Hobson was aware of the Boy Scout movement, fronted by the Boer War commander Robert Baden-Powell. The idea of an organization of young boys, well disciplined and in readiness for all eventualities, was close to both men's hearts. 'King and Country' was high on Powell's list. For Hobson, with the scent of Home Rule wafting in the wind, the king had no role to play. The new republican youth movement was headed by Countess Constance Markievicz, who recalled watching Boy Scouts parading before the Lord Lieutenant to pledge allegiance to the crown: 'I could see these children growing into manhood and gaily enlisting in the British Army and being used to batter their own class into submission. Surely, nothing could be sadder than to see these boys saluting a flag that flew in triumph over every defeat their nation had known.'

She later remarked how George V had made Baden-Powell a baronet for stimulating patriotism in his country, but had given her a prison sentence with hard labour for doing similar work in hers.

'It makes sense,' I said to my friend, as we wheeled passed the croquet lawn and down to the handball alley.

'Think about it,' he said, 'and we'll talk again next week. Tell no one we've spoken about this.'

In the coming weeks and months I would learn more about the history of Fianna Éireann. In a quiet corner of the Low Field I secretly read from a battered manual, handwritten in Irish, how to give and take orders, stand to attention and stand at ease.

'Aire!' I shouted to the wind. 'Seasaigí ar ais!'

The cows were already standing at ease.

'Go mear máirseáil!' I said, for it was time to march them home for the milking.

I learned secret codes for the passing of information and my heart began to pump with excitement now that I was playing a part in freeing Ireland once and for all. Then at last the great day came.

'Here is your passport to Crumlin Road prison,' my friend whispered sternly, handing me the official membership card of the outlawed Fianna Éireann. 'And here is your badge.' On a green disc, an orange sun was crossed by a pike.

'Now go to ——,' he said. 'He's a member of the seniors, and inform him you will be setting up a unit of Fianna Éireann in the area.'

I knew the man in question, but I had no idea he was an active republican. That same evening he looked me up and down.

'I know you,' he said slowly. 'I have no problems with your credentials, but who is the fella who sent you here?'

I was astonished to learn that people in the same organization didn't know each other.

For a time I began to see policemen and Protestants in general in a different light. They may have been decent people, but they were supporting and upholding the British occupation of our country and 'Ireland unfree shall never be at peace'. What would my Protestant neighbours think if they knew I belonged to an outlawed organization hell-bent on overthrowing this 'ancient yoke of oppression'? Perhaps they were in illegal societies too, on the unionist side. Many, of course, were committed members of the Orange Order, which had been set up, after all, to maintain British domination over Catholics.

If Ireland were to be peaceful and free, then the British would have to go. But what about my pro-British neighbours? Would they have to go too? I didn't want them to go anywhere. They were part of my place and part of me. Could a way be found so that we could live together and both feel free? Most had a simple answer to that question: it was impossible. We were living side by side, but they were opposing sides. The march ditch that divided our fields was higher than the new wall they had just built in the city of Berlin. We were christened in different churches, chastened by different rules, bred in vying cultures and buttered with different history. All this would have to be explored and the demons within confronted, and that would only come about when the demons on the surface became more difficult to deal with than the demons below. On the surface we were friends, but below there was a dark cave we were afraid or unwilling to explore.

I came to believe that if I read less and thought less about these things, life would be simple again. It was easier to deal with the present by talking only of the weather, crops and fields – that's where we could reach agreement. But in the end, I decided to read everything I could get my hands on that would shed light on the dark place we had been landed in. A place, I was beginning to realize, which had been cleverly constructed to keep us all at each other's throats. The winners – the British – wrote the history, but the losers had all the good songs, and since both sides in the North were losers, we had a fair share of good songs between us.

My career as oc, however, was short lived. In fact, it was over before it really began. During the morning break of 17 May 1962, near the grotto where the statue of Our Lady was slowly ascending towards heaven by virtue of the volume of coins being placed beneath her, my contact and comrade confidentially broke the news.

'The IRA has called a ceasefire,' he announced.

I can't say that I wasn't relieved. Most of the volunteers were in jail, north and south of the border, and the people were fed up with the campaign. Although there was still sympathy for the eternal cause of gaining freedom for all of Ireland, and thousands had turned out to the funeral of Seán South, both the methods used and the meaning of freedom itself were seriously being called into question. Instead of uniting our people, which was the utopian aim, the campaign was causing a more bitter division amongst them. Most serious of all for me, was being involved in a war, albeit theoretically, against my own neighbours.

My friend instructed me to be always on standby for the call-up when the right time came. As it happened there would be another call-up to deal with, not from earthly beings this time, but from a higher authority.

Was it a picture in the post of a favourite and friendly smiling Uncle Tom under a banana tree in the Philippines, surrounded by beautiful girls and eternal sunshine, that influenced my thoughts on a cold grey winter morning in Ryan? Was it the sacred spell of Uncle Ben's charisma, even from beyond his grave in Jos, where thousands of Nigerian pilgrims were gathering each year? Was it the adventures and sufferings of Uncle Hugh as Mao Tse-tung's personal hostage in a cruel Chinese prison that blew some strange seeds of defiance my way to sail against the wind? Or was it feeling anxious to make the best of my life and the desire to give perfect happiness to traditional Irish Catholic parents?

Perhaps a mixture of all these things would send me off, prim and pimply faced, to proud St Patrick's College in Carlow. During the next five years, Ireland's oldest institute of philosophy and theology would leave me reasonably accomplished on five-string banjo, passable on guitar and mandolin, arm me with a thousand songs, spiritual, traditional and radical, and train me in the art of logic to prove beyond a shadow of reasonable doubt that a black pig was white. And my holidays at home would be filled with ploughing, praying, singing and playing with The Sands Family Folk Group.

Mary was now a qualified teacher and getting married to Queen's University graduate and the 'smartest man in Dungannon', Séamus Mac Pairc. Jimmy, as we called him, had a student colleague who was in the Nationalist Party. Austin Currie had been elected to Stormont and on his invitation I accompanied Jimmy to the visitors' gallery to watch a debate in the House.

The Nationalist Party had abandoned its abstentionist policy and agreed to be the official Opposition in the Northern parliament. Eddie Richardson, Nationalist member for South Armagh, was on his feet when we walked into the gallery. He had been an All-Ireland cycling champion in his youth and when he first came to Stormont Castle had ridden his bicycle up all of the sixty ceremonial stone steps that led to the great entrance hall. Now, however, his powers seemed extremely limited. He was complaining about discrimination against Catholics and the gerrymandering of constituencies to ensure Unionist votes but he was getting nowhere with his complaints. Loud shouts of derision were rising from the other side and I recognized prominent Unionists like Brian Faulkner and Ivan O'Neill leading the laughter. I remember being shocked and mesmerized. Perhaps this was the way politicians behaved with each other but I couldn't imagine such a scenario to be sustainable. One group was withholding decent living conditions from another simply because they were the majority group and had the power to do so. In all the years of Unionist rule only one measure proposed by the Opposition had ever passed into law, the rather uncontroversial 'wild bird act' of 1932. It seemed farcical. As I looked around the chamber, the powerlessness and frustration in the Nationalist ranks seemed evident on every face.

Although Catholics were having bigger families, few houses were being built in Catholic areas. They were also met with discrimination in the workplace, with jobs in the heavy industries traditionally reserved for Protestants. And most positions of power were filled by Protestants. In 1964, for example, the Youth Employment Board had only 3 Catholic members out of a total of 33; the Hospitals' Board had 2 Catholics out of 22; and the General Health and Services' Board had 2 out of 24.

I tackled my neighbour Tom Wilson about this worrying situation when I was helping him build a dry-stone wall at Davy Wright's place in Desert.

Tom was frank and honest with me, as he always was. 'If you were building a house,' he said, 'would you employ someone who would want to undermine its foundations? Catholics never wanted this house called Northern Ireland to be built. This house was for God and Ulster.'

His explanation made some sense, but what about God and Ireland? Our God wanted an Irish house for Irish people.

I decided to look into the whole franchise issue. In 1946 the Northern Ireland government passed the Elections and Franchise Act, which gave as much as six votes to one individual provided he satisfied the property qualification. Those who owned no property had no vote at all in local government elections. More Protestants owned property than Catholics, so the results were fairly clear-cut. Derry, for example, had a large Catholic majority, yet it was ruled by a Protestant council. It was also the case that not all Protestants were property owners and many of them were also deprived of the vote in local elections.

History had shown that it was in the interests of rich unionist landowners to keep both Catholic and Protestant working-class people in their place and this was best achieved by keeping them divided. At St Patrick's I was beginning to wonder if God really did give a damn what colour flag hung from a chimney. I soon concluded that whatever doubt there was about God's attitude to flags, there was no doubt whatsoever about the importance of flags to politicians when it came to election time.

Since the IRA had hung up their arms in 1962, there was now an opportunity to examine the lack of democracy in Northern Ireland without the distraction of republican violence. New methods of protest were being sought both within and without the republican movement.

During the 1963 bicentenary anniversary of the birth of United Irishman leader Theobald Wolfe Tone, a push began for democratic reform, which was taken up the following year by branches of the Connolly Association in London. In 1965 the mainly Protestant Belfast and District Trade Union Council called for one man, one vote and the repeal of the Special Powers Act.

In 1966 the fiftieth anniversary of the 1916 Rising was widely celebrated in the Irish Republic. Eamon de Valera, the Irish president and one of the leaders of the rebellion who had escaped execution because of his American citizenship, arrived at St Patrick's College and shook hands with us all. An Irish tricolour flew from his English Rolls Royce.

I noticed in the *Newry Reporter*, sent to me from home, that the Rising commemorations had been held in Newry too, and Dan Moore had got the usual prison sentence for carrying the tricolour at the head of the parade. Every year, if it wasn't Dan carrying the flag, it was his brother Gene, and one or the other was arrested and imprisoned for the offence on an annual basis. The Flags and Emblems Act had made it illegal to display the Irish flag or to interfere with the flying of the Union Jack.

I wrote a song called 'Ireland unfree shall never be at peace', which would be recorded by others and attributed to 'traditional' on future record sleeves. I didn't object. It wasn't safe to declare authorship of such sentiments and, besides, for your composition to be accepted as part of the tradition was more important than the few pounds of royalties it would earn.

Meanwhile people just kept getting on with their lives like they always did. Stormont kept on arguing about politics and The Sands Family kept on singing at wakes, weddings, pubs and concert halls. In so doing we would soon be meeting politicians of the future, but in the most unlikely of places.

The Fifteenth of August, the Feast of the Assumption, was our equivalent of the Twelfth of July, the turn of Catholics to celebrate, you might say. If we milked their Protestant cows on the Twelfth to give them a holiday, then, in return, they milked our Catholic cows on the Fifteenth. 'Make a day of it,' we would say to each other.

We hoped it wouldn't rain. If they got a good Twelfth, it would be all the more humiliating for us if it rained on the Fifteenth. If it did rain, however, we could always secretly rejoice in the fact that, unlike them, we hadn't lost a good day at the harvest due to the holiday. Like good Christians, we always saw the bright side to everything and it renewed our faith, if it needed any renewing, to know that God was still on our side and working in mysterious ways.

We marched behind the Hibernians and the Foresters not knowing much why, but when Big Barney Fitzpatrick of the Thomas Davis Pipe Band signalled the opening roll after high mass in Newry cathedral, something stirred deep inside. We were celebrating the Assumption of the Blessed Virgin, as the priest had said, but there was something more. It was the month of Lúnasa.

After mass we marched boldly in the direction of Warrenpoint – everyone from miles around went to the Point on the Fifteenth. There was a cure in the water if you went in before midday. Few swam, of course, but we took off our shoes and socks and rolled up our trousers and went for a paddle. If you happened to be a woman you pulled up your skirt instead, for few women wore trousers in those times. If you happened to be a woman wanting a baby, you stayed in until seven waves had passed around you. My mother already had seven children, so she didn't stay in the water any longer than was necessary.

'Were you in yet?' you'd say to a neighbour you met along the front. It was like being asked, 'Did you do your Easter duty?'

Christie McGuigan, the boatman, handed out a bottle of seawater to Auntie Maggie. She never went into the water, nor into a boat either. The memory of her uncle and aunt being drowned in the lough when the *Connemara and Retriever* crashed in 1919 may have been a reason.

'That'll be sixpence, Maggie,' shouted Christie with a chuckle.

Noticing that the tide was now well out, Maggie had her answer ready. 'Do you not think you have sold enough of it for one day, Christie?' she shouted back. 'There's hardly any water left.'

She thanked him well and headed home to wash her feet in the privacy of her own house, for no one underestimated the power of the tide on the Fifteenth.

Lúnasa was named after the ancient Celtic sun god, Lugh. County Louth was also named after Lugh and that's where we would be drawn to before the end of the day – over the salted border to Omeath. We'd take Christie McGuigan's boat across the lough and then head down the Carlingford Road to Calvary by horse and trap. A Celtic cross, with its circle of sun in the centre celebrating the meeting of old and new, stood quietly by as we whispered our way around the stations of the cross.

Now, ready for anything, we sucked on sugar sticks and bought butter to smuggle home. Swirling seagulls watched as white-skulled customs men in Warrenpoint searched the handbags of honest women, so innocent that butter wouldn't melt in their mouths. Some were so nervous that occasionally it did melt in their drawers. Laughing and giggling, young and old, we scrambled out of the small boat, up the shore and back to the amusements of the town.

The men headed for the pub. For some, it was the only day they drank strong liquor all year and their lack of practice often left trails of regurgitated Guinness and undigested sugar sticks to mark their progress around the town. In 1966 many headed for The Ship, a new singing pub owned by Christy Mallon from Dungannon. A young group played there that people were talking about. They were called The Sands Family.

The Sands Family, 1966: Ben, Tommy, Anne, Piper, Col and Dino (photo John Boyle)

That day The Ship was full and all who sailed in her were full too. There were two barmen keeping an eye on the proceedings and making sure that everyone was satisfied and no one was surpassing such satisfaction. One was called Séamus Mallon, a fine big man who was a teacher and an Armagh county footballer. Another equally fine strapping fellow was lending a hand, for with drink in and wit out there might be some bouncing to be done. He was from the Dungannon direction, we were told, and his name was Ken Maginnis. Both men were dressed in white shirts and red ties and they could have passed as brothers to the unfocused eye. Many's an eye was unfocused on the Fifteenth of August.

We had launched into 'The rocks of bonnie Gibraltar', and Ben was singing it with the fiddle under his chin. Jamie O'Hara, who taught us the song from the back of his Ford Ferguson tractor, was proudly standing in front of the bar, righteously rinsing his palate with Black Bush. My father was dancing with Aggie McConville, the thresherman's wife, and Christy Gilmore, known to the world as Gilly, was doing cartwheels up and down between the tables as Dino banjoed into 'The mason's apron'.

I scanned the crowd. We knew our audience, most of them personally. Many were neighbours' faces with a fortune of stories to tell and as many more that would never be told. The man they called Baldy Gribben was there with more hair on his head than anyone else, and so was Wee Hughie O'Hare, who would later do his party piece, standing on his head. Other neighbours included Bow Wow Butterfield, who spoke in a low gruff voice; Liam Daly, who spoke only internally when he was out; and a man they called the 'Human Dog'. That name had stuck to him since the time the circus had come to town thirty years before. As a finale that year, the circus management, in their wisdom, had offered a pound note to any man who would fight the brown bear. The bear and his Russian trainer had been standing at the side of the ring during the performance weighing up any possible opposition. He seldom had any. Some men, drunk or badly in need of a pound or both, would sign up but quickly scurry out of the ring as soon as the bear came within roaring distance. Not so the Human Dog. He stayed his ground and shocked the crowd, the Russian and, more importantly, the brown bear, with a sudden wellington boot up between the legs. The bear went down with a grunt and a groan and was further surprised to find itself pinned to the ground with a dungareed knee on its Adam's apple. The trainer, thinking his bear was going to be choked entirely, declared above roars of man and beast, 'Stop zee fight, stop zee fight, that eez not a man, truly that eez the human dog.' The Russian, the bear and the circus people packed up in a hurry and headed down the Dublin Road in search of less threatening opposition. No one knew precisely what a 'human dog' was but the name stuck.

The Human Dog had a reputation to defend and the Fifteenth might be as good a day as any. Given the clientele in The Ship and the day that was in it, a rumpus of some sort was not to be unexpected and we had prepared accordingly with a ready mixture of music, story and song to appease here and cajole there. What we did not expect, however, was that the trouble would come from the quietest man in the house.

Liam Daly was drinking whiskey as we struck up 'Skibbereen'. The Famine song awakened a native emotion, deep and unresolved, within Liam's breast, and he began accusing some big man, 'with your fancy English accent', of having stolen his land. The poor man was not English nor had he an English accent. His only mistake, it seems, was to have chosen the wrong weekend to try out a new pair of dentures. Admittedly he did sound different but for Liam, it was as close to an English accent as was necessary at that moment of time.

It was one of those days, I suppose, when ordinary decent men get a bit twisty with whiskey and form wrong conclusions. Soon two good Christians were rolling on the floor and three good tables of Christian drink were flying in the air. The big man got to his feet, quite toothless now but much more articulate in his vernacular. The string of curses that followed would have brought blushes from a trouper. Ken Maginnis heard the commotion and felt spits landing on his red tie. He saw what looked like a lunatic cursing the world in general. There were no visible signs of an object for such bile, for Liam, having done his bit for Ireland, had slipped into some kind of satisfied coma under Bow Wow Butterfield's table, one of the few still standing.

'That's enough out of you, ye boy ye,' shouted Ken, 'or you'll be looking in through that window from the other side.'

Ken Maginnis moved quickly. He grabbed the big man by the scruff of the neck and the backsides of the trousers and bellied him out on to the street like a busted bale of badly saved hay. 'And don't ever come back within a drunkard's gowl of this place with your fighting and your spilling of good drink.'

The man slowly gathered himself up, or whatever he could find of himself. He

In The Ship: (standing) *Dino, Ben, Colum, Anne, Tommy*
(sitting) *Christy Mallon, Séamus Mallon, Mick Sands, Jamie O'Hara*
(photo John Boyle)

was beginning to look like a bad cowboy in the Savoy cinema on a Saturday night who would do damage before the credits came up. He grinned a ghastly grin through emancipated gums. 'I'll get you again, ye boy ye, for throwing me out in the wrong. I might be drunk but I never forget a face.' He staggered up the street like a man whose time had not yet come, with the suspicious eye of Ken Maginnis still trained on the back of his head.

It was during Anne's rendition of 'The quiet land of Erin' that the attention of the audience seemed to wander once again, this time down towards the door where another wrecking match was beginning to get into its stride. Séamus was on the ground, apparently having been surprised by a rabbit punch from a certain returnee, full on revenge and short on teeth. 'I never forget a face,' he was shouting.

Séamus got to his feet and did whatever had to be done at the door. Slowly he walked back in with a smile on his face and to great applause from the Bridge boys, whose glasses were now happily full and out of harm's way.

'Will you come up and give us a song, Séamus?' I shouted, sensing the focus of the crowd's desire.

'I haven't the wind for a song,' he said, 'but I'll give you a recitation instead.'

He stood at the microphone and a silence fell over the place. Even Liam Daly, senseless now for the best part of an hour, opened one eye.

Séamus whipped off the offending red tie that had become the millstone round his neck, flung it at the chuckling Ken, and reminisced empathetically and dramatically with a poet called Robert Service.

> A bunch of the boys were whooping it up in the Malamute saloon;
> The kid that handles the music-box was hitting a jag-time tune;
> Back of the bar, in a solo game, sat Dangerous Dan McGrew,
> And watching his luck was his light-o'-love, the lady that's known as Lou.

Maybe events like this one cemented both the friendship and the rivalry between the two barmen and would stand them in good stead for the days of deep division that lay ahead.

Maginnis, like any good law-abiding Protestant unionist, would soon join the Ulster Defence Regiment, become the deputy leader of the Ulster Unionist Party, and would eventually sit as Lord Maginnis in the British House of Lords.

Mallon, like any good justice-seeking Catholic nationalist, would join the emerging civil rights movement. Later he would be elected MP for Armagh, become deputy leader of the Social Democratic and Labour Party and eventually become Deputy First Minister in the new Northern Ireland Assembly in 1998.

On the Fifteenth of August 1966, such developments were far from our minds. There were more immediate tasks at hand.

'Ken, give no more drink to that man under the table!'

'All right, Séamus!'

'And you, Sands Family! Keep singing for God's sake.'

> Here's to the boys who are happy and gay
> Singing and dancing and tearing away
> Rollick some frolicsome frisky and free
> We're the rollicking boys around Tanderagee.

8

Record Time

'He near put the heart crossways in me, to tell you the truth, landing in on top of me and me sitting in the middle of my dinner at the time.' That was the gist of my mother's announcement and we all knew it had been the sudden arrival of a telegram boy that she was talking about.

The very sight of a telegram boy was enough to fill any house with dread. Just an innocent anonymous boy on a bike, you might say, but the tidings he bore were sometimes shattering and life-changing. The death of someone in America, perhaps, or God knows what.

'It says, "Ring Mark",' she said.

I got on the bike and rode the three miles to the public phone box at May-obridge. I would have arrived in record time too, if I hadn't been forced to stop at Mooney's Corner and Fegan's Close to inflate the back tyre. When I did arrive I discovered the phone was out of order.

'Try the one outside the Orchard bar,' suggested Big Patsy Finnegan and Wee Tarry Flanagan, who were witnessing my bare-knuckled quarrel with Button 'A' through the missing windowpane of the red telephone box. I had lost the guts of half a crown in that box. The Orchard Bar was five miles away. It would be five miles of wondering what the news from Mark McLoughlin might be.

It was difficult to guess – Mark was a man of many parts with a finger in many pies. He owned a pub in Dundalk, hosted great music sessions, and his place had become our favourite haunt. None of us drank alcohol at the time, except 'the eldest of the boys', as our father, the Chief, described himself, who drank enough for us all. People walked in as strangers and walked out as friends, united by the rhythm and warmth of Peter McArdle's fiddle and the many music-makers happily gathered around him. Regular visitors included the Clancys, Tommy Makem, the Dubliners, the Fureys, Judy Felix, Maeve Mulvenny, Butch Moore, and every guest musician who performed in Dundalk town hall, for Mark's was the place to be for the famous session afterwards. When Peter died, hundreds of musicians attended his funeral and I wrote a song to help raise some money for a special headstone:

> There was Peter sitting in the corner, fiddle in his hand,
> Playing away like you never did hear and you'll never hear again,
> Charlie on the banjo, Shorty on the bodhrán, everything was grand,
> Come on Mark and let me in, I want to join the band.

> But then the time said 'Gentlemen please' and the gentlemen did go,
> Some of us might stay a while and sing songs very low.
> Then Peter he'd play one last tune and put away the bow
> But his fiddle is still playing no matter where you go.

Closing time at eleven-thirty was very strict, but not if you happened to be a friend of the house and heard Mark's whisper in your ear, 'Just go to the toilet and wait there and keep very quiet.' And when you squeezed into the toilet, you discovered maybe forty others, all jammed in there and waiting for the two or three 'outsiders' at the bar to leave. There was a secret knock to gain admission after hours, which gave shape to a tune composed by Olcan Masterson called 'The knock on the door'.

Mark could justifiably be called a character. He could have fitted nicely into the role of the big lad in that Blues Brothers film if there hadn't been so much running about to be done or as many high notes to hit. Mark moved more slowly and sang with a deep voice, especially late at night when the pub was closed and the bar was open. He was the eldest of twenty children and when he was young, to make ends meet, his father and himself had taken over a run-down factory in the west of Ireland that was full of unsold statues of Blessed Martin de Porres. There would be those who would tell you that it was partly as a result of the Vatican being leaned upon by the McLoughlins that Blessed Martin suddenly out of the blue became St Martin. In no time there wasn't a parish priest or a reverend mother in the thirty-two counties of Ireland who wouldn't give an eye tooth or more importantly, its equivalent in cash, to have a statue of the new saint standing proudly and piously in their midst. Others said that the McLoughlins were just lucky and that good people make their own luck. Certainly Mark was a kind man and if he hadn't anything good to say he would say nothing. That's why the pedals drove me onwards, down the Newry Road, past Edenmore (the brow of the hill), Derryleckagh (the stony oak-wood), and round by Crown Mound (the fort of the Cruithin), to hear what it was he would say.

When the conflict started and the border town of Dundalk was labelled El Paso by the media because of the many political activists and mysterious strays who gathered there, Mark had the old door of Dundalk jail house put onto his pub, just for safety. The door had a peephole, to check the suitability of would-be customers. One night a bullet came through that peephole and buried itself in the stairs. It was meant for the man who was in the process of re-forming the Official Republican Movement into a left-wing, working-class political party. Cathal Goulding, a friend of Mark's, was having a drink at the bar that night. When the gunman was arrested, it was Mark who found a lawyer to defend him. He was that kind of man and it was that kind of pub. I often saw embittered enemies eyeing each other over tables crowded with drink, while their toes tapped in unison to a jig as impulsive as themselves and as old as the trouble that engulfed us.

Mark liked our songs and had introduced us to many friends of music and intrigue who then invited us to play in all sorts of places. That's how we met John Joe McGirl, for example, and later played in his town of Ballinamore. John Joe was not only a well-known publican but a well-known republican too. He was also a well-known undertaker and the contents of his coffins, which often had occasion to cross the border, sometimes attracted the attention of customs men.

In Mark's we met with Tom Slevin, who brought us to his 'Oul' House' in Belfast's Albert Street, where we first befriended the great McPeake Family and Seán McGuire, the fiddler. Through Mark we played for the National Graves Association in Dublin's Gresham Hotel and Liberty Hall, and in Mick McCarthy's famous Embankment we did concerts in memory of a dead patriot called 'Skin the Goat'. We were all mostly skint ourselves, but money was rarely talked about. We just wanted to play and meet the other singers and musicians. In Dublin every pub was buzzing with the music of what was and what could be.

At Liberty Hall there was always a great sense of political awareness. One night at a Skin the Goat concert Kathleen Behan came up on stage with a pint of Guinness and sang with us. Her brother Peadar Kearney had written 'The soldier's song', the Irish national anthem, and her son Dominic had written 'The patriot game'. Her other wild son, Brendan, had written *The Hostage* and *The Quare Fellow*. Seán Garland, who had been part of the 'patriot game' on the night Fergal O'Hanlon and Seán South were shot, still had a limp from his bullet wounds. 'Any fool can learn from his own mistakes,' he told us, 'but it takes a wise one to learn from someone else's.' He was standing beside Cathal Goulding and they were sharing lessons learned in prison and speaking about international socialism and the importance of uniting the working classes. Songs that reflected that hope were much to the fore at those sessions, but for Mark any song that sang of love for a common place was itself an indication of shared pride and unity. He was anxious that such songs be taken down and handed on to a new generation. As I rode onwards I could feel a litany of local ballads leaping out of the hedges and ditches that ran alongside, behind and before me. 'The maid of Ballydoo', 'The ghost of Edenmore', 'Rathfriland on the hill', 'Mourne rambler' – all with a story to tell of a living tradition and many more that were hardly known outside the neighbourhood and might well fade away if left unnourished.

Five miles, four tyrefuls of air and tenpence later, outside the Orchard Bar in Saval, I heard Mark pick up the phone in Dundalk. 'Billy McBurney of Outlet

The Sands Family in the Long Field. In the background left is Tom and Nora Wilson's house; to the right of it is Wee Willy Wilson and Willie McMullan's (photo John Boyle)

records in Belfast wants you to send him a tape of yourselves,' he said. 'He wants to make an LP of The Sands Family.'

I couldn't believe it. We were going to make a record. It would be a record of this stony, storied land that grew us. I couldn't wait to bring home the news. The bike was on the rims as I freewheeled into the street.

'We just have to find a tape recorder,' I announced the next day as we sat for a sober meeting on the cement seat where the roses grew in the summer.

'We'll have to find electricity too,' said Ben. There was still no electricity in the townland of Ryan.

'What about the engine of thon thing Pat and Mary Ann have for milking the cows?' suggested the Chief. 'It can run a milking machine, so it might run the tape recorder.'

In a few days we were walking along the Crossan Road, loaded down with a big Grundig tape recorder, a microphone and a reel of recording tape, just in time for the milking.

McBurney told us later that he had never heard a sound quite like it. 'Rathfriland on the hill', 'Mourne Maggie' and 'The rocks of bonnie Gibraltar' were not only accompanied by the high-pitched strains of fiddle, whistle and guitar, but also the low purring noise of an AC generator, the rattling of chains, the shaking of hay, and cows bawing inquisitively in the background.

'That's a good wee girl,' Mary Ann's coaxing voice could be heard on the tape from time to time, more interested in releasing the milk yield than with her mad cousins releasing records. The idea of making a living from this music was fairly unbelievable to the neighbours and, if the truth were told, it was fairly unbelievable to us as well.

When we went to record in Belfast, it was a very different experience. The studio was not prepared for us and we were even less prepared for a studio. We had to record the musical backing for the songs first, without singing, and then sing to the musical backing coming out of a loudspeaker, without playing.

'This is the new way of doing things,' said Cel Fay, the engineer, wrestling with the first sixteen-track tape-recorder in the city. Things had been more homely in Brennan's byre. This was all too new for us, and although the results were not quite what either Cel or ourselves would have wanted, we were now recording stars and *Folk from the Mournes* was in the shops.

A big night was planned for The Ship. Séamus Mallon brought along Birdy Sweeney, the comedian from Dungannon to be MC, and with relations, friends and neighbours raring for any excuse for a hooley, there was very little drink left to be spilt when the cry, 'Have youse no homes to go to?' split the salted air.

We heard ourselves on the radio, on the very same wireless that broadcast the voices of Mícheál Ó Hehir, Count John McCormack, Lonnie Donegan, Dinjo, Mary O'Hara, The Clancy Brothers, President Kennedy and Pope John XXIII. Dolly McMahon, the singer, was speaking about us and playing our music and my mother was so happy to hear it, she was speechless. The Chief was delighted too. He went out, pulled a hen's neck and made soup 'for all hands'. Meanwhile people all around Ireland were listening with no little surprise as melodies of Mayobridge, Hiltown and Rathfriland landed in on top of them and they maybe 'sitting in the middle of their dinner at the time'.

9
Civil Rights

One January night in 1969 Louis Boyle, the taxi man, gave my father a lift home from Newry. 'Come on in, Louis, ye oul' rascal ye, till you hear some good music,' the Chief said.

The invitation suited Louis fine and he landed in the kitchen with a pipe in one hand and the Chief's carry-out in the other. It suited my father even better. He didn't want to be asked about pigs, at least not straightaway. A human shield would come in useful.

The previous night we had washed five pigs in buttermilk to make them look clean and gleaming for the fair in Camlough. It had all been very businesslike. Ginger Graham had come in good time with tractor and small trailer. The idea was to sell the pigs and bring home the money. A song, however, of past woes to divert attention from present trivialities was the first sure sign of where much of the pig money had gone.

> Ah, the Banshee cried when young Donal died,
> At the Valley of Knockanure.

'Would somebody give Louis Boyle a drink, for God's sake,' said my father, as if it was part of the song, 'for Louis Boyle is a gentleman, a scholar and a judge of good whiskey.'

Roughly translated, that meant, 'Would Louis Boyle give me a drink quick, for I'm parched.'

As Louis looked into the brown paper bag, the door opened and Liam Daly and Tom Wilson slowly entered at a safe speed.

'You left your beef in the taxi, Mick,' they said, helpfully handing over a blood-stained parcel.

'Swing the pan, Anne,' said the Chief. 'There's enough grub here for the townland. We're going to celebrate tonight, for Louis's son is going to be the next prime minister.' If you can't beat them, join them, thought Anne, reaching for the pan, and Dino began reluctantly to tune the mandolin.

Louis Boyle, junior, had joined the Unionist Party. He was bright, intelligent and represented a new generation of educated Catholics. Ever since Terence O'Neill had become prime minister and had met with Seán Lemass, the Republic's taoiseach, in 1965, a new mood was in the air. The Nationalist Party was the Opposition in Stormont and many Catholics, rather than pushing for a united Ireland, felt they could be content in the North, provided power was shared with their politicians in a reformed Northern state.

Many Unionists were against such change, and some feared it. Ultra-Unionist Ian Paisley warned that power-sharing with nationalists was a road to a united Ireland under the influence of the Pope of Rome. The Ulster Volunteer Force, which had ceased its activities in 1920, re-formed to target republicans, but soon settled for an any-Catholic-will-do policy. In 1966 UVF leader Gusty Spence, whose very name struck dread into many of us, was sentenced to life imprisonment for the shooting dead of Peter Ward, a young Catholic barman, in Belfast.

Louis didn't join in the liquid celebrations. He was driving, he said, 'and the breathalyser might be on the road'. He took a mug of tea instead and lit up his pipe.

'Aye, young Louis,' he said. 'He wants to try to change things from the inside. The second lad wouldn't have the same patience though.'

Louis's second son, Kevin, was in the radical People's Democracy, which was involved in the organization of a big civil-rights march planned for the end of the week in Newry. The campaign for change had been brewing for a long time. The previous June another straw had been added to the camel's back in Caledon, County Tyrone, when a house was allocated to a nineteen-year-old single Protestant woman in preference to a family of Catholics. Austin Currie had raised the issue in Stormont, but when he got no satisfaction, he took his protest, with a Brantry republican group, to squat in the house in question. Suddenly it seemed that all the pressure groupings had come together and the Northern Ireland Civil Rights Association was launched. Initially it was concerned with housing issues. There was a joke going round that Christmas.

'Why was Jesus born in a stable?'

'Because the Protestants had all the houses, that's why.'

The mention of civil rights was a source of silent contention in mixed company. I looked at Tom Wilson. Troublemakers, he could have said, but he said nothing. Peacemakers, would have been my father's description, but he too said nothing.

'Give us a rake o' reels,' he said at last, and before you knew it, toes were tapping to the lively rhythm of 'The pigeon on the gate' and 'The loanin with no turning'.

They were both right perhaps. On the journey to peace there would be a lot of trouble. It would last much longer than we feared and begin much sooner than we expected.

All the drink was gone now and so was everyone else, except the Chief and I.

'What about the pigs?' I asked.

'It's a long story,' he said, with his head in his hands. 'Will you give that plug of tobacco to one of Louis's lads at the march on Saturday?' he added. 'He might be needing it.'

'I will,' I said, 'if they've time to take it from me.'

'Nobody has time nowadays,' he said. 'Nobody has time for nobody.'

On the day of the march, I met Frank Feely, my old history teacher, outside the Boulevard Hotel in Newry. He seemed younger now than he was when he taught me.

'Are you coming to write some history?' he asked, as we headed towards Monaghan Street and the starting-point for the march. Hundreds were walking in the same direction, in ones and twos, and threes and fours, all with a common purpose. Like going to a football match. There were no flags but many different colours of opinion. Some stood in a huddle and wondered if they should be seen marching at all. Some didn't want to offend Protestant neighbours. Some were Protestant neighbours.

It was the second Saturday in the new year and it looked like rain.

'It's hard to trust it,' said Frank, looking doubtfully at the sky.

I recalled the story of an old woman watching the rain as it began to fall on a Corpus Christi procession in Mayobridge. She shrugged her shoulders with reverence but without sympathy. 'He's only bringing it on himself, you know,' says she, 'and him the only one who can stop it.'

Feely laughed. 'It's like this government we have,' he said. 'They have no idea how to deal with legitimate protest.'

He talked about the first civil-rights march from Coalisland to Dungannon, the previous August. 'A small group of people, fed up with writing to government ministers and newspaper editors about unfair housing, decided to take to the streets instead. And what does the government do? Instead of dealing with the message that's obvious to everyone, they simply brand the messengers subversives.'

It was like being back in his class again, except that history had now sneaked up behind us.

Paddy O'Hanlon was just ahead of us. He used to sing at the back of the bus going to school and had also been taught by Frank. He looked round, 'You're not in Colman's now, Frank,' he teased, 'but you're right, you know. If their bigotry was not surpassed by their stupidity, they would have made a move years ago.'

Gary Mills, a Protestant from Belfast, was with Paddy. 'It's easy to say that,' he said, 'but O'Neill can't rush this with Craig and the rest around his neck. The government must be given time.'

'What! Another fifty years, you mean?' said Séamus Ruddy. 'The government doesn't have time. If peaceful revolution is attacked, then violent revolution will defend.'

'Maybe violence is the only answer after all,' someone said. 'I doubt if they understand anything else.'

'Or maybe they do,' said O'Hanlon. 'Perhaps the government *wants* trouble to happen. They are well equipped to deal with violence, but ill equipped to deal with peace.'

'It's all about strategy,' said Sean Hollywood emphatically. 'I can see the script writing itself.' Sean taught English in St Colman's, played hurling and wrote plays.

After the Coalisland–Dungannon march, the protest had been taken to Derry in October, and the march there had been banned by the government and attacked by the police. Six long years of O'Neill diplomacy in Stormont were undone by six minutes of swinging police truncheons on television. Gerry Fitt, the West Belfast Labour MP, had brought his injuries with him to Westminster and repercussions were already under way.

The Derry campaigners had reacted by forming the Derry Citizens' Action Committee under the chairmanship of Ivan Cooper, a Protestant businessman, with John Hume, a Catholic schoolteacher, as his deputy. Shocked students just back from the holidays at Queen's University spontaneously marched around the city hall in Belfast and staged a sit-down in Linenhall Street. They had formed themselves into the People's Democracy. Their views were articulated by people like Bernadette Devlin, Michael Farrell, Cyril Toman and Kevin Boyle.

We were well used to marches, both Orange and green. Usually government ministers marched in the Orange parades and banned the green ones, which didn't impress the nationalists, of course. Unionists viewed any organization with a tint of green as being subversive and intent on overthrowing the state. The first civil-rights march was of neither colour. It was about housing reform, not the abolition of the state.

In Newry that day there were Catholics from south Armagh, Irish and proud, who wanted a job, any job. There were Protestants of no property from Portadown, British and true, who wanted a vote, 'one man, one vote'. Graduates from Queen's, whose qualifications had been won by ability rather than privilege, chanted, 'Revolution, revolution!' And I recognized a few of the lads from threshers at home, who just liked the excitement and maybe a bottle of stout at the end of it all. A huge crowd had already gathered at the far end of Monaghan Street. There were old and young, men and women, rich and poor, and some were singing as if it were a festival. The atmosphere was great.

'How will it turn out, do you think?' I asked Tom Moore.

Tom was the quiet one in the Moore family – it was his brothers Dan and Gene who took their turn in prison from year to year for carrying the tricolour at the Easter parades. But quiet and all as Tom was, he would end up in Long Kesh when internment was introduced, just for being a Moore.

'I hope there's no trouble,' he said. 'That's the last thing we want.'

We marched up the street in our thousands, holding hands and singing 'We shall overcome', all inspired by the pacifism of Martin Luther King. It was great to be young and up against authority. It was even better to challenge authority and know we were right.

The plan was to walk around the Savoy cinema, down Merchant's Quay and round by Sugar Island. That had been the route of a smaller march a few months earlier. It had been confronted by Protestant youths singing 'The sash' and marchers had taken up the Orange anthem, believing they were campaigning for the benefit of working-class Protestants as well. But we knew this time that the route would be out of bounds. A hardline loyalist and ex-British army Major from Belfast called Ronald Bunting had threatened a counter demonstration if the march was allowed in that part of Newry. A line of police tenders and barricades were drawn up beside the Savoy and a sea of police officers and B Specials were spread out behind it in full riot gear. We could walk no further, so we sat down instead, the whole length of Monaghan Street sat down, and began to sing.

John Hume stood up and called for order; then Éamonn McCann stood up and called for disorder. Bernadette Devlin, Paddy Devlin and Gerry Fitt all had their own things to say, but in the end they were united in demanding a new beginning.

It rained and we sang 'We shall not be moved'. We sat there, an army dressed in faded jeans and sandals, with the world at our feet and the might of the British Empire watching and waiting. It was getting dark now and the traffic lights painted us green and red, with a brief orange in-between, reflecting the political affiliations of the crowd fairly accurately. On the other side of the cordon, orange was the prevailing politic among the darkened uniforms of the RUC and B men. The air was becoming dense with tension and waiting.

'SS RUC,' someone began to shout, and then the chant was taken up by the crowd. 'SS RUC!' It had been well practised in Derry when the marchers were beaten with batons.

Later people would say that the government had wanted the police to be attacked in Newry that day, to show the world that the civil rights movement was not a peaceful organization, as it claimed, but full of militant republicans and wild anarchists. High above Kevin Boyle's head, on a telegraph pole, hung the remnants of a red and black flag, the traditional colours of anarchy. For Newry, though, they were the colours of County Down, who were the current All-Ireland Gaelic football champions. I wanted to say to Kevin that I had his father's tobacco in my pocket, but it didn't seem the right moment.

Everything looked different now and unfamiliar. Perhaps it was the mixture of the lights, the growing darkness and the rain. Monaghan Street wasn't Monaghan Street. The wee corner café where we got soup on Saturdays seemed lost behind the strangers sitting on its window sill and leaning against its wall. It was like a movie in some far-off place. The Savoy cinema, where we had watched cowboys and Indians battling it out, now looked like the setting for another battle about to be played out much closer to home.

Then someone threw a stone. I turned my head to see where it came from and only saw more heads turning for the same reason. The clunk of the stone on the policeman's shield echoed around in the still air. Everyone feared that a night of trouble was brewing. The police and B Specials stood unmoving behind the barricades, their pale faces coloured only with a mixture of fear and fury. We all knew they would charge, sooner or later.

'No!' shouted O'Hanlon. 'They have better sticks and stones than we have. We cannot win that way. We can only win by peaceful methods.'

Someone shouted, 'We have tried peace for years and it has got us nowhere. No one listens to peace.'

What happened next would be reported in predictable versions in rival morning papers, but the first casualty – truth – had already been wrestled to the ground long before a stone was flung or a baton flew. All I remember is running and running, everywhere, nowhere and anywhere, to avoid the head blows of a B man's baton. To remonstrate with a threshing truncheon would have been as useful as talking to a flying stone and there were now plenty of both bouncing about in abundance. Hostile greetings of 'Orange bastard!' and 'Fenian bastard!' were now being traded in the old traditional way. I could smell smoke. Police tenders had been seized beside the canal and set alight. They ran on diesel and they didn't burn quickly enough, so they were pushed into the canal instead. The police made no attempt to rescue them.

On television people watched as a cameraman zoomed in on a burning tyre and suddenly the whole world was on fire. The government could now claim that this was a violent movement. They were as right as they were wrong. On that cold January, we students returned to college with the first page of a new chapter of history to discuss. The remaining pages were still blank.

IO

Walking On

Professor P.J. (Pa) Brophy swept in like a bald 6′2″ eagle, his flowing toga, beaded and braided, brushed scoldingly against the door cheeks of Carlow's main lecture hall. He preferred open spaces.

'We know what we are, but know not what we may be.' He was quoting from Shakespeare and speaking of change.

P.J. Curley beside me whispered under his breath, 'If thou lookest for change, search thee not in the new vending machine.'

Pa didn't hear. He didn't like coffee much either. He had other ways of getting high. He was just getting into his stride. 'It seems there is no one more anti-clerical than a clerical student,' he said. 'Like many radical university students, however, who will soon become establishment lawyers and conservative doctors, you, in your turn, will become fat parish priests insisting that things should be done your way and your way only. You will become like little institutions bowing and scraping to man-made rules which have got nothing to do with your calling. Gentlemen, it is time to cast aside meaningless power structures and get back to where it began.'

He was talking about Vatican Two. Wasn't everybody? Back home, they were talking about the Second Vatican Council as well. Pope John xxiii had made a big impression. Even the Protestant neighbours were saying, 'He's not a bad wee man,' and coming from that quarter, that was a compliment and a half.

'If the people won't come to the Church,' Pa was saying, 'then the Church must be brought to the people, for the people are the Church.' He looked around the hall, scrutinizing our faces. 'I don't intend to detain you long,' he said finally.

'As Henry the Eighth said to the wife,' somebody muttered.

Lectures from Pa at times provoked such responses but always sent us out meandering with a mindful of questions.

'For as St Francis said,' he continued, 'one should preach the gospel but only speak when necessary.'

He seemed such a rebel yet managed to remain personally content within such unloved confines and structures. Perhaps he enjoyed the discipline of it all. He spoke of the early Irish church living not within walls but outside of walls with the wind and the rain, the grass and the waves and the places where people were. Then cardinals and kings had tried to capture religion and control it indoors and people were left out in the cold. Vatican Two wanted to bring the laity back in again. For those long gone the shock was too much.

Some didn't want to come in – they wanted the mystery of it all to continue. But now the altar was facing the people. The men at home were especially sceptical about that move. Not only could the priest see you coming in late, he could see you going out early as well. They harkened back to when they could kneel on their caps at the back of the chapel, near the holy water font, say their beads in peace and slip out for the odd Woodbine to help them with their nerves in between decades. The new liturgy was putting an end to all that sort of carry-on. Reason was encroaching upon mystery. Some thought that reason could make but a poor stab at understanding religion. It was like going to the well with a pitchfork.

'We're getting more like Protestants every day,' mumbled Buster Lyons, as he was herded up the chapel, like a Christian walking the plank. Buster was even asked to participate, along with the priest, in the lifting of the collection. 'I will,' says he, 'providing I get half of the gate.'

'I am the Good Shepherd. I know mine and mine know me,' Pa was saying. 'The Church must be meaningful to the world and you must be meaningful to the people. We can no longer stand on ceremony. The Christian message is about love, everything else is irrelevant. All you need is love. You can fill libraries with Theology and fight wars about Dogma. Princes and kings can clamour for the high ground of righteousness but at the end of the day all you need is love.'

Such a musical parting seemed a good cue for the next lecturer, piano-playing history professor Joseph Coulter. He was a cool dude who talked out of the side of his mouth, like any good Derry man, almost conspiratorially. His brother Phil's song 'Puppet on a string' had just won the Eurovision song contest for a long-legged English girl, in bare feet, called Sandy Shaw. Joe's job was to lay bare the hands that had long pulled the strings of power, both religious and political, in Ireland and elsewhere.

'History comes from the Greek word *historia*,' he said. 'It is not just a collection of facts that have been passed on, nor, for that matter' – this out of the side of his mouth – 'a collaboration of lies that have been agreed upon. *Historia* means an "enquiry into".'

Inspired, I decided to enquire a little myself. I went to the library and was closing the door quietly behind me when I noticed a yellowing piece of paper pinned rustily to the back of it. It read: 'To remove a book from this library is an offence punishable by excommunication from the Church.' A little on the extreme side, I thought, especially now that Vatican Two had arrived. Some archaic rules and traditions lingered on no matter what else had changed in the process of time.

I thought about Aunt Sally's story about tradition.

'I always cut the roast in two before cooking it', she said, 'because it was a tradition in the family to do it that way.'

One day she asked her mother, 'Why do we always cut the roast in two at Christmas?'

'Because your granny always did it like that,' came the reply.

Then Aunt Sally asked her granny about it.

'Child dear, I cut it in half because the dish I had was too small, that's why,' she said. In a few short years, practical actions had become sacred traditions.

I reached for an old book covered in cobwebs and started to read. It told of years stretching back to the early days of the Irish Church.

When fifth-century Romans went hammer and tongs at battering out rules for Christianity, the sparks that flew were both colourful and contentious. Augustine of Hippo, a product of the Roman Empire, thought hierarchical thoughts, and for him all power came from on high. For Pelagius, the Celt, however, the sacred power of Nature and the presence of God were to be seen and felt all around us. The two views clashed but Augustine's prevailed and held sway wherever the Romans reigned supreme. Since the Romans never made it to Ireland to interfere with the traditional ways, the Church in Ireland quietly found its own ways in the well-ploughed furrows of Celtic spirituality. There were no Christian martyrs in Ireland when Patrick came. The druids found they were able to accept the new religion without any great shock to the system. Gods and goddesses of nature were quietly canonized. Pelagius had more relevance here than Augustine. Columba's chants, which referred to God as the 'Great White Sun' and to Christ as 'My druid', were as natural as morning turning to day.

But slowly the day wore on and there was very little sign of money making its way back to the coffers of Rome from the Christians of Ireland. The bishop's lofty mitre carried less weight among the earthy Irish than the well-grounded monasteries, and Rome was not amused. Crusades had already been unleashed to rein in the wayward, but it was only when an Englishman became Pope that plans to bring Ireland into the fold began to emerge.

In 1154 Nicholas Breakspear, an Englishman of Saxon extraction, had croziered his way through the ranks of his Norman betters to reach Rome and when the whiff of white Vatican smoke curled towards the heavens, he would become known to the world as Pope Adrian IV.

Now was the time to solve the 'Irish question' once and for all. In 1156 he issued a *Laudabiliter*, a papal bull approving Henry II's planned conquest of Ireland in the name of God. When Dermott McMurragh of Leinster invited the Anglo-Norman Strongbow to help him out in a local row in 1170, the final pieces of the jigsaw began to fall into place. Soon Ireland would be Roman Catholic, thanks to the English, and would remain so until another Henry would cast a roving eye on Anne Boleyn.

Then they would try to impose Protestantism on the country, but that would be another story.

I left the old library, making sure to leave the book behind me. I didn't want to be excommunicated. I walked along the corridor and heard Odetta and Harry Belafonte sing 'the hole in the bucket' through a crack in Pa Brophy's door. I would later sing with them both. 'Well fix it dear Henry, dear Henry fix it.'

The sad September wind sent a gentle shiver through the honeysuckle, bucky briars and robin-run-the-hedge, which were bunching together along the roadside as far as the eye could see. I didn't want to see that far. I looked down at my black shoes. Sometimes they seemed to slow down, fearful of the freedom that lay ahead; and sometimes they speeded up, as if being followed by a ghost. The future had deserted me.

Another car stopped. 'Would you like a lift?' a voice said.

Isn't it always the way that whenever you want a lift no one will stop, but as soon as you don't want a lift, you get offers all round?

'Thanks all the same,' I said again. 'I want to walk.'

The road nodded in a northerly direction for seventy-odd miles. I had a lot of thinking to do before I reached County Down. Not a step must be wasted.

There was always a smell of sugar round Carlow. The sugar-beet factory, 'on the road to Sweet Athy', made sure of that. When the frost stiffened the grass on the fields and the wind dropped down in December, the syrupy scent would just hang around waiting for someone to breathe it in. Then it would gladly soak into the heart. Its bittersweet taste often brought a tear to the eye, sometimes of joy, sometimes of sorrow, sometimes of both. I had no way of knowing why. Maybe it was that time of year when I thought of the Ryan Road, my parents, brothers and sisters, and the music at night, the neighbours coming in and the lovely young girls. A long time ago, it seemed, I had turned my back on all that for something greater. But it was my choice.

At the college young strangers had gradually become grown and trusted friends. They would all be lying prostrate on the high altar right now and the Gregorian chant and incense would be wafting up through the rafters of St Patrick's Cathedral on its way to heaven. Maurice Costello would be first. Then it would be Ronnie Madden, Buffalo Bill Leahy, El Daltono, Rory McDonald, then a space where I should be, and then Willie O'Byrne, Brendan Moloney, Jim O'Donovan and Jarlath Cushenan and all the other lads by order of seniority. It was Subdiaconate Day. They would be taking vows of celibacy and obedience. They would have noticed my absence by now.

Had it been the inspiration of my three clerical uncles that had sent me scurry-

Sampling the new apple juice: Tommy on couch with (standing) *Jarlath Cushenan, Maurice Costello, Jim O'Donovan and Willie O'Byrne*

ing on this spiritual adventure? Or was it just the dream of a child for something better that lightened my weekly three-mile race up past the mass rock to the Bridge of Mayo breathlessly rehearsing everything from 'Introibo ad altare Dei' to 'Deo gratias'? I felt that I would be unscrambling reasons for my entrance into this world and my exit from it for the rest of my life. And I already suspected that I would regret neither. Now I was progressing in reverse, proceeding against the current like a singing tribe I would later meet in India called the Bengal Bauls. They respected all religions but felt that churches often blocked the Divine path and scriptures sometimes confused rather than enlightened. I was forsaking the boundaries and challenges of the promised land for the borderless and less charted *tir taingiri*, the land of promise.

Perhaps the dream changed or the child changed, and it would be a long time before the answer to that riddle would emerge, but I was fond of the college and everyone in it, and it would have been much easier to stay than to leave. Sure, there were run-ins with the powers that be and recantations of articles I had written in my alternative college magazine, the *Bulbino Baaz*. The long road to perfection has many turnings. Joyless Jensen had left his mark on us all. Once in a fit of rare continence, our table, went off sugar for Lent. Gradually, however, we came to suspect that such deprivation was of itself giving our souls undue satisfaction. So we went back on to it again. But there had been plenty of craic as well, and new ideas being born and friendships that would never die.

I had learned a lot from students and professors alike. I'd got new reels and jigs

On the banjo in Carlow

from Fergal McAuliffe and had mastered the lethal art of logic under the guidance of P.J. McGrath. I'd learned the doubtful intrigues of Church history from Joe Coulter, and Pa Brophy had introduced me to the inspiration of the new liberation theology in Latin America, reflected in the words of the Brazilian Archbishop of Recife, Dom Helder Camara: 'When I give food to the poor, they call me a saint. When I ask why the poor have no food, they call me a Communist.' A young ex-seminarian called Victor Jara, raised on the heavenly wings of Gregorian Chant at Redeemer College, San Bernardo, had landed with guitar in hand and was singing of poverty and injustice in his native Chile. That struck a chord with me and the closest hymn I could find to parallel such sentiments was Pete Seeger's socialist anthem 'The banks are made of marble':

> The banks are made of marble with a guard on every door
> And the vaults are stuffed with silver that the people sweated for.

Seeger's songs taught me lessons about the struggle of poor people the whole world over. I had a good friend in Tommy Groome and we talked of these things and sang together. He took delight in complicating the most simple of theories and simplifying the most complicated. He once took the melody of a republican song, which had itself taken the melody of an English folksong called 'The jolly ploughboy', and threw back his head and sang:

> We're all off to Carlow in the black in the black
> To a life that's free from sin
> Where no birds nor booze nor living loose
> Will ever enter in.

We'd sit night after night, talking and philosophizing and wondering would we meet again after we left Carlow and were scattered all around the globe. (Thirty years later, I would meet Groome in a small club in Weston, Massachusetts, and we would have dinner together. That would be after he would have done his doctorate with Paulo Freiri, written a best-seller on Christian Education, humbly declined the offer of being Bishop of Dodge City and married the Irish step-dance champion of North America, Colleen Griffith.)

St Patrick's College didn't care much for worldly pursuits. We weren't encouraged to read newspapers and radios were banned altogether. I once managed to construct a piece of apparatus inside a tape recorder that made it possible to hear the *Gay Byrne Show*. I huddled closely to the forbidden appliance to listen to the Brian McCollum Folk Group sing 'I hate to hear people cry'. I already knew the words of that song, because I had written it six months earlier, during a social etiquette lecture by a reverend professor we called The Mow.

> I hate to hear people cry,
> One is for sorrow, two is for joy
> And love is a dove
> That needs two wings to fly.

It was the first of my songs ever recorded and behind a locked door in the oldest ecclesiastical establishment in Ireland, I was filled with a curious, illegal thrill.

Yesterday, my future course had seemed obvious and clear – I was 'in the world but not of it'. Today, I was in the world, and of it, I knew little. I had been in touch with the outside world, of course, during holidays and in correspondence. I was keenly aware of political developments and I had gone on the march in Newry during my holidays in January of that year. The attack on the first civil-rights march in Derry had shocked me deeply. For a sermon, I had quoted from *Holy War in Belfast* by the label-defying historian Andy Boyd, in which he lambasted both Orange and green sectarian traditions, and all positions that led to conflict without resolution. Later I would meet Andy, and court his lovely daughter, but at that moment in time, dressed in a long black soutane, such things were far from my mind. I too was supportive of the idea of uniting the working class of both traditions to create better conditions for everyone. There was a revolution in progress, and maybe I wanted to be a part of it. In 1968 students had come out on the streets of Paris and in the US demonstrations against the war in Vietnam were in full swing.

Now, as I walked homewards, a lot of vehicles coming towards me were piled high with luggage on roof-racks. They didn't look like holiday-makers. I had stayed in a Balbriggan bed and breakfast overnight and was now nearing Dunleer.

I passed a man clipping a hedge. 'You're heading the wrong road, ga'sun,' he said. Residuals of old Norman French still had residence in the language of the Louth people.

'I'm heading home,' I replied.

'You're not heading north of the border, surely?' he said, the French r's rolling in his mouth like a mouthful of stout. He had recognized my northern accent. 'War has broken out in Belfast,' he said. 'They're killing each other up there.'

'Violence is not the way forward,' I said.

'You can tell that to those people clearing out in their hundreds, ga'sun.

Catholics being burnt out of Belfast and not a one to defend them. The IRA used to mean Irish Republican Army, now it means "I Ran Away", according to what I hear.' He shook his head despairingly and went back to trimming the hedge.

The Northern traffic heading south was getting heavier now. We were going in opposite directions – both in search of refuge, in search of freedom. Some vehicles had beds strapped to the roof and chairs in the boot. Dundalk was full of Belfast accents hushing each other on nervous corners as I walked down Clanbrassil Street and slowly headed for the border. I knew the Newry Road well. Hidden birds sang out of hedges and bushes as unapproved border roads smuggled and furrowed deep into the rising hills of south Armagh.

At least, from here on, I thought, I won't be short of someone to talk to. First it was An Garda Síochána, the Southern police, asking questions; then the Southern customs; next it was the Northern customs and then the RUC. They got little information, however, from the lone stranger dressed in black and heading north. Confusion was all I had to declare. In truth, I didn't know where I was going or what I intended to do.

It was just south of the Cloghoge Bridge outside Newry that a clarity emerged. There was a sudden sound of squealing brakes as a black taxi came to a stop. I heard my name being called. It was Anne, Colum, Ben and Dino. They could have asked, What in the name of God are you doing out walking like a pilgrim in the wilderness? But Colum said, 'The people of Bombay Street in Belfast have been burned out. We're going to play for them in the Gormanstown refugee centre. Your guitar's in the boot. Will you come with us?'

I clambered into the back of the car, happy to be with them all again.

We sped sweetly down the road I had so slowly and painstakingly trudged up, and played all the night and into the morning amid the tears of the homeless and the birth pangs of the Provisional IRA.

II

Vying for Light

Generally speaking, 1970 was a dirty year for spuds in our part of Ireland, particularly so in the Low Field. Whatever agreement the rain, sun and grey-backed crow had reached, there would be few people in Ryan, Protestant or Catholic, to agree that the humble potato had much to boast about that year as a result of their negotiations. Father Hugh told us it was the Year of the Dog in China. He'd read it out of last night's *Evening Press* for breakfast. In Ryan it was the Year of the Weed. Every weed that the Latin language could tag a name upon sprang up before us. We had even more colourful names to call them by as we hunkered backwards down the long drills that led from the foot-rig of the low field to the head-rig at the top. Gilgowans, redshanks, yellow grass, dockens, nettles by the score to keep us alert and the odd thistle 'to smarten us up' stood in the way of our reversing progress, strangling our wellingtons and catching our ankles until we could hardly fall upon our backsides even if our weariness warranted it and God's gravity craved it. To clear a way for growing was our work as innocent budding eyes below the clay vyed for the right to light. That's how my father and his father before him had struggled to make a living, so what was there to complain about? Just get on with it and thank God for the spud that makes it through to fill the belly and pay the bills.

'What do you think?' shouted Dino from the fourth drill.

Ben and I were reversing together and Colum and Dino were on the next two drills. I knew what he was talking about. It had been the main topic of conversation all day.

We'd been wakened by another article in the *Evening Press* that morning. There was a competition in the Old Shieling in Dublin. It was open to ballad groups all over Ireland and the winner would go to America.

Dino had been serving his time working as a plasterer, but his mandolin work was more precious to him. Colum was working at the tax office in Newry. It had been blown up once already. The guard, an ex-soldier who had vowed he would devour any IRA man who trespassed on his territory, had changed his mind when a pistol had been put in his mouth.

'Yes, why not?' Anne replied. She had arrived with a bottle of milk corked by another page of the *Evening Press* and a basket of egg sandwiches.

But what chance would a Northern group have in Dublin? The South was full of great musicians and, besides, people from the North meant trouble.

Colum had bought an old Austin A40 from Pat on the Hill for a fiver. 'It isn't the best in the world,' Pat admitted, 'but it might do a turn.'

'Would she make it to Dublin?' I asked.

Col shook his head and thought for a bit. 'Petie Breen from Croan has a purple Morris Minor for sale. She's dear, though,' he said slowly, examining a thistle thorn in the index finger of his left hand. Just what a fiddle player needed. 'She's thirty-six pounds.' Then he looked up quickly with a smile and added, 'But she's got a hand-brake.'

One week later, like Hannibal facing the Alps, we hoisted the double bass on the roof and the five of us boarded the 'new' Morris Minor and headed for the bright lights of Dublin in the quest for fame, fortune and survival. Our father came too as a kind of non-playing captain and advisor.

The Old Shieling in Raheny on 7 June 1970 looked white and shining but as we fell out of the car we felt a match for anything. Inside, the legendary Bill Fuller, a man who seemed to own everything and everybody, smiled kindly and made us welcome.

We were starving, but all our money had been invested. To buy a meal in such an expensive place was out of the question. To buy a loaf of bread in a local corner shop wasn't on the cards either. We didn't have a bean. Every last penny had been spent on petrol for the journey.

'My belly thinks my throat's cut,' moaned Anne, the youngest and hungriest.

'I could drink out of a dead man's boot,' said the Chief, the oldest and thirstiest.

Then we thought of a plan as if heaven-sent. I stood outside a phone box and battered my pockets like a smoker wondering if he had a cigarette. 'Would you have tuppence for the phone?' I asked a passing woman. 'I have no change.'

Any busker will tell you that the most generous people in the world are middle-aged women who see their own son looking out of every young lad's eyes.

'Surely to God, son,' said the first woman, for tuppence was no big strain on most people, unless they had just bought a Morris Minor. Nor was it a strain on the second, or the third or the fourth, and soon we were savaging a sliced pan loaf, without butter and without jam, but with a passion that was binding us together for the task ahead.

There were six groups on the first night and two would go through to the semi-finals, Dolly McMahon explained. Her husband Ciarán Mac Mathúna nodded in agreement. He was one of the judges. We would be judged on our ability to entertain not just an Irish audience in Dublin but one in a New York nightclub as well. We knew little of Dublin and nothing of New York, but we had a good idea of what an audience in a Ryan kitchen wanted. We stared at a line-up of possible songs.

'Never thin your own turnips,' said my father, 'or they'll never grow. Let me have an outsider's look at that list. If you can entertain people in your own kitchen you can entertain them anywhere.'

That was the answer. We had to make the audience believe they were in our kitchen. We had to make them feel welcome with chat, jokes and stories; let them laugh and cry and sing, just like at home. Most important of all, at the end of our set they would have to feel better than at the beginning.

I still remember the set we played that night for we used it in the semi-final and final also. A slow but strong song by Tommy Makem called 'Sally-o', followed by a funny one called 'The reluctant patriot' by Dominic Behan, which captured the audience almost immediately. Then Anne sang the traditional 'Month of January', which she had learned from Tommy Makem's mother, Sarah. After that, we gave a sprinkling of reels and jigs and only when we felt that the audience had something to hold on to did we take them along less familiar winding roads with our own songs of the North.

Around home they still talk about the night of the final. Some neighbours arrived as if out of nowhere to cheer us on and were just as nervous as ourselves. A coin was spun to see which of the four finalists should be first to take to the stage. We didn't want it to be us. The coin eventually came down and Dolly made the announcement. The Sands Family would go on first. Wonderful groups from the other three provinces followed.

We couldn't bear to wait for the results and went outside for a walk, just to be together and talk. Someone suggested a decade of the rosary to prop up our chances. I gave it out, 'Hail Mary full of grace …' And the others answered out of the Raheny darkness, 'Holy Mary Mother of God …'

'In the name of Christ,' whispered Ciarán Mac Mathúna to my father and Bill Fuller, as they paced nervously backstage. 'Where is The Sands Family? We have to make the announcement.'

We arrived at the door just as Dolly took to the stage.

'And the winners … the group who will go to America and play in New York's famous Old Shieling in the Bronx is …'

She paused, enjoying her moment of suspense, and we stood close together now, arms reaching unconsciously around each other's shoulders.

'… The Sands Family,' she announced warmly.

We were jumping up and down, we were back on the stage, we were hugging Dolly, we were being clapped on the back, we were getting kisses from people we had never seen before. We were sitting at Bill Fuller's table. He was pouring red wine out of a bottle in a basket.

'You'll have a glass,' he said.

'Thanks, but we don't drink,' I replied.

He smiled. 'What about Mister Sands? Will he have a drink?'

'Yes, Mister Fuller,' said the Chief, licking his lips. 'Mister Sands most certainly will have a drink.'

Our trip to America couldn't come quickly enough, but it wouldn't come as quickly as we thought. There were visas to be sorted out and we were constantly shoving pennies into telephone boxes and waiting endlessly for the word to go.

In the meantime, life went on. Anne went back to school, Dino to the plastering, Col to the tax office. I took on some temporary teaching in the town of Aughagallon and Ben announced he had fallen in love with Barbara, daughter of the famous Nan Sands of Tormore. Nan had ten daughters, who were not only beautiful girls but were camogie players as well. When their talents weren't being sufficiently recognized by the County Down Camogie Board, Nan decided to run for the chair herself and take over the county team. In less than a year, with the power of her daughters on the field and Nan on the sideline, Down swept aside all in its path. First Derry, then Antrim, then the All-Ireland semi-final against the girls of Wexford, and finally the sacred All-Ireland crown itself, beating the mighty County Cork. Barbara was in the top ten of Ireland's best players that year. Her celebrity status increased all the more when, as a Sands marrying a Sands, she inherited the cure for the whooping cough. That went down well with the neighbourhood and the parish priest in particular, who dreamed of future sermons being uninterrupted by sudden whoops, sprays and splutters. Beyond the parish, however, there was less reason to celebrate.

The political situation in the North was rapidly deteriorating. Hopes of peaceful advance were being strangled. There was rioting in Belfast and Derry in June 1970 following the imprisonment of Bernadette Devlin for her part in the Battle of the Bogside in 1969. In July, a curfew was imposed on the Lower Falls Road in Belfast, and tension continued to mount throughout the province. By the end of the year twenty-five people were dead.

In August 1971 Brian Faulkner introduced internment. I knew nothing about the measure until I arrived back from a holiday on the Aran Islands on the morning after with Pat and Angela Treanor to find Newry in flames. Internment meant imprisonment without trial and although there was violence coming from all sides, there were no Protestants among the 300 lifted in the first dawn raid. All were Catholics and most of them were innocent. The flames continued and the premises of many innocent Protestant shopkeepers paid the price. Lockhart's, where we bought our gramophone needles, was gutted. Radcliffe's, another famous old Newry business, was burned, and the two young men who started the blaze were trapped inside. The fact that fire-fighters were prevented by stone-throwers from reaching the blaze was indicative of the madness that was spreading everywhere.

Amongst the many innocent pulled out of bed that night and interned without trial was Tom Moore. I went to Long Kesh to see him. I was searched and led through doors, which were unlocked before me and locked behind me. Even in prison he was without bitterness but determined to continue the struggle to unite the Catholic and Protestant workers. The Protestant workers guarding him at the time didn't think much of his chances.

Since so many household breadwinners were behind bars, we helped to organize events to raise money for their dependants. Massive concerts were held in Newry, Belfast and Dundalk. We tried to have a new song written for each one. It wasn't difficult – there were so many things happening.

One night on our way to Newry we were stopped by a British army patrol. We little knew at the time that for the next twenty-five years such occurrences would become part of everyday life. We were taken out of the car, put against a wall, our legs kicked apart. Soldiers with Birmingham and Glasgow working-class accents looked at us with a mixture of hate, fear and confusion. We were held for over an hour. The audience was still there when we walked onstage in our overcoats and began to sing 'Right will conquer might', a ballad we had composed during the wait.

> We've just been stopped by British soldiers on the way to town,
> They took us all out of the car and searched us up and down,
> Where are you from? Where do you go? We may not let you through,
> Must we put up with foreign troops who tell us what to do?
> But right will conquer might
> We'll let the whole world know
> And we must work together
> And we'll reap the land we sow.

These were songs of the moment and songs of the times, and many years later I would meet ex-soldiers in Civvy Street and hear them talk about the strange and terrifying borderland that they had found themselves in.

The army claimed one night that three young men were trying to rob a night safe in Newry's Hill Street. No one really knew if they were or not. They weren't asked. They were shot dead by soldiers positioned on the roof of Woolworth's. Their names were read out on the radio. One was Seanie Ruddy, whom I remembered from the first day at St Joseph's. The town went mad. Woolworth's was burned to the ground and after the funerals, a riot broke out. There were rubber bullets flying and cs gas hung in the air. Any young man walking the streets at night was in danger of being beaten by soldiers. People were terrified to go out. A virtual curfew had been imposed and the town was kept in darkness. NICRA (Northern Ireland Civil Rights Association) in Newry sent word to us that they wanted music. Would we play in the town centre to lift the people's morale and give them some hope?

It was pitch black and the streets were deserted. The traffic lights changed from red to amber to green but there was no traffic on the roads. We opened our cases and began to play. It was an eerie feeling, like playing to an empty world. The music echoed down Hill Street and up Margaret Street. There was not another sound.

Slowly some figures appeared at the top of the street, then some more. People came to hear the music, and soon we were joined by other musicians. The street was now crowded, a *céilí* was in full swing and people were dancing. The following night, the lights were back on again.

We believed in bright new tomorrows and often at night after marches and rallies we would meet in special places to divine for the waters of wisdom sometimes assisted by the 'waters of life'. Gatherings had representatives from many shades of revolutionary thinking. There were Marxists, Trotskyites, anarchists and humanists. There were devout agnostics and confident Christians; there were Official Republicans, named 'Stickies', who had gone modern by sticking 1970 Easter lilies on their breasts with gum; and Provisional Republicans, called 'Pin-Heads', who had gone traditional by fastening theirs on with a pin. There were International Socialists and locals too. Some had gone so far to the Left they had become Right. Still we sat and sang, argued and laughed, with a oneness that little foresaw the varied paths that would inevitably lead forward. Some dreams would lead to mainstream politics, some would lead to prisons and graveyards. In the semi-darkness of pub corners, ideals were sung and quotes flew, and if a row started, there were more coats held than blows struck.

Sometimes it was little bits of madness that helped maintain the sanity. One night, after a visit to many hostelries of diversion and enlightenment, our old history teacher, who had once come into class with a hangover and two ties on him and would later become Lord Mayor of the City of Newry, declared, 'Let's go for a dacent drink.'

He took off down the street like Good King Wenceslas gone bad and a crowd of good friends in his stead. He was heading home with a brown paper bag under his arm. After several unsuccessful attempts to get the key into the lock in the dark, he looked around for inspiration.

O'Hanlon shouted, 'Would someone hold the house till Frank gets the key in the door!'

No one did. So Frank, followed by his loyal ever-growing band, climbed through the window instead and settled themselves down for a good night's session in the comforts of the sitting room. Drink was drunk and songs were sung and Gerry Doherty sat at a piano and played boogie woogie until the dawn looked through the curtains and a strange woman in a nightgown looked down the stairs. No one seemed to know who she was.

'Get out, you crowd of hallions,' she shouted. 'You kept me wakened all night and only yer man there is half decent on the piano, I would have flung yiz out hours ago.'

It was the wrong house.

Chastened guests, rail-roaded with bent heads, made bolts for the door and Frank buttoned his shirt, tightened his tie and headed off to continue his 100 per cent success rate in the teaching of A-Level history.

12

All the Little Children

Bloody Sunday changed everything. The news spread like wildfire. It was 30 January 1972 and in Derry the Paratroopers had opened up on the civil-rights marchers with live ammunition. It was hard to take in. The Paras were always dreaded when they came to Newry. They didn't care whom they hit or where they hit. They wanted to flush out the terrorists, they said. Now they had shot dead thirteen innocent people, and another lay fatally wounded.

Before Bloody Sunday people had believed that the peaceful demonstrations with marches and sit-downs were getting somewhere. The world was watching and listening. Britain would not permit inequality and injustice to reign unabated in her own backyard. Now the mother of democracies had answered back. Bloody Sunday was her reply. British politicians' attempts to excuse and deny what had happened added insult to injury. In Westminster the next day, they upheld the army's story. They had shot in self-defence.

A march was due to take place in Newry the following Saturday. It was banned. We didn't care. A hundred thousand people gathered at Derrybeg. Loudspeakers from roaring helicopters buzzing overhead warned that we were breaking the law and to desist immediately. Those who at one time would have returned learned quotations from Socrates, Acquinas or King about the people's duty to disobey unjust laws settled now for much less articulate retorts. Surface to air 'F' sounds spat skywards and upwardly mobile finger signs spoke louder than words could thunder. Sean Hollywood was in charge of the march. He was cool and calm. It was all well planned. No matter where the army would herd us, we had a contingency plan for the meeting. We knew we wouldn't get far. At the Monaghan Street roundabout, instead of heading towards the town, we turned left into Rooney's Meadow. The world's media were there and famous people, like Vanessa Redgrave, were lending their support. Newry residents would have many stories to tell about taking them in and giving them cups of tea.

I met Bernadette Devlin, now the Mid-Ulster MP, in the Bit and Bridle. When Home Secretary Reginald Maudling made his 'acceptable levels of violence' statement on Bloody Sunday in the Commons, Bernadette had grabbed him by the collar.

'I'm sorry I didn't get him by the throat,' she told me.

That's how many felt. People were now saying that the IRA had been right all along. The only way to talk to Britain was down the barrel of a gun. The old clichés were coming back with the sad ring of truth. The Northern state had been set up by force and it could only be dismantled by force. Some friends I knew had already decided what to do.

It seemed for many of us unpatriotic not to get involved in the fight. Conscience rather than any proclivity for violence was driving young men into the arms of the IRA. I went to see D.M.

'I want to join up,' I said.

'You mean the army?' he asked.

'Yes,' I replied. 'What do I do?'

He told me to go to a bar near the border at two o'clock the following Tuesday. 'There'll be a man to meet you there,' he said. 'You can have a chat over a glass of beer.'

The next time I would see this D.M., he would be burned like raw meat. Burnt by his own bomb.

I got to the bar in good time. There was no one there but the barman and a friend of mine called Joe. Joe was a like a father to me. He loved my songs and would always request a peaceful one before the end of the night. He was a gentle kind of person and I hoped he would leave. I didn't want him to be around when some cold-blooded killer walked in the door. He seemed in no hurry, though.

I sat down in the far corner. I looked into the beer that we were to talk over. Two o'clock came and went but no one turned up. I'll give him another half-hour, I thought. There were roadblocks around the town and maybe he was avoiding them.

At three o'clock I decided to go. I felt relieved in a way, my conscience some-how sated. I left my empty glass on the bar like a chalice that had been removed from my lips. 'All the best, boys!' I said.

'What's your hurry?' asked Joe.

'I was expecting someone,' I said, 'but he hasn't turned up. I have to head on.'

'You're looking at him,' said Joe quietly.

I couldn't believe it. Not only was Joe in the army, he was running recruitment. I knew lots of people who had spouted in bars about what they would do. I was now realizing that the people who say the least are perhaps the ones who do the most and vice versa.

'You mean the army?' I said cautiously.

Joe became deadly serious. 'So you want a gun?' he said.

'Is there another way?' I answered.

'Do you want to kill people?' he asked flatly.

'I want to stop people being killed,' I said.

'Could you kill?' he asked again.

'I don't know,' I admitted.

A strange look came into his eye. 'It's much easier than you think,' he said. 'Too easy.'

'I want the killing to stop,' I repeated.

'That's why I joined,' he said. 'I didn't want my children to go through all this, and you know, that's why my da joined too, so that I wouldn't have to go through all this. There's maybe another way, but I don't know what it is. I was hoping people like you might, though.' He sounded tired and disappointed.

Perhaps he was protecting me; perhaps he knew I had neither heart nor head for such methods; perhaps he was fed up being overcrowded by young recruits who had no idea of what they were getting into and what the cost would be. Perhaps his whole life had been overwhelmed by the struggle and he had come to believe that nothing was worth the taking of another life. Perhaps, deep inside, he believed there was another way, somewhere. For the moment, the present was going nowhere.

He went behind the bar and poured a large *uisce beatha* and set it down. 'Take that effing whiskey,' he said, 'and go into that corner there and write a song.'

He walked out through the door and left me standing there. I sat down filled with anger and frustration. I wasn't sure of anything any more. I looked at the *Irish News* on the counter and stared at the blank spaces between the huge, ominous headline: 'All Ireland or Nothing'. But one thing I did know – I would never point a finger of condemnation at those caught up in the conflict, without seeing one pointing back at myself.

How many joined that weekend, I don't know. How many would be later killed or spend years in a prison or die on hunger strike and be called rabble and scum and terrorists? Perhaps if they had seen another way at that moment, they would have grasped it. How can you tell a person to stop struggling if he's lying with his back on the ground? I tried to imagine a distant time when all this hatred and anger would be past, when children of a future generation would be skipping in the sunshine. And as I sat, I watched my pent-up feelings begin to slowly flow onto the page:

Little children hiding in the shadows
Waiting for the changing of the day,
Watching for a break between the showers
When they can come out and start to play.

And we're singing of the times
When the sun will always shine
And armoured cars and tanks will fade away,
People will be one and the fighting will be done
And all the little children, they can play.

I don't suppose a man will stop his struggling
If he's lying with his back upon the ground

It's only when everyone is standing
That peace and justice can be found.

This song would shortly join the popular song chart in East Berlin and would be reproduced in German schoolbooks as a plea for peace.

Atrocities like Bloody Sunday, presumably intended to defeat violence, would in fact provoke much more. I would see pain staring out of many eyes as a result of that day for a long time to come. Like Karl Bosley, for example, many years later at a concert in Glencree Reconciliation Centre in Wicklow. I was singing 'All the little children' and he was sitting near the front. I was told he wanted to talk to me. He sounded English and looked like a soldier. 'Yes,' he said, 'an ex-Para actually.' I knew he could only have been a child when Bloody Sunday happened yet I would soon learn how that tragic event destroyed his life too.

'Why did you join up?' I asked.

'To kill any Irish I could find,' he said matter-of-factly.

I could sense he had much more to say and I was in no hurry. The concert was over and people were sitting around having a drink and talking.

'And did you kill any of us?' I asked.

He took a sip from his glass and looked me in the eye. 'No,' he said. 'When the time came for my unit to go to Ireland, they wouldn't let me go. I was furious. They had trained me to kill and I had learned well. Now they wouldn't let me go and do my job. It was because of Brixton,' he said, in answer to my unspoken question. 'I burned down an Irish pub there.'

'Why?' I asked, wanting to understand his motivation.

'They had thrown me out of there once when I objected to the collecting of money for the IRA.'

'And you hated the IRA?' I said.

His face became dark. 'Bloody Sunday,' he said. 'It happened three weeks after Bloody Sunday. I was just fourteen then and at school. My mum was Irish and was very disturbed by the death of her country people but she kept her sorrows to herself. She just got on with her job as a cleaner in the local army barracks.

'I'll never forget that last morning with my mum. We had a bit of a fight over packing my PE gear for school. We parted on bad terms. I will never be able to make up for that.

'I was sitting in the school canteen when the bang went off. The windows came in around us. I didn't know then that the bomb had been two miles away, outside the officers' mess in Aldershot barracks. I was to meet mum there after school. I'll never forget it. I can still smell the cement, the rubble. The IRA planted it. It was in revenge for Bloody Sunday. Later they said they were sorry for not having killed any British soldiers in that blast, but they didn't apologize for killing seven civilians, two men and five women. They never apologized for killing my mother. The bastards.'

His fists clenched tightly as he stared at the ceiling, tears breaking in his eyes. 'I left home. It was no home any more. I vowed I'd join the Paras and avenge my mother's death. I dedicated myself to the job like no one else. Then they wouldn't let me go to Ireland. I was livid. I took to alcohol. I was in and out of trouble for years. My life was ruined.

'The twenty-fifth anniversary of Bloody Sunday was marked with TV programmes and memorials, but no one remembered my mother. I had been drinking heavily. I just flipped. It was twenty-five years of pent-up emotion being released. It was like I was watching everything from another place. I was dressed in my Para gear again, the red beret, the lot. Suddenly I was holding two grenades and there were guns pointing at me. The guy at the front shouted something. He was scared. I could see how his gun was shaking. I shouted back, "If I drop these, we all go up." His gun shook even more.

'An army officer asked why I felt like this. It was the first time anyone had asked me how I felt since my mother died.

'I did nine months in Wormwood Scrubs for that offence. When I came out again, my mind was no less easy. It took only the sound of an Irish accent and I would freak. Then one night I was down in the pub and met Patricia. Just being with that girl seemed to heal my pain. Until the night she brought me home to meet her parents. I couldn't believe it. The father was from Belfast and the mother from Dublin. I froze. I hadn't realized that she was Irish.

'That's her sitting over there. We have children now, a little girl, Karla. She looks like my mother. And a son called Max. In this remarkable way I have come to slowly learn who Irish people really are. It's ironic too that the most help I have had has come from Ireland, and believe me, I still need help. That's why your songs have been important to me.'

Francie Molloy from Sinn Féin was at Glencree that night. People like him were the Paras' targets on Bloody Sunday. David Ervine, leader of the loyalist Progressive Unionist Party, was there too. He had joined the UVF after Bloody Friday, when the Provisionals set off 26 explosions in Belfast on 21 July 1972, killing 11 people and injuring 130.

'Maybe we're all victims,' said Karl.

Such conclusions would take many years to emerge. In 1972, all we could do was dream of a light at the end of a long dark tunnel 'when all the little children they can play'.

It was later in that year of '72 that we got word about our long-awaited trip to America.

'Don't separate, whatever you do,' warned my mother, hiding her tears with the hug that she gave us.

'We won't,' I promised, for I was the oldest.

The car boiled up going to the airport and we missed the plane. We arrived in New York a day late, just an hour or two before we were due onstage for our first appearance in America.

13

Let Ye All Be Irish Tonight

'Fresh from Ireland' said the front page of the *Irish Echo* at JFK airport as we sleep-walked off the plane in March of 1971. New York was New York, though, and the chemistry and energy in the air had us champing at the bit to get at it, when Tom Griffith announced us at 207th Street in the Bronx. Our special guest was Paddy Reilly. We knew Paddy from home and felt at ease in his company.

The audience ranged from tough drinkers standing at the bar and hiding their homesickness to the nostalgic soft-hearted punters sitting at the tables and crying out for a bit of craic. Every county in Ireland was represented and on the first night we even met O'Hares from Mayobridge and Doyles from Saval, and some people whose American wake we had attended before they left Ireland because they were never expected to return. Now here they were like spirits from the otherworld. This wasn't America, this was home. The Big Apple was full of the Irish and full of Irish musicians too. Charlie Magee, who had played his guitar on the Walton's radio pro-gramme at home, dropped in. Big Jesse Owens, Joe Burke, and Johnny Cronin all came to bid us welcome and cheer us on. We met people who had never been to Ire-land but whose great-grandparents had left at the time of the Famine, and they were full of love for the old country. Some wanted to give us money for the IRA and some wanted to join the IRA. They could tell from our songs that we were involved with the civil rights movement. 'What the hell's going on over there?' they'd ask.

Then one evening a frisson of excitement ran through the bar staff. Bill Fuller was coming. He arrived with an entourage and sat at the front with arms folded and feet spread. After the show, we were summoned to his table. It was like going before God. He was surrounded by shiny-faced women and big men.

He came straight to the point. 'How would you like to play in Carnegie Hall?'

We had heard of that place all right. A famous concert hall. It was somewhere in America, wasn't it?

'Yes,' said Fuller. 'Right here in New York.'

His wife Carmel Quinn was presenting a St Patrick's Day show there and we were invited as the special guests. There would be an audience of 2000, including the press and impresarios looking for new talent. A big mover called Mike Broadbine might be in attendance. We couldn't wait for 17 March.

The taxi pulled up outside our hotel on 44th Street.

'Where you guys wanna go?'

'Take us to Carnegie Hall,' I said calmly, trying to hide my excitement.

The driver's brown Puerto Rican eyes looked the five of us up and down. Col was holding the double bass like a drunken shig of hay.

'I'll take three of you,' he said, clearly excluding Col and his bundle of troubles. 'The rest of you can get another cab.'

'No, we all go together,' I said firmly, remembering the promise we made before leaving home.

'Not in my cab, buddy,' he shouted and sped off in the direction of a pale-faced man in a black suit, whose hand was up in the air like the Statue of Liberty.

Back home, cars half the size could hold anything up to ten or twelve at a push.

'Will we walk it?' said Ben. 'It's not a bad day.'

It was freezing cold but at least it wasn't raining and, as they say, that was the main thing.

'It might snow,' said Anne, whose fingers were blue.

'Does anybody know where we're going?' panted Col, bellying the bass in front of him and trying to avoid a serious collision with the constant flow of people crowding along the footpaths of Manhattan.

'We're going to Carnegie Hall,' said Dino, 'and surely to God everybody should know where that is.'

But many a smart-ass New Yorker had waited all their lives to reply to just such a question.

The first suggestion about how to get to Carnegie Hall would come as soon as we had the courage to interrupt the race of humanity tearing up and down and all around us. Streets were snarled with yellow taxis horning each other through traffic lights, and sidewalks were crammed with all shapes, sizes, colours and creeds. We were adding our own contribution to the chaos by constantly bumping into one another. Sometimes we ran when it said 'Don't Walk' and sometimes we walked when we felt like lying down. But it wasn't a place for lying down, unless you had just returned from Vietnam with a leg missing and were waiting for a nickel to be thrown in an empty coffee cup.

A thin, black-faced man, who looked like he needed a week's sleep, shouted over the roar of traffic, 'Would you like to buy some shit?'

'Not just at the moment,' Col shouted back, not wanting to offend him unduly.

'They'd sell you anything here,' said Dino, giving him a wide berth, and we smiled and wondered if it would be any good for fertilizing the rhubarb in the back garden at home.

Tommy Makem welcomes The Sands Family to New York, 1971

A man was parked with his back against a window full of cameras. He had a face like a cat, and stood eating a hot dog and drinking a Coke.

'How do we get to Carnegie Hall?' said Col, very out of breath now and glad of a chance to rest for a moment.

The man looked at five bright-eyed waifs, faces blue with the cold, and stopped masticating for a moment. Ask me that again? he seemed to want to say, if his mouth hadn't been so full.

'How do we get to Carnegie Hall?' I repeated.

The explosive *p* of his sudden reply liberated a portion of salivated side-salad. 'Practice, practice, practice,' he spat, seizing the moment and emptying his mouth. 'Well I'll be doggone!' he said, choking on the tears of a long-lost laugh.

'So is your hot dog,' muttered Dino.

Peppered amongst other suggestions about getting to Carnegie Hall included: 'Get a good agent!' 'Get three taxis,' and 'Are you sure you don't want shit, man?' but eventually a big black man, realizing we weren't joking at all, not only led us to 'the corner of 57th and 7th', but carried the double bass as well. 'Sock it to him, you guys,' were his final parting words.

Carnegie Hall was gracious and palatial, with a foyer of marble columns, embracing arches and deep red carpets. The house manager, whose name was Stewart

Warkow, told us that the dressing rooms were on 56th, one whole street away, as he led us out and in through the stage door instead. He showed us dressing room A, where Tchaikovsky had spruced himself up in 1891 and where the Beatles had tuned up in 1964. We tightened our strings in dressing room B, until Colum gave a gasp. The D string had snapped. We had no spare fiddle strings. 'You'll have to use the wee finger high up on the G tonight,' whispered Dino hopefully. There was a photo of the Rat Pack on the wall looking down, laughing, and another of Yehudi Menuhin looking up. He had been here too, as well as the Great Caruso and Count John McCormack.

If only they could see us back home right now. I felt like shouting over the ditch to Bob Dodds or Mary Ann Brennan but they wouldn't have heard and they wouldn't have time to listen. The crows would be eyeing the new seed spud in the alleys now and they would have to be hopped up or it would be a heart scald of a dibbling match to replace the seed that was sucked into the trees.

'It takes $3000 to have that Carnegie Hall curtain pulled open,' Warkow was saying.

Who would believe that at home? Imagine the look Nora Wilson would give you, as she pulled her curtain to see who was knocking on her door, if you told her that. People had returned from far-off places before with stories no sensible human could take in.

We stood on the stage and looked out into the dark auditorium. We couldn't see a solitary face, but we knew people were out there, for they applauded politely at first and their affection grew as we relaxed into our set. Our songs from home were going down well, especially 'Everything must be used' and 'Right will conquer might'.

At the end of the concert we sat in the dressing room, enchanted and breathless. There was a knock on the door. A big man in a white suit walked into the room. It was Mick Broadbine.

'I'd like to handle you kids,' he announced, tapping his cigar into the ashtray. I took it he meant to manage us. We followed him to a restaurant called John Barleycorn.

Col spoke up. 'We would like to be guaranteed a few years here at least, if we were to leave our jobs in Ireland.'

'I'm not talking about a few years,' said Broadbine. 'I'm talking twenty, thirty years.'

It was hard to picture ourselves at the age of ninety-two gumming out 'Her eyes they shone like the diamonds'.

'Hell,' he said, 'why don't you come up to Boston and try it out for six months?'

He reached into his pocket and produced a card, like an ace of hearts in a game of forty-fives, and flicked it at the waitress. 'Take it out of that, baby,' he drawled.

It was the first time I had seen a credit card.

The sun was brightly beating around the Boston suburbs as we headed for Norwood, Massachusetts, and the home of the Harp and Bard. It was one of the most prestigious Irish music clubs in America, we were told. We would be paid $100 each a week with food, accommodation and a car thrown in. 'It's steady,' advised Tommy Makem, 'and then you will also be doing outside concerts too. Many a young musician in the States would give their eye teeth for such a deal.'

Other musicians and singers were in residence: Billy Connolly, already a famed folksinger from Glasgow with his hilarious patter; Shay Healy, a writer, wit and singer from Dublin; Eugene Byrne and the Blarney Folk; the McTaggarts; the Sweeneys from Omagh; Robbie O'Connell from Carrick-on-Suir; the Cochrane Brothers, and many others, all champing at the bit in the stableyard of Mike Broadbine.

Boston people had a different way of talking from New Yorkers. For 'Harp and Bard', they said 'Hap and Bad'. Shay Healy and I wrote a chorus they could join so we could hear the way they dropped their r's:

Let's get away from it all, my love
From the reading and writing and washing,
Pa'k the ca' in the ya'd at the Ha'p and Ba'd
And sing like a la'k in the mo'ning.

We were given a big wooden house in Norwood, at the corner of the car park, and it soon became a gathering place for some of the most unlikely but likable characters that God had planted on this planet. There were dancers from New York, drug addicts from Vietnam, a Marlboro cowboy from Cambridge, a nurse from Dublin, two witches from Salem, singers from everywhere, and a ghost named Emma, who threw pots and pans around at night whenever we eventually decided to sleep.

One day Broadbine said, 'Make a bit of room in that house. Hamish Imlach will be staying with you for the next few months.'

The Scotsman, who was conceived in Melbourne and born in Calcutta, was a legend in folk-music circles and well known to us for many years. We remembered him from the Castle Tavern in Dublin, where he had been mistakenly billed as the great Séamus Hemlock.

It took a lot of room to house Hamish and it wasn't just his 300-pound weight that demanded space. He was larger than life and had a laugh that sounded like a lorry load of stones being tipped on a tin roof. He told the funniest of stories and sang the saddest of songs, with a mean Guild guitar, whose neck chain-smoked his cigarettes. Many of his songs came from the blues tradition and most of his stories had a distinctive blue tint as well. He was fond of a bottle too, in fact many bottles. One morning he awoke with a bad dose of the shakes. 'It's the only exercise I get,' he told us as we brought him to the hospital. When asked by the doctor if he drank anything, he replied, 'Yes! Anything!'

Hamish was excessive in everything and loved every minute of living. He was often told that his pace of life was leading him to an early grave and he knew that. 'Isn't it terrible to see people dying of a bad heart,' he said, 'when all the other parts have hardly been used at all. When I go I want everything to be used up.' They were. But there were many wonderful years still before him. When the time came an old comedian colleague, Danny Kyle, asked the chapel full of mourners back in Glasgow to give Hamish one last round of applause before his body went down. The type of applause we should have given him in life. People began to applaud and they wouldn't stop. There would be no encores. We knew if we stopped the Hamish concert of life would be over forever. We just wanted him to stay with us a little while longer. The Sands Family clapped to the end for we would always remember those days in Boston, his shining talent, his humour and generosity, his kindness to a fault.

The Harp and Bard was proud of its fine food and quality music. It attracted a well-heeled clientele, powerful politicians and lofty bishops, as well as low-down lawyers and people who just liked the music. To gain admission, a jacket and tie and proper shoes were the rule. Such formal attire was often foreign matter in the bohemian wardrobes of our growing gang of new-found friends and often they just gathered in our house for private music sessions when the gig was over.

Mo McQuade, the hard-shoe dancer from New York with a soft smile and loving heart, arrived with her cousins and friends and livened up the wee small hours in a way never to be forgotten. 'Mad' Peter Johnson, the early model for Marlboro with a foot on a corral rail and a scar on his cheek, came in a Saville Row suit, a torn pair of sneakers, a bunch of flowers and a proposal of marriage for my sister Anne. An heir of some sort to the Johnson's Baby Powder millions, Peter was required to be either married to someone sensible or declared legally sane before his inheritance would kick in. Anne, seventeen now, immediately declared herself as 'not that sensible', but like the rest of us, she took to Peter's warm eccentricity and soon he became a good friend of the family and a constant visitor.

With the danger of marriage safely out of the way, he could now concentrate on being as mad as ever. He got a job as the 'turkey man' for a Boston radio station. The theory was that he would go round houses, dressed as a turkey, handing out frozen turkeys to those who were able to tell him the secret code word, which had been given out on the radio that day. This was all too boring for the mad Peter. Instead, he climbed up on roofs, flapped his wings from chimney pots and gave out free turkeys to all and sundry, with delighted Cambridge Street people in tow applauding his every gobble and squawk.

His sacking was as amusing to Peter as it was inevitable to everyone else. He had been thrown out of better establishments, the US Navy, for example. Members of his family had been admirals and vice-admirals before he followed suit and joined the force, but it soon transpired that Peter's ambitions lay elsewhere. It all came to a head after he had been given 'safe job, to keep him out of harm's way', painting his vessel a traditional battleship grey, with a marine red lead undercoat. When the job was finished, it was discovered that he had indeed painted the battleship, but in a less traditional grey and covered with red lead candy stripes and polka dots. His dishonourable discharge was followed by an equally swift disownment by his family, who wrote him out of their fortune. One little detail that was overlooked, however, was his account with various Saville Row tailors and Peter would arrive in a spanking new suit every day until the error was rectified.

Later he would marry the 76-year-old street singer Maggie Barry from Cork, not with the intention to inherit worldly goods, but to contribute to the cause of Irish musicians in particular and American music in general by landing her with a green card.

Scotty, a Sergeant just returned from Vietnam, and his battalion of survivors malodorous with marijuana, were constant callers and often stayed in our Norwood demesne. Many late nights were shortened with long and woeful stories from that sorrowful, beautiful land.

'I used to dream about being in a war with bullets whistling by,' I said one evening, 'and to escape I would lie down and pretend I was dead. Would that work over there?'

Big Steve, a heroin addict who would later end his own life, shook his head. 'Not really,' he sighed, measuring out portions of his drastic medicine. 'You go around those guys and you make darn sure they're dead as hell. Then you search 'em.'

'What did you search for?' I asked.

'Papers, documents, something that might be useful,' he said.

'What did you find?' I asked.

'Only pictures of their parents or girlfriends. Just the type of thing we were carrying ourselves,' he said, and began to cry inconsolably like a child. Scotty came over very slowly and put his arms tightly around him.

Kurt had a necklace of Viet Cong ears. He said he had to hate, in order to keep going; now it was himself he hated.

As the night wore on, their survivor status blurred as their victim-hood became more apparent.

'Dino,' Scotty said, 'please play your mandolin.'

Col joined in on fiddle and Anne on the bodhrán.

It was nearly time for breakfast and it was my turn to fry the frankfurters.

The role of the musician in most music clubs in America is relatively straightforward. You put backsides on seats and keep them there – on the edge of it, if possible. If the music in some way contributes to audience thirst, like the salted peanuts freely available at each elbow, and adds an extra and essential harmonic to the till, then you've made it. You're as right as rain.

If people walk out, however, the musician is in trouble.

'Why in the name of sweet Christ of Almighty did that table full of good whiskey drinkers walk out on you?' Chris Mitchell, the manager at the Harp and Bard, was always religious in his line of enquiry. 'Change your effing set,' he added angrily, 'and don't let your audience leave.'

No matter what you might say in your own defence, you knew it wouldn't cut much ice.

One night Mitchell hissed to us from the wings, 'Who in the name of sweet Christ of Almighty let that crowd of lunatics past the door?'

We looked down into the audience and spied a motley crew of punters stepping up the aisle, as innocent-looking as if they were going to the rails for their First Holy Communion.

Scotty and his mates had found a way to beat the dress code. Two of Peter's Saville Row suits had been commandeered and Hamish's wardrobe had been rifled as well. Wide shirts adorned long lanky bodies and trousers stopped just below the knees of the big Vietnam vets. They looked like the walking wounded, hunkering down to hide hairy calves and bare ankles and limping along in shoes several sizes too tight. But they were shoes, all the same, and their ties and jackets, in theory at least, complied with every regulation.

'Has Chippe'field's gaddam ci'cus come to town?' shouted a fat, shiny-faced man at the back.

The boys laughed and sat down a little self-consciously, but they gradually felt more at ease and began to listen to the music and shout out occasional requests.

Some of the regular clientele, well-fed on their large T-bones, eyed the newcomers with disdain. The people who stayed that night were the ones who liked our music; those who left clearly did not, at least not enough to share it with Scotty and company. The problem was, they were the big spenders, and Mitchell was not a happy man.

'Why not throw "Danny Boy" into the set? To let people know you really come from Ireland,' he said.

'Danny Boy' was as much meat to the listener as it was poison to the performer. Some customers would just sit back, wet-eyed, and think of Ireland. Other, less sentimental, would listen cynically to see how the singer would cope with the famous high note in the second part, like wily old punters watching an outsider facing Beecher's Brook. If you fell at that fence, you might never recover for the rest of the night. Unless you were someone like Shay Healy, that is. He'd stop just before the high note, drop his head and say, 'It's too emotional.' Then he'd be besieged by drink and dollar bills, more by far than if he had cleared the jump with the soaring tonsils of a Count McCormack.

The 'Derry air', or the 'Londonderry air', depending on the caller's political persuasion, had a beauty that was accepted by both camps at home and abroad. And here in Boston the two sides of Ireland were in view in the pews of the Harp and Bard.

'Give us that song again,' came a voice from a dark corner as the mics went off, the lights went down and the barmaids began to count their tips tiredly. We were tired too but an entertainer in the Harp and Bard was never off the stage.

'Come over here to meet some real Irish,' came a second voice.

'He's Scotch–Irish actually,' corrected the first, 'but I'm the real thing.'

Neither had ever been to Ireland but one said that his folks had come over with the Potato Famine.

'Mine were here before that,' said the second. It was Jack Murphy and Sam Maharg from the two sides of yesterday, now Boston business partners and drinking together like they knew no difference. In a funny way it was mindful of the farm at home where my father, in bringing together the warring piglets of different litters, would sprinkle their tails and the walls of their common sty with large handfuls of Jeyes Fluid. 'They'll never know who they are now, I houl ye,' he would say. The scent of time, space, money and whiskey had dulled all divisions between Jack and Sam and with their wives Kate and Rebecca they were out celebrating their commonality.

'You betcha,' said Jack Murphy. 'Have you ever heard of south Armagh? Border country, I believe. That's my country.'

'I know it well,' I said. 'No flies on them boys.'

'You betcha,' said Jack Murphy. 'They gotta live by their wits, that's why, there's nothing but rocks. Good Rebel IRA country I believe,' he added with a chuckle, 'At the head of the column.'

'A land of poets,' I said, 'McCooey and O'Doirnin, and a land of rebels too, long before there was an IRA. It's in the gap of the north, no man's land.'

'Sounds like "the debatable land",' said Sam Maharg, suddenly.

'Sounds interesting,' I said.

Glasses were refilled and Sam Maharg closed his eyes as if looking for something in the dark. Having found it, he seemed satisfied and took a long sucking swig of Scotch.

'My people, I gather, came from the borderland between England and Scotland,' he began. ' "The Debatable lands". Have you heard of the Reivers?'

Welcoming our silence as a signal to proceed, he sat up in his chair and brought us back to the turning of the fourteenth century and the stirrings of a people who in time would number in Ireland as Ulster Scots and in America as Scotch–Irish.

'In fact you could go back further than that', he said, 'to the Roman General Hadrian who built a wall to keep them out. When Robert the Bruce gained independence for Scotland these people belonged to neither England or Scotland and the only allegiance they had was to their own clan chiefs. "Reiver" means "plunderer",' he said, 'and no wonder as they were well plundered themselves and trampled upon when the Scots and English went into battle with each other. They learned their trade well and became the greatest shower of cutthroats and gangsters that ever inhabited the island of Britain. Their main contribution to English culture were the words "blackmail" (which was protection money paid to them, rather than "greenmail", which was paid to the landowner) and "bereaved" (which was what you became when your loved one was killed by a Reiver).'

There was little love lost between his grace the Archbishop of Glasgow, Gavin Dunbar and the Reivers. In fact in 1528 he put a curse on them that would make hair stand on the head of the bald:

By the auctorite of Almichty God, the Fader of hevin, his Son, our Saviour, Jhesu Crist, and of the Halygaist; I curse their heid and all the haris of thair heid; I curse thair face, thair ene, thair mouth, thair neise, thair tongue, thair teeth, thair crag, thair shoulderis, thair breist, thair hert, thair stomok, thair bak, thair wame, thair armes, thair leggis, thair handis, thair feit, and everilk part of thair body, frae the top of their heid to the soill of thair feet, befoir and behind, within and without ... And, finally, I condemn thaim perpetualie to the deip pit of hell, the remain with Lucifer and all his fallowis ...

Their main season for sculduggery lay between the Lammas time of August and the reopening of the courts. That was a three-month period when judges were nowhere to be seen and kidnapped cattle and sheep were healthy enough to be coaxed at a high speed over solid ground from one clan to another. Apart from burning each others' houses and villages, however, there was occasionally time for the odd football match. One such match, documented in 1599 between the Armstrongs from the Scottish side and the Ridleys from the English, turned out to be a bit on the rough side. Three Ridleys were killed, thirty taken prisoner and many were badly injured including one John Whyfield whose injuries were such that 'his bowels came out but are sowed up again'.

These clans were such a thorn in the side of both England and Scotland that when the chance of land came up in Ulster after the Flight of the Earls in 1607 many of the Reivers were deported or cajoled into emigrating there. Famous Reiver names that had Viking, Norman, Anglo-Saxon and Pictish origins were Armstrong, Graham, Kerr, Johnston, Nixon, Scott, Foster, Hume and Tromble.

'The English were always very generous about making gifts of land which belonged to someone else,' cut in Jack Murphy.

'What about your own name, Sam?' I asked. 'You haven't mentioned Maharg.'

'It sounds strange,' he said, 'but it's what I have always been told. Our name was Graham, but we were hunted and hounded so much that we reversed the letters and the name became Maharg.'

'I won't tell,' I said.

'Would that turn the curse into a blessing?' asked Jack Murphy with a tongue in his cheek.

'I doubt it,' said Maharg, 'but we're a stubborn bunch, we survived, went to Ulster and when it came to taming a frontier, there was none better than we, be it in England, Ireland or later, America.'

I readied myself for a song of the Reivers in return for his story. It was a bloodthirsty one called 'Twa corbies', which we had learned from Hamish Imlach. Before I had time to wet my lips, however, Sam's wife Rebecca had broken her silence. 'If we survived,' she said, 'it was not because of our stubbornness but rather in spite of it.' She then quietly began to sing another song from that period but one of great tenderness. It was called 'The lament of the Border widow'.

I sew'd his sheet, making my name
I watch'd the corpse, myself alane;
I watch'd his body, night and day;
No living creature came that way.

I took his body on my back,
And whiles I gaed, and whiles I sat;
I digg'd a grave, and laid him in,
And happ'd him with the sod sae green.

'When people are savaged they become savages,' said Maharg. 'Isn't that right, Jack Murphy?'

'At least our cutthroats were more humane than your cutthroats,' said Murphy. 'We were cursed too you know,' continued Jack, 'by Macha, the woman who was forced to race against the horses of the king of Ulster and gave her name to the city of Armagh. Did you know that? Is it any wonder we are the way we are? There's a curse on both our houses.'

'I believe they're knocking hell out of each other in the old country these days,' said Maharg.

'Killing each other to get at each other,' said Murphy.

They drank a toast to friendship, smiled and then put their arms around each other like dancers about to swing in a four-hand reel.

People of all nationalities frequented the Harp and Bard: English, German, Jew and Palestinian, all wanting to be Irish for the night. The old 78 rpm record by the Flanagan Brothers, which had so often played at home on a gramophone, was now making better sense.

Let ye all be Irish tonight,
Let ye all be Irish tonight,
You French, Scots and Germans, Italians and Jews
Act like McKennas, O'Sheas and O'Tooles
And I'll shake you all by the hand, as if you come from Ireland.
Forget all your troubles, your cares and your woes,
Imagine you're one of the Macs or the Os,
Do everything Irish except start a fight,
Let you all be Irish tonight,
Let you all be Irish tonight.

One day I went down to Albany to visit old Mike Flanagan, the only surviving Flanagan. 'We played in the Bucket of Blood,' he said, 'so called because of all the rows and ructions on a Saturday night, but the one thing that took a tear to their eye was the music.'

Interviewing Mike Flanagan, the last survivor of The Flanagan Brothers

Our journeys took us up to Canada's capital, Ottawa. We'll give our brother Hugh a surprise, we said. We were due to do a TV chat programme on arriving and we knew he lived around there somewhere. It was we who were surprised though for the host of the programme was none other than Hugh himself.

'What takes you out here anyway and me thinking I had got clear of you all?' was the first question he squeezed out amid stunned embraces. 'Is Paddy Breen still baling hay in Ryan?' and, 'Has Nora Wilson still got the green bike?' were his next two.

'Is the Pope still a Catholic?' said Colum, attempting to answer the question and internationalize the moment. But there was no need, for the audience, although open mouthed at our regionalism, understood well that the musings of a small townland is no less universal than the wonderings of a whole world. It was an unforgettable programme of memories and togetherness and wonderful was the time we spent afterwards too, playing in the Ottawa Arts Center with The Clancy Brothers and in a club called The Molly Maguires with the talented Charles de Lint and Nathan Curry. The Arts Center was state of the art, the Mollies was in another state. A few broken tables on the morning after was a sure sign that a good night of high dancing was had by all. The name "Molly Maguire", infamously associated with the rebelling miners of Pennsylvania in the 1860s and 70s had an earlier origin back home in Ireland where legends of such origins are legion. During the penal times when a poor Catholic tenant farmer died, his widow and family were duly evicted

With the Clancys – Paddy, Bobby and Tom

from their humble abode. Molly Maguire was one such widow and the night after her eviction the landlord responsible discovered his own thatch being lit by a whin bush. It was a present from the sons of Molly Maguire. He knew that and everyone else did too but when the law came looking for Molly they found dozens of people, all claiming to be Molly Maguire. Molly lived to fight another day and her legend crossed the Atlantic with the dispossessed Irish to fight somewhat similar fights and contribute to the ultimate setting up of organized labour in the USA.

During the time we were in the States, we learned all the songs we needed to know and wrote some new ones as well, but there were other songs we wanted to sing, songs that reflected the here and now of Ireland. We had sung our share of pretty fair maids in the month of May and also June, but at home it was becoming July and August and pretty fair maids were among those being maimed and murdered by petrol bombs and rubber bullets. We had sung 'the songs our fathers loved' and loved them too, but another day was dawning and new songs were crying to be sung. Such songs were not for simply making people happy, nor were they for filling rooms in bars.

We had been in America for a long time. We had made many friends and some would always remain closer though farther away like Denise, Ginny, Jack and Michaela and none more than Declan and Maureen, in ways they would never imagine. It was like emigrating in reverse now. Our parents and friends from across the Atlantic would write and say, 'Are yiz never coming back?' They were lonely for us and so were we for them. Our six months were up and it felt more like six years. We were going home.

Coming into Shannon half-asleep and half-awake, a fond and misty green dawn blinked up through the clouds. Suddenly tears began to fall, secretly and surprisingly.

We arrived back in Ryan Road amidst great welcoming and jubilation with enough money to pay the bills still hanging from hungrier days. Celebrations were planned and six chickens – our version of the proverbial fatted calf – were quickly earmarked for sacrifice, but not quite yet. The hay, commanded the Chief, would have to be mowed, turned, baled and taken in, first and foremost.

'Gadammit,' said Dino in a fake American accent, 'will we never get away from turning hay?'

It had been another wet summer and as neighbours gathered to join the battle, stories were soon being swapped between the big snows of Boston and the big slaps of rain in the land of Ryan.

'This would be a great wee country,' said the Chief, 'if there was a roof on it.'

'The ground was that wet, you could stir it with a spoon,' added John O'Hare, kneeing a heavy bale onto the trailer.

John Campbell told about a neighbour of his who couldn't get the hay saved, for every time he went out to turn it, it was sure to rain. One morning he got up very early, hoping the rain wouldn't see him, and tiptoed out through the gap, with the pitchfork up the leg of his trousers. He wasn't in the field two minutes, when a big wet spit plopped down from heaven and landed on his nose. In disgust, he looked up to the sky and said, 'You needn't bother your backside, sure I was only looking at it.'

John stood back, pulled out his pipe and positioned as if to say, Put one of your American yarns up against that one, ye boy ye.

Soon we took off on a kind of homecoming tour not only to cheer up our neighbours and relations but to recharge our batteries with their stories and songs. Auntie Maggie in Burren was happy but not surprised to see us. The cat had been washing its face all morning, she said, and a couple of knives and forks had dropped on the floor, all obvious signs of impending visitors. As well as that, our initials had been 'as clear as the heavens' in the tea leaves, and so she had been to Terence's for groceries, to the well for water and already the kettle was boiling on the hot coals when we walked in the door.

Uncle Patrick arrived with his black bicycle at the same time. He travelled everywhere by bike and when he became older and not fit to ride, he took it with him anyway just for company and for leaning on its handlebars, like a gate, to converse with his neighbours. He had been over giving some advice to the schoolmaster that day. Observing schoolmasters seemed to be a pastime in the family. Eoghain Connolly, his father and our grandfather, had written a poem fifty years before about the same schoolhouse.

> It's well I remember that day in September
> I took a short stroll to the Pound
> As round me I gazed
> I soon was amazed

When towards the schoolhouse I looked down,
And there Master Austin,
The ditch he was tossing
I wondered what made him do that,
Till I met with the eye
Of one passerby
Who said, 'He's in search of a rat.'
Then up came McGraw
With a slate in his claw
And he swore he would soon root him out
But the rat got away
Without further delay
With the loss of his tail no doubt.

Uncle Patrick seldom returned from anywhere without a story to tell. He was laughing and saying what a good sport the schoolmaster was to be listening to the likes of himself.

'And why wouldn't he be listening to the likes of yourself?' said Uncle Tom, having recently returned from his teachings and missionings in the Philippine Islands and enjoying every minute of being home. 'You know,' he said, with half-closed eyes, 'a man needs to leave home to realize that he doesn't need to leave home at all.'

This stopped the conversation for a while until he told the story of a student who was trying to cross a river one time to learn about the important things in life from the old village master who lived on the other side.

'What do you want?' shouted the old master.

'I want to get to the other side,' replied the student.

'You're already at the other side,' said the master, and the student was happy to have learned such a good lesson.

We all laughed, both knowingly and unknowingly, but as sure as more tea was being made we all knew that a Big Night was in the brewing. They asked us about America and if we had changed much or become Yankified in any way. The songs began and the verses sung were defiantly and lovingly the same as always and as each in turn did a 'turn', all in the room seemed closer together.

Auntie Maggie's favourite was 'The garden where the praties grow'.

Have you ever been in love boys, or did you ever feel the pain?
I'd rather be in gaol myself than be in love again.
Though the girl I loved was beautiful, I'd have you all to know
That I met her in the garden where the praties grow.

Auntie Maggie sang it with a great sadness. Maybe it was because of her own singleness or maybe she was sensing the fate of its author, who gave his very life in trying to bring people together.

Johnny Patterson, the famous uilleann piper and singing clown, had composed countless ballads like 'The stone outside Dan Murphy's door', 'Goodbye Johnny dear', 'Shake hands with your Uncle Dan' and 'Brigid Donoghue' to name but a few. In 1889 in Tralee, County Kerry, he sang a song urging nationalists and unionists to put their differences aside. It was called 'Do your best for one and other' and it was the last song he would ever sing. A section of the audience took unkindly to its sentiments; he was struck on the head by an iron bar and kicked to death. He was only forty-nine and Ireland had lost one of its greatest entertainers.

'Give us one to liven things up, for God's sake!' shouted the Chief to Tommy O'Rourke. He was the husband of Auntie Katie, my mother's other sister who lived on the side of Cnoc Shee mountain, and he only performed after a few bottles.

'I can't sing,' he protested.

'You can sing rightly,' called his wife.

'Well, if you can't sing, you can tell us how it happened surely,' said the Chief, who had assumed his usual mantle of MC.

'There was three coorse girls,' began O'Rourke, 'and they came out of a dance one night in Hilltown. "I never enjoyed a night no better," said the first. "So did I neither," said the second. "Neither did I too," said the third.'

'Keep her going,' shouted the Chief, in the midst of the laughter.

'Anyway, their father was fed up with them coming in so late,' O'Rourke went on, 'and the following morning he gave out one last roar of a warning. "You three are a pair if ever there was one," he said. "Last night you came in this morning and if you come in tonight, tomorrow, you better find some other place to stay if you want to live here."'

And so it went on with songs and stories, many of which we'd all heard before but just like good Shakespearean plays, they were listened to again and again and respectfully enjoyed anew.

Then all too early it was all too late.

'The man that made the bed wasn't sleeping,' sounded my Uncle Patrick.

Nobody really knew what that meant exactly but my father was tired anyway – it was a hectic time. 'I suppose it's time we were all spitting in our own ashes,' he said, reaching for his hat.

We were all parting again, closer than ever.

14

Beyond the Curtain

One day a man with a strange voice and a strange name drove down our road. He had a strange car too. The steering wheel was on the left, which attracted a lot of attention. No doubt, the faces that looked from behind curtains, over gates and through hedges would have been strange to him too, but Willy Schwenken was used to unusual people. He had managed Hamish Imlach in Germany for one thing, and there was no one more out of the ordinary than Hamish. Back in Boston, Hamish had told us that Herr Schwenken had a weekly radio programme and often played the record we'd demoed in Brennan's byre when the cows were being milked.

'I would like to bring you to Germany,' he was saying, as he drank my mother's tea and took a slice of soda farl she had baked on the griddle.

'We'd love to go,' we said.

'After the harvest's in,' added my father quickly.

So after Hallowe'en when the hay was in and the corn was threshed and the spuds were dug, we began to make plans. We bought a second-hand Humber Hawk from a man in Ballyholland for £50. It was a big stately car, chosen especially to hold the four of us plus the double bass. Ben had opted to stay behind to be with Barbara and their two delightful new arrivals, Michael and Kellie.

We put the bass in head first and belly to the back. Its great stomach squeezed the two back-seat passengers against the doors on either side. When we said goodbye to those at home we said goodbye to each other too, because the presence of the bass allowed very little communication between us until we boarded the boat in Dublin.

'Are you there?' Col would shout to Dino.

'I'm here,' said Dino. 'Are you there, Anne?'

It was like a roll call.

On the crossing from Harwich, England, to Cuxhaven, Germany, we inhaled the accents and languages from many European nations. It took some time to feel at ease with English accents. Such accents had become synonymous with fear and control. 'Up against the wall, Mate!' 'Spread your legs, Paddy!' 'Where's your identification then?' The more cultured English accents had their own negative connotations of pompous politicians pointing fingers of righteousness. Once we had admired the English accent so much on the lips of our cousins, the O'Connors who came on holidays each year, and the likes of The Beatles and Jimmy Saville. The Troubles had twisted us all.

We listened for familiar words in the German we heard. The movie world had translated the voice of an entire nation into 'Seig Heil' and 'Heil Hitler', the obscene speak of the Third Reich. We had no experience of Germany beyond the screens of Hollywood. Soon, however, with growing expectancy, through a window dimmed with rain and saltwater we saw the shape of a German port slide slowly towards us.

We were a day late but time-wise that was no problem. We had a day to spare. Money-wise it was, for we had spent practically all of it on and in the only hotel we could find back in Harwich and we were strapped for ready cash. We did have sixpence though, which we discovered looked very much like a Deutschmark. We also discovered that it fitted perfectly into a German phone box.

'We're in Bremerhaven, Willy,' Col shouted down the line, 'but we've no money for petrol.'

Willy Schwenken was well experienced in dealing with disorganized musicians. He didn't hesitate. 'Go to Herr Werner Puckhaber at the Jugend Centrum,' he said. 'He owes me forty marks.'

With the help of a hitch-hiking Turkish man, we found Herr Puckhaber at home celebrating his daughter's birthday. We ate more than our share of the cake and the Turk took the rest. Puckhaber couldn't recall owing Schwenken money, but he lent us 110 marks all the same.

Later a belly dancer came from behind a drape and began to dance.

'You must dance with her and put 10 marks into her bra, that's the tradition,' our Turkish friend said to me.

I did my bit for tradition's sake, but made the mistake of tucking in the 100 mark note instead of the 10.

'You have nice long fingers,' she said.

We were left with ten marks.

'You better dance with her again,' whispered Col, pushing me forward, 'only this time put the 10 mark note in and take the 100 mark note out.'

It wasn't easy, but I managed it, for necessity is the mother of invention, and I have nice long fingers, thank God.

We stayed with Willy and his wife, Chris. Our bedroom was wallpapered with posters of Derrol Adams, a singer who was no longer managed by Willy so his posters had to be used for something.

Then we began our first tour in Germany. We went from middle to north, north to south and from west to east, at least as far east as we could get in West Germany.

East Germany would come later. We discovered an audience interested in every tune and song. Some already had our record and many were familiar with recordings of the Clancys, the Dubliners and the Fureys. They liked the music and were keen to uncover the secrets that lay behind it. We played in youth clubs, folk clubs, jazz clubs, blues clubs, rock clubs and beer cellars. Sometimes we slept on floors with half our audience, and were kept awake by questions from blue-eyed northern blondes and brown-eyed southern brunettes.

We were booked for the Osnabrück Festival with Na Filí and The Boys of the Lough.

'Don't feel you have to sing well-known songs like "The wild rover",' said Chris. 'We want your own songs, from your own place.'

This was heaven – an audience with no preconceived ideas of who or what we should be. No need to be or pretend to be half-drunk Irishmen. This was an altogether different experience from the nightclubs of America or even the singing pubs of home. This was virgin soil in a fertile land and we sang ancient songs, learned from our parents and neighbours, songs like 'As I was going to Newry, riding on a plough', which had scarcely been heard outside of Ryan. And we sang our own new songs – the audience wanted more and *Zugabe!* rang out throughout the 2000-strong crowd.

'Germans don't sing their own songs any more. The folk tradition has been broken,' said Gisella Sticht from Reutlingen.

'Why is that?' I asked.

'The Nazis desecrated many noble traditions. They highjacked the swastika, that ancient emblem of well-being for centuries, and turned it into a symbol of hatred. Many of the beautiful old folk melodies were used by the Nazis for their goose-stepping propaganda and now this music is reviled and despised by young Germans.'

'It's difficult to like music so much identified with those you hate,' said Dagmar Sieg from the Ruhrgebiet.

I thought about the Protestants at home. Had they abandoned their own music just because we Catholics had embraced it?

The Germans liked the wild abandon and spirit of our music – something that seemed to be missing in the German character. Did they covet the soft mist of our unspoilt 'green island', compared to their own hard and heavily industrialized Ruhrgebiet? Soon German groups would emerge playing and singing Irish songs. The Rambling Pitchforkers, Beda Folk, and Tramps and Hawkers were becoming well known. They recognized the worth and significance of our music and their production values in staging events were legendary. Back home the music was taken for granted. Every pub and alehouse was bursting at the seams with musicians playing for pints. It may have been good for the music, but those playing it found it difficult to make ends meet. For many years Germany would provide the bread and butter to keep body and soul together.

In time German musicians would adapt Irish music and make it their own. By this route, they gradually eased their way back into their own folk traditions. The Rambling Pitchforkers would become Fidel Michel; Beda Folk would change to Moin; and Tramps and Hawkers would become Liederjahn – all leaders in the German folksong revival. We felt honoured by their interest in our music and impressed by their knowledge of English.

We quickly learned that a working knowledge of a second language was a useful key into a new world. We had to learn new ways to deal with our linguistic problems. The French, for example, even if they can speak English are often very reluctant to do so, especially if *l'étranger* is disinclined to attempt some French first. We found that by asking a question like, 'An bhfhuil Gaelige agat?' (Irish for 'Do you speak Irish?'), we could bring a balance to the situation. When the answer was 'Non,' we could mutually agree on a compromise – 'Well, I suppose then we'll just have to settle for the bloody *anglais*'. After that we got on like a house on fire.

Back in Ryan, late in 1973, we received a telegram from Willy, who was not only economical with money, but with words too.

'You have been invited to the Röte Lieder Festival in East Berlin ... Please be in London to catch the Interflug flight to Berlin on the afternoon of next February 9th. Your tickets are in the post.' End of message.

Col's German was best. '*Röte Lieder* means "red songs",' he said quietly. He didn't want Father Hugh to hear. He had heard enough red songs to last him a lifetime.

We had never been 'behind the wall' before. Newry's Rowan Hand, a reporter with RTÉ, arrived out to our house to ask if we were nervous about going. We told him that we were, but we were excited too. What would they know about Irish songs or Ireland behind the Iron Curtain? We wondered. We would soon learn that they knew much more about us than we knew about them.

There were two Interflug flights going east that afternoon. One was aimed at Berlin; the other at Prague. They were both red.

At 30,000 feet I said to the air hostess, 'It won't be long till we're in Berlin now.'

'The worst chat up line I've heard in years,' whispered Dino.

'Not Berlin today,' the young woman said as she handed me a beer.

'You what?' put in Col. 'Sure, aren't we playing in Berlin tonight!'

'This plane is going to Prague,' she answered, throwing her weight behind the trolly and leaving us light-headed in her wake.

'How did that happen?' we asked each other in a panic.

When we arrived in Prague with no entry visas in our pockets, we were put in a small room. A Russian movie with Czech subtitles was showing on a television in the corner. Anne took a fit of laughing, and we all joined.

The next day we made the headlines at the festival without striking a chord: 'Lost Family Finally Found'.

The authorities were very cautious about Westerners and the adventures of capitalism. Some would call it paranoia and the idea of the secret *Stasi* reporting upon and betraying even members of their own family seemed so treacherous. Rarely, however, is there smoke without fire, and in the plush lounge of our hotel we would hear many solid reasons being offered as to why the East should be concerned about the intentions of a US-led West.

'We must be very careful,' said Dr Jack Mitchell, a singing Scotsman who was professor of English in Humboldt University. He had hopped the wall eastwards to escape a British military call-up to kill or be killed in Korea. 'I didn't want to be killed at that particular time,' he said.

'Socialism is like a fragile flower,' he explained. 'It must be protected against those who want to trample and destroy it. Sadly sometimes that necessitates the building of a wall. It's only through socialism that we can achieve equality and justice for all, and that is the only real basis for peace. Without peace there can't be socialism but without socialism there can't be peace. There is enough wealth in this world to go around for everyone. Socialism sets out to ensure that the loaf is divided equally, in order that all at the table may eat. Capitalism says we should be "free" to grab as much as we can from the table, and tough luck on the weak ones who fail. To protect the livelihood of the weak, we must be prepared to take on the aggression of the greedy. That is what this festival is all about, giving a platform to those countries seeking a progressive path forward from the slavery of greed and corruption. No matter how small or downtrodden an individual person or nation might feel, they are never alone because working-class people are everywhere.'

Sounds like a good cue for a song, I thought. I shouted across to the next table to Elke Bitterhof, the festival leader and member of the Oktober Klub, a song group set up to remember the Bolshevik revolution in October 1917. She had been sitting quietly with the Minister for Culture, Herr Krenz, listening to the conversation.

'How about "Wir sind uberall", Elke?'

'Only if you Sands Family will sing with me,' she said, lowering her glass and rising to her feet.

> *Wir sind überall*
> *Auf der Erde, auf der Erde ...*

'We are everywhere,' whispered Birgit Kühn, our interpreter, 'on the earth, on the earth ...'

'Now it's your turn,' Elke said. 'How about "All the little children"?'

Soon we were on our feet, singing songs that had gained popularity in the German Democratic Republic, songs like 'All the little children', 'The winds of freedom' and 'Daughters and sons'.

Each year we went to the festival the solidarity and camaraderie grew. Everyone was singing and harmonies came from all directions and from many countries. Here, songs of freedom were relevant and profound. Many of the artists had personally suffered from the ravages and greed of foreign aggressors. Mikis Theodorakis, who wrote the music for *Zorba the Greek* and *Z*, was tortured under three regimes, German, Italian and British. 'The British were the worst,' he said.

Later we played together the music he had composed for a Greek adaptation of Brendan Behan's *The Hostage*.

'Did you know Behan?' he asked.

'No,' said Dino, 'but we know his mother.'

Mikis was fascinated by our stories of Kathleen Behan swigging Guinness in Dublin and singing songs in the Embankment. 'You know,' he said, 'the Greeks and the Irish are cousins – we love to drink, we love to play music and we love to love!'

Joan Jara, a dancer from England, told us about her husband Victor. I remembered that name. He had been a driving force in Nueva Canción, the great song movement in the Chile of the democratically elected president, Salvador Allende. On 11 September 1973, when the US-backed military junta of Pinochet took over and assassinated Allende, Victor, like thousands of others, was herded into a sports stadium. There, he did what he always did. He took out his guitar and began to sing songs of freedom and peace to his people. When he ignored orders from the military to stop playing, they broke his fingers one by one. When he continued to disobey, they shot him dead. His songs were not forgotten, however, and exiled musicians like Inti Illimani, Quilapayun and songwriter Sergio Ortega were keeping that spirit alive at the Röte Lieder Festival.

Valuable performances of American greats like Harry Belafonte and Pete Seeger graced that stage, along with the rare raw talents of Ewan McColl, Peggy Seeger, Dick Gaughan, Dolores Keane, The James Connolly Group and many others.

The festival fostered a feeling of hope, mounting to euphoria at times. These young people had a vision of what life could become, the world over.

Birgit Kühn shared that vision. 'Our land has already seen too much hatred,' she said.

Sometimes at night we walked through the silent streets of her native Dresden hand in hand, East and West, gazing upon relics of ancient glory, power and punishment. In the Zwinger Palast we saw magnificent monuments to Augustus the Strong, depicting the might of past days when people were ruled by the powerful. And in Lenin Square we saw bright pictures of strong working men and women, depicting the socialism of the present. We stopped beside a large heap of sandstone rubble surrounded by a fence.

'That's the Frauenkirche,' Birgit said. 'The church of Our Lady.'

A full moon filled the place where the spire had once stood, the effect was both eerie and sacred.

'They didn't rebuild it,' she went on. 'They just put this fence around it and left it as a monument to war. No one from Dresden will ever forget the night the British

The Sands Family in Germany, 1974

bombers came. Our city was always considered a centre of art, not a target for war.
Thirty thousand are known to have perished. A revenge raid, because of Coventry,
they said. People were on fire. Their bodies were burning. They jumped into the Elbe
to extinguish themselves but instead it was the water that was set alight. The bombs
were made of phosphorous. Those who had escaped to the surrounding hills returned
to find their historic city devastated. Miraculously, the Frauenkirche was still standing. It was red hot from the fire of the bombs. It stood like that for a time, proud and
defiant, and then suddenly tumbled into rubble. It has lain in that state since 1945.'

The rest of the city had slowly risen from the ashes. Shoulder to shoulder,
women and men cleaned the cement from the slates with their bare hands. The people had rebuilt Dresden and now the people ruled it.

'We want no more wars, no more Hitlers, no more imperialism, no more
bombers,' she said.

'Are you happy with communism?' I asked.

'We can never be complacent,' she replied. 'I believe in the ideals of socialism and
we must continue to find ways to make it better. Unfortunately our leaders are conservative, just like yours. They like power, they like to keep things the way they are.'

Birgit left me to the airport.

'I'll see you,' I said lamely. I knew I would miss her.

'When?' she asked.

'When your leaders invite me back,' I said.

'If they don't,' she said, 'and if the wall doesn't come down, then I'll see you in
thirty-seven years.'

'That long?' I said, feeling her soft blond hair touch my cheek as we embraced.

'Yes,' she whispered. 'I will be permitted to travel to the West when I'm sixty, after I've retired. May I come?' she asked.

'Yes.' I smiled, 'The invitation will never expire.'

'And will you take me to America?' she asked.

'I'll take you to America.' I nodded and smiled again.

'Why do you smile?'

'Are you or have you ever been a member of the Communist Party?'

She laughed and we kissed before I left her for passport control.

As the plane took off for the 'Free World' I looked out the window and she was standing on top of the departure building, waving without restraint.

When we arrived back home in Ireland, a message awaited. It was a note from the local Carmelite monastery written neatly in blue ink.

'Sister Josephine would like you to teach her the guitar,' said my mother. 'She wants to play it for midnight mass.'

I liked going to midnight mass in Glenvale and hearing the nuns sing 'Tantum ergo' and 'Adeste fidelis'. They sounded like angels from another world. And indeed they were from another world. They never went beyond the monastery walls. When they were hungry, they rang a bell and people would bring food. We always brought eggs and were received with a gentle grace, gratitude and promises of prayer, and we frequently arrived home with more food than we had given.

Anne came with me to see Sister Josephine. We rang the bell and slowly the door opened, pulled by a rope from somewhere deep inside the monastery. We went through to the next door and it opened too. This was always a moment of magic for us, as technology was embraced by sanctifying grace. We stood shyly before a large steel-framed curtain and waited with a nervous reverence. The more serious and silent the situation, the more Anne was inclined to threaten a titter.

Soon we heard footsteps. 'Yes?' came a sudden whisper, like the voice of a strange invisible spirit that made me jump a little.

'It's the Sandses, Sister,' I said. 'Bridie's ones.'

'Oh, how welcome you are,' Sister Josephine said. 'And how is your mother? She's a saint on this earth, you know.'

The nun didn't refer to my father's saintliness, but she asked about him anyway and also about Father Hugh and Father Tom.

'They're all doing the best, thank God,' I said.

'And how is the music going? The parish priest tells us all about you.' Then she paused, taking a significant intake of breath for a question that she seemed hesitant to ask. 'And just what is it like behind the Iron Curtain?' she said.

Anne, biting her lower lip and sticking her toenails into the soles of her shoes, pinched my arm and furiously pointed at the brown curtain. 'You ask *her*!' she whispered.

'It was very interesting,' I said to Sister Josephine, still out of sight beyond the curtain.

'Indeed,' said the nun, 'and you certainly seemed to have enjoyed yourselves, thank God.'

Anne and I were laughing by now, for I knew that there is no one in the world, East or West, smarter than a nun when it comes to irony.

'Indeed,' she said again, 'and is it not a holy and a sacred thing to laugh?'

I could see the outline of her face against the curtain, still subtly moving in mirth.

'The communist ideal is to share what the community produces. Human nature often stands in the way of that goal, but it's what they strive for,' I said at last.

'Go on,' said Sister Josephine.

'Christians dream of an ideal world in the next life, in heaven. The communists dream of an ideal world in this life, on earth. It may not be perfect, but they want to give it a try.'

'To find perfection in community is what we all strive for,' she said more seriously, 'but perhaps a little music can help. And you're going to teach me the guitar, I believe?'

'Have you a guitar there, Sister?' I asked.

'I have that,' she answered enthusiastically.

This is going to be a job and a half, I said to myself.

'Will you sound your E string, please,' I asked. 'The thinnest one that you can see,' I added, sensing that she had never handled a guitar before. 'That way we'll have our two guitars in tune.'

A plonk from behind the curtain suggested her E string was flat. I could see Anne's shoulders start to shake again.

'Do you see the peg which is nearest to you on the bottom of the neck?' I asked. 'Please turn it to the right with your left hand, that's if you're right-handed and have the guitar neck pointing to your left.'

'I am that,' she said happily.

The next sound was now dangerously high. Anne began to pace about with her fist in her mouth.

'Maybe you should hand it out to me, Sister,' I said.

I knew the procedure very well. We'd been exchanging things through that hatch for the past twenty years. She lifted the hatch, put the guitar in, then pulled down the hatch on her side and I lifted it out on my side. In two minutes the guitar was tuned and ready for the return journey. Throughout the ritual, neither of us clapped an eye upon the other.

'We'll start with something simple,' I said. The only song that came to mind that could be sung using only two chords was 'Tom Dooley'.

'Is this a song about Dr Tom Dooley, the man who did good things in Vietnam?' Sister Josephine asked.

I had to be honest, this was a different man and none too good. 'He killed his wife, I'm afraid.'

'Glory be to God!' she whispered softly. 'God forgive his soul.'

'We'll start with the D chord,' I said slowly. I had to figure this out.

'Ready when you are', came the answer from the dark.

'Right,' I said. 'Put your first finger behind the second fret on the third string. Then put your second finger behind the third fret of the second string. And next, put your third finger between the second fret of the first string. Have you got that, Sister?' I asked, awaiting the appropriate twang.

'What's a fret?' she said.

That finished Anne off, and she disappeared through the door with a suppressed howl to wait for me outside.

From various corners of the globe, I would send postcards to Sister Josephine with a little more information each time on the technique of guitar playing. She was a gentle kind soul and if she's above in heaven, and I can't imagine her being any-where else, I would say that herself and the two Tom Dooleys are having a good laugh at all the goings on, on this side of the human curtain.

15

There Were Roses

My mother planted them and my father trained them and the Heavens Above, never the ones to be outdone in the springtime of an Irish townland, rained softly upon them. We, in our growing, watched them bud, blossom and trustingly open their pink petals, for the sacred golden thrusts of a shy northern summer.

For me those roses were like no others. Their scent-coloured breath had brushed our childhood's pale canvas and eased deep within us the entwined mysteries of love, life and death. Certainly their presence embraced many a wake, wedding or christening, evoking the appropriate emotion from a throne in a button hole, a bouquet or a well-washed jam jar. If you were far away they reminded you of home and if you were at home they reminded you of some secret room within it, long forgotten or as yet undiscovered.

Round about home big nights were rarely planned. People seemed to gather, without knowing and without asking, like starlings would at the edge of winter on the byre roof. It was only in the glow of warmth and friendship that old songs would slowly rise; songs of love, longing, home and belonging reintroducing us to ourselves and to each other, all over again.

Friends and neighbours' children would gather in our yard to talk, play marbles, pitch-and-toss or traditional games in feats of strength. Then when the night came down and the midges came out, we would go into the house, and soon the parlour would fill with music and merriment. My father would play the 'Oul' clap reel' on the fiddle, shouting out dances, 'Hook before ye, hook behind ye, rag men in the middle, now go to sea.'

Neighbours of all persuasions, Protestant, Catholic and those unsure, Orange and green and the many in-between, took part in the merrymaking, for if we were all able to work together in the fields by day, why shouldn't we dance together at night? Isaac Scott from Benagh was one of 'the other sort' and there was no better dancer and lover of reels and jigs. Amongst the many who often came were singing

Da and Ma on fiddle and box beside where the roses grew

neighbours like Jamie O'Hara from down the road and Mary Murphy from up the road. She would sing 'My Morris 10 and me' and her husband, John, the hardest working farmer in Ryan, would give us an old Scottish ballad called 'Caroline from Edinburgh town'. John's sister, Rosie, who made the best flan cakes in Ryan, would sing 'The faded coat of blue', and Agnes, Rosie's lovely daughter and a pal of my sister Anne, would be there too, laughing and passing round sandwiches 'to beat the band'. Agnes's boyfriend, Seán McDonald, was a quiet gentle lad from up the country around south Armagh and the word was out that he and Agnes had dreams of getting married soon.

In 1973 sectarian murders were on the increase and the sound of drums, guns and explosions could often be heard ever closer to the Ryan Road. One night in the late summer, after a particularly cruel spate of killings, we sat talking in our yard. The roses were in full bloom and their scent seemed to hold us together. 'No matter how close the Troubles get to us here,' someone said, 'it won't change us, for we're friends and we know each other.' One year from that day almost everything had changed.

It was John Murphy who brought us the news on that July morning.

'Wasn't that desperate about Isaac Scott?' he said.

We had already heard on the radio that there had been a shooting outside a singing pub near Newry but we had no idea who was dead. It pains me to admit that such shootings had become so common that they had begun to shock us less. No names had been reported. Now we were hearing that the victim was someone we knew very well, and suddenly everything was different.

My father looked over the fields towards Benagh. 'Lord have mercy on him,' he whispered. 'Lord have mercy on him.'

Just a week before, Isaac had left my father home from town, both of them 'well on' and singing their heads off like there was no tomorrow. Now for Isaac, there would be no tomorrows. There were claims and counter-claims about who was responsible for the killing and why it was carried out, and no one seemed to be certain of anything.

I remember Isaac's funeral. It was raining. We gathered round the grave at the Presbyterian church in Newry, the same graveyard where John Mitchel, the Irish patriot, is buried. I could see all the neighbours standing there, heads bowed. The minister was saying that there should be no revenge killing and we prayed quietly with him. But we would soon learn that not everyone in the vicinity was saying the same prayer. Before long we began to sense some strange unfamiliar fear gripping at our community. There were rumours of suspicious cars, prowling around late at night.

One evening my friend Peggy Johnston and I had gone out on the moonlit road for a quiet walk. She had come from the besieged Unity Flats in Belfast in search of a peaceful weekend.

To see a car every half-hour on the Ryan Road was perhaps the norm, but that night the road seemed to be much busier. Then it dawned on us that what we had thought was a stream of traffic was in fact just two cars, constantly circling. Maybe some people, not familiar with the area, had innocently lost their way in the maze of narrow country roads, but somehow our instincts told us different.

A car driving towards us with full headlights on stopped just before us. We heard the doors opening. That was enough. Like two racehorses, we jumped the stone wall and bolted through the dark fields, over hedges and ditches, running for our lives. Peggy was terrified. She knew the streets around Unity Flats like the back of her hand but this inky wilderness was a different world. I knew every hill, hump, hollow and guttery gap and we ran through dozing cattle and sleepy sheep without stopping to look back until we reached the Rushy Bottom.

'We're safe in this glen,' I panted. 'We're practically surrounded by bog.'

We lay there, feeling safer now in each other's arms, listening and waiting until we thought we heard doors closing and cars moving. Eventually we made our way home, not knowing whether we had fled from friend or foe, but shocked and wounded by the fact that we hadn't dared to wait and find out.

But days passed and somehow life went on. Local families went back to the fields and The Sands Family went back on the road.

In August we were invited to the Merrymass festival in Irvine, Scotland. The way to Larne Harbour was well littered with road blocks and bomb scares but the sea before us, we would soon learn, was no less treacherous and would reflect some of the worst of what we had thought we were leaving behind. On the Stranraer boat we found ourselves a cosy corner, or so we thought, to sit and play a few reels and jigs. We didn't know, however, that Rangers and Celtic were playing that weekend in Glasgow and the audience closing in around us consisted almost exclusively of Rangers fans. They were well jarred, in a fighting mood, and they didn't like the sound of fiddles.

'Play "The Queen",' one of them shouted.

'We don't play party songs,' I answered naïvely.

'Well you've just played "The soldier's song", haven't you, you Fenian bastard?' the man roared back.

'That was "Lucy Campbell", a Scottish reel,' I answered accurately but quite hopelessly.

'Sing "God save the Queen" or youse Fenian bastards and your IRA instruments are going over-fucking-board,' snarled a shaven-headed giant glaring down at me. He had tattooed arms, massive and muscular, and a mouthful of teeth like the Ten Commandments – mostly broken. Right now I wanted to be at home. This was no joke. Then suddenly, just as I feared that the Fifth Commandment might be next on his list for the chop, two policemen appeared. I was never as glad to see the RUC in my life.

We reached bonnie Scotland's shore in one piece, and Stan and Jean Robertson, Mary Canning, Joyce Pyper, and all the gang from the Irvine festival were soon introducing us to the other guests, many of whom we knew. The warmth and wit of Billy Connolly, Hamish Imlach and Danny Kyle soon transported us far from the worries of warring to a world of song and laughter. The Fisher Family of Edinburgh, the Stewarts of Blairgowrie, Dick Gaughan, Iain McIntosh, the Vind Screen Vipers, Eddie and Finbar Furey, the Buskers, and many others, inspired our music and reignited our energy.

It was when we were all on a high, sitting in the green room of the Eglinton Hotel in downtown Irvine, awaiting our turn in the final concert that the word came through. The news seemed to inch slowly towards our consciousness. Another killing has taken place in County Down ... on the outskirts of Newry ... near the village of Mayobridge ... in a lonely country lane. And then we realized it was the Ryan Road they were talking about.

The full story came to us soon enough. My father had heard the automatic gun-fire close by and he knew there was 'bad work' being done. He also saw the night sky lighting to the flames of a car being burned.

Seán McDonald and Agnes O'Hare had been sitting in their car when two other cars drew up, one in front and one behind. Two masked men pulled their doors open. They ordered Agnes into the house and Seán out of the car.

'We're going to shoot you for Isaac Scott,' they said.

That was the last time she saw Seán. They took him down the Ryan Road to a quiet lane, where lovers often met, and shot him in the head.

I can't recall the music we played that night in Irvine, but I do remember Anne crying quietly on stage. The ghastly cycle was complete, two people were dead and Ryan had loved them both.

It would be a long time before I would find words to express such sorrow. When I did they came on the wings of a song and with a memory of roses that straddled a summer seat where we so often sat. And they came in the shape of a lament: not one to bring sorrow, but to bring out the sorrow and leave a space in the soul where love might return.

It was a song for Ryan, to give a voice to a gentle people who bore pain without words. I wanted them to be the first to hear it sung. Later the families of those who died requested, for various reasons, that I change the names. They had suffered enough. Sadly there are all too many from the loved and lost, the named and nameless, to take their place in verses such as these. Such events sum up war anywhere. How often countless ordinary people like ourselves get divided up into little groups, be we of different religion, colour or nation, and be told by the few who find it useful that we are different human beings.

> My song for you this evening is not to make you sad
> Nor for adding to the sorrows of this troubled Northern land,
> But lately I've been thinking and it just won't leave my mind
> To tell you of two friends one time who were both good friends of mine.
> Allan Bell from Benagh, he lived just across the fields
> A great man for the music and the dancing and the reels
> O'Malley came from South Armagh to court young Alice fair
> And we'd often meet on the Ryan Road and the laughter filled the air

> There were roses, roses, there were roses
> And the tears of the people ran together.

> Though Allan he was Protestant and Seán was Catholic born
> It never made a difference for the friendship it was strong
> And sometimes in the evening when we heard the sound of drums
> We said it won't divide us, we will always be the one
> For the ground our father's ploughed in, the soil it is the same
> And the places where we say our prayers have just got different names
> We talked about the friends who died and we hoped there'd be no more
> It's little then we realized the tragedy in store

There were roses, roses, there were roses
And the tears of the people ran together.

It was on a Sunday morning when the awful news came round
Another killing has been done just outside Newry town
We knew that Allan danced up there, we knew he liked the band
But when we heard that he was dead we just could not understand
We gathered at the graveside on that sad and rainy day
And the minister he closed his eyes and he prayed for no revenge
And all the ones who knew him from along the Ryan Road
We bowed our heads and we sayed a prayer for the resting of his soul

There were roses, roses, there were roses
And the tears of the people ran together.

Well fear it filled the countryside there was fear in every home
When a car of death came prowling round the lonely Ryan Road
A Catholic would be killed tonight to even up the score
Oh Christ it's young O'Malley that they're taking from the door
Allan was my friend, he cried, he begged them with his fear
But centuries of hatred have ears that cannot hear
An eye for an eye was all that filled their mind
And another eye for another eye till everyone is blind

There were roses, roses, there were roses
And the tears of the people ran together.

So my song for you this evening it's not to make you sad
Nor for adding to the sorrows of this troubled Northern land
But lately I've been thinking and it just won't leave my mind
To tell you of two friends one time who were both good friends of mine.
I don't know where the moral is or where this song should end
But I wonder just how many wars are fought between good friends
And those that give the orders are not the ones to die
It's Bell and O'Malley and the likes of you and I.

There were roses, roses, there were roses
And the tears of the people ran together.

16

Tour de France

Even though we had beds, we got little sleep that night on the Orient Express from Tubingen in Germany to Paris. Adrenalin from the road behind us, anticipation of the one before us, and snoring from the bunks around us kept the land of nod well beyond our reach.

When we arrived at La Maison de la Mutualité, we were half-dead with exhaustion. It was the first time that the feet went from under me after a concert. I fainted. We had been on the road for months, night and day. I opened my eyes on a narrow Paris street and a man said, '*Nous voudrions vous inviter au festival de Cassel*. Will you come?'

I opened my mouth and without hesitation I said, 'Yes.'

Col, Anne and Dino had already accepted the invitation. You never turn down gigs. If you're ill or weary in most other professions, you call in sick. Not musicians. But despite the exhaustion, we loved what we were doing.

'It's better this, I houl' ye,' said Dino, 'than knocking the frost off a shovel at eight in the morning on McMahon's building site.'

'Or getting a gun shoved in your mouth in Newry tax office,' said Col.

'Or throwing a mop at the ceiling in a chip shop,' said Anne. She was remembering her swansong in a 'real job', when she got fed up washing the floor in a Newry café.

Or looking over the hedge wondering what you're going to be doing next, I thought. The gig at Cassel would mean just a few days at home, then we'd be back on the road again. We were already booked for the Lorient festival and a tour of Brittany, and our LP *First Day and Second Day* was being released by Arfolk Records in Lorient.

'How about taking Ma and Da with us to see the great mainland of Europe?' suggested Anne when we got back home.

Great idea, we thought, but would they come?

'Sure, what would take us away over there?' my mother protested, but I could see she was tempted and knew she only needed a little coaxing. The Chief was raring to go. He missed us when we were away and longed for the good old times, the big nights at home and playing around all the local pubs. Petesy on the Hill and his wife Eileen would come too. There was great excitement in Ryan.

Two friends from Germany, Werner and Didi, whom the Chief had met in Mark's bar, offered to fit out the blue Ford Transit with a few extra seats.

'We might never be back,' shouted the Chief to the neighbours who had gathered to see us off.

'All the best now!' they called.

My mother had packed tea bags because Bernadette Lennon, who had been to Lourdes, told her that you couldn't get a 'dacent cup of tay over there'.

'At least,' said Eileen, 'we can get mass on Sunday, for they're Catholics in France, aren't they?'

'Yes,' said Father Hugh, who had overheard the commotion, 'but French Catholics.'

At last we were off. Up to the end of the lane past the Wee Field gap and turned right at the fairy thorn. That was the best way to go to France. It was also the way we always turned when going to England, Scotland, Wales, Germany or America. In truth, however, it wouldn't have mattered what way we turned. The distance from Ryan crossroads to Newry was exactly the same no matter which of the four roads we took and we had to go to Newry to go anywhere. It certainly mattered little to the Chief as he sang from Newry to Dublin and from Rosslare to Le Havre. His spirit was already in France, singing 'Bonaparte' and 'The bonny bunch of roseso' long before the rest of us rolled off St Patrick's ferry and straightened out along the auto route.

Claude Flagel was at Cassel, a rare and rhythmic exponent of the French hurdy-gurdy. Alan Stivell was there too, and I wanted to meet him, but he was surrounded by so many well-wishers it was impossible to get near him.

'We'll meet in Lorient,' he shouted over the crowd. 'We're both playing there.'

In that warm summer festival I remember great performances from Holly Tanner, Tom Rush and Dave Bromberg from the United States, and the crowd, in a beautiful blaze of bathing suits, loved them all. When the sun shone even brighter, a different colour began to reveal itself on the big hill. It happened slowly at first but soon gained momentum. We had hardly finished 'Twa corbies', a dramatic, shut-eyed song that wedded fourteenth-century Scottish lyrics to an ancient Breton melody called 'À larc', when we became aware that a change had come over our audience. They were all stark naked. That's what it was. Not a sock on any of them and no one batting an eyelid. Well, almost no one.

I looked at my mother. So these are the sort of places you've been travelling to, she seemed to say, but then she and Eileen took a fit of the giggles and Petesy on the Hill took his first ever glass of alcohol.

'There's damn all wrong with this,' he said, looking around, seriously considering the thought of converting to French Catholicism himself.

After a mighty weekend of music, song and dance, it was time to take them to Le Havre and the boat home. They didn't want to leave at all. Eileen said that this was the best holiday they had ever had. Petesy and the Chief had cemented themselves in the corner of a pub, telling yarns and singing songs to young French women, declaring that France was 'the best wee country in the world' and wondering if they should go to Lourdes on the next trip from the parish of Saval.

With waves and hugs we said our goodbyes at the French port as if it was America itself they were going to and we'd never see them again.

The four of us had a long journey ahead. Early next morning we piled into the Ford Transit and straightened out on the road for Brittany. Somewhere between Le Havre and Caen a strange rattle developed in the engine of the van. Col, who was the technical adviser in the family, jumped out and put his head under the bonnet. Then he looked back in through the perspiring windscreen and shook his head slowly.

'Bad news,' he said. 'She's bust her boilers.'

We were to take part in a pre-festival session that night in Lorient, and knew that the breakdown would make us miss the start time. We didn't realize then, however, that without the breakdown other great events would have been missed.

We sat at the side of the hot Normandy road, the sun scorching and the van fuming, not knowing what to do.

'We'll make some tay,' said Anne. 'We've still got Ma's tea bags and the Primus stove.'

As mugs slowly emptied of tea and minds filled with ideas, a definite two-pronged strategy of action began to emerge. Dino and Anne would hitch onwards to Caen with mandolin and bodhrán, catch a train and try to make the opening in Lorient. Col and I would head back towards Le Havre, hire a car, tow the van to a garage, leave it to be repaired, and head for Lorient in the rented car with the rest of the gear.

It is said that young women get lifts easier than young men. Certainly Anne's presence seemed to ensure a swift journey south. They were scooped up in no time by a white Renault and disappeared in a cloud of dust, waving and laughing. For Col and myself, going north, it was another matter.

We stood with upbeat smiles and upturned thumbs but Citroëns – both DS and 2CV – flashed by. Instead of slowing down they seemed to speed up as they approached our position. Finally we came up with a plan. It turned out to be a masterstroke. We walked to a petrol station and bought an empty petrol can. Instead of thumbing now, we just stood at the side of the road with a mildly embarrassed smile, finger pointing at the can. And before you knew it, there was a scream of brakes that frightened a gathering of crows that had been having a quiet caw on a nearby tree.

'Venez, messieurs, mais c'est mon plaisir ...'

Now we were regarded as brethren in trouble and we had our choice of a BMW or a Citroën Dyane. We took the BMW purely for reasons of comfort, and had great difficulty explaining, in rather rusty school French, that the fuel we needed was so special it wouldn't be available at the next station, or the one after that. Nevertheless, with the help of several generous, if totally confused, members of the driving fraternity, we reached Le Havre, hired a car, towed the van to the garage and headed for Lorient as planned, with the empty petrol can stowed safely in the back, just in case.

The next day we joined Anne and Dino, who had already met up with old friends from home, John Watterson and Dessie Wilkinson, and a local group of wild seafaring singers called Djiboujeb. They were playing on the street and drinking Ricard.

'This is the life,' said Watterson, as he rifled into a Breton dance tune they had learned the previous night. It was a tune drawn from the same well as our own but with quite a different bucket. The word 'Celtic', which adorned shop windows, was rarely used in Ireland at that time and, for us, a new door to a common ancestral history was suddenly ajar.

We met Alan Stivell. Born in Paris as Alan Cochevelou, of Breton parents, he took the name Stivell, meaning 'spring or source'. He more than anyone was rejuvenating and energizing the wonderful Breton music and dance tradition with harp, *biniou* and bombarde. Beside him was Dan Ar Braz, a wonderful guitar player who, together with Stivell, was bringing a new pride and modernity to an ancient Celtic culture. They were acutely aware of how much their country's past was mirrored in Ireland's history and they drew inspiration from the Irish music revival back home. Stivell was familiar with the music of Turlough O'Carolan and almost every harpist since the seventeenth century. We talked about Mary O'Hara, a frequent guest on Raidió Éireann's *Take the Floor* many years ago. After her young husband's death, she had disappeared into a monastery. Someone said she had returned to the world again but no one seemed sure. A sense of pride and wish for cultural freedom and recognition was evident in the words and music of Gilles Servat, Les Soeurs Goadec, and Glen Mor.

The seven Celtic nations of the world – Ireland, Scotland, Wales, Cornwall, the Isle of Man, Galicia and Brittany – were all represented at the festival. The Bothy Band and ourselves, amongst others, represented Ireland. The concerts in the big halls were formal and dignified; the sessions in the small pubs were cosy and wild.

One night down by the Port de Pêche, in a place called Teeptoe, a row broke out. That was nothing new in the Teeptoe. Michel from Djiboujeb was quite capable of going after a French soldier with his clog. And many sailors gathered there, a little worse for wear. On this occasion, however, it wasn't Michel or the sailors who were the troublemakers. Paddy Keenan, the peerless piper with the Bothy Band, had lost his balance and taken half a table of drink with him. That was fine, anyone could make a mistake. He got up, however, which was his downfall, and came up with an encore that brought down any beer that had been missed the first time.

Donal Lunny tried to calm things and got a punch in the jaw for his trouble, and in no time a battle royal began to develop. A big bouzouki fan was asking for his coat to be held so that he could throw a punch somewhere, and the drunken, beerless opposition were flinging off clothing left, right and centre. They say in times past it was traditional for the Celts to go naked into battle and Mícheál Ó Domhnaill rolled up a shirtsleeve in anticipation. 'Do you think,' says he to me, 'will we have to die for Ireland yet again?'

Whether it was our new pal Michel's ominous removal of his clog that did the trick, or Big Mama, the black barmaid, who cooled the bucks down with a bucket of slop beer she saved for such occasions, I'm not sure, but it was all over before it started and we were soon swaying back and forward with fresh beer in our fists, singing 'Jean Français'.

A trip to Paris brought us to the Gare du Nord, where we met John Keane and Gerry McAlinden. They had arrived to do a university lecture tour, explaining the socialist and anti-sectarian hopes behind new republican thinking. We travelled together from Morlaix to Rennes. John said that an important aspect of Ireland's history could be summed up in a single observation: the Anglo-Normans had invaded Ireland in the twelfth century under the leadership of Strongbow, the Earl of Pembroke. Eight hundred years later, Leinster House, the seat of the Irish parliament, was still paying ground rent to the estate of the Earl of Pembroke. Both Gerry and John were clear thinkers and impressive speakers. Anne in particular was impressed, for herself and John would later be married in Sheeptown chapel back home in County Down. There was a long road to travel, though, before that happy event would take place. Right now the problem was to get the van fixed. French motor mechanics were not equipped to deal with Ford Transits, so we towed it onto the boat and sailed for Southampton. Our engagement after Brittany was at the Edinburgh Festival.

We had a good friend near Southampton called Patsy O'Toole, from the Aran Islands, who put us up and found a mechanic.

'I see you're Irish musicians,' said the man in the garage. 'There's an Irish musician living just up the road there.'

We pictured a bearded fiddler perhaps, or a box player.

'No, actually, she's a woman,' he said, 'very quiet and dignified like. She passes this way on her bicycle sometimes.'

She lived in a small cottage on the edge of a large estate belonging, he thought, to the Guinness family. We had time. It would take a day or so to fix the van. In the afternoon we were knocking on her door. It was opened by Mary O'Hara, just out of the monastery she had lived in for twelve years. Soon she had us drinking tea and eating hot scones, dripping with butter.

'How about a song, Mary?' I asked after a while.

'Och sure, who would want to listen to me?' She smiled. 'I'm out of date.'

'We would,' we said in unison, and to get things going we sang a few songs ourselves.

'I'll give you one from your own part of the world,' she said at last. 'It was written by a man called McCambridge from the Glens of Antrim. He had decided to emigrate but by the time he reached the boat, he was so full of love for his native place that he couldn't bear to leave at all, and so he turned on his heel and went back home again. The song he wrote about it, though, has travelled to many places. It's called "*Aird tí cuain*". This is my sister Joan's translation.' She straightened her back in the chair and set her gaze somewhere far away.

> By myself I'd be in Aird tí cuain
> Where the mountains stand away
> And 'tis I would watch the Sundays go
> In the cuckoo's glen across the bay.

> *Agus och, och ar lig's o*
> *Ar a liom dibh's o*
> *S'é mo chroí tá troim agus bróna*

> I would travel back the winding years
> In the bitter wasted wind
> If the Lord above would let me lie
> In a quiet place above the whins ...

Never was such a round of applause heard in the quiet house of Guinness.

'What about the harp?' I asked.

'Oh, it's upstairs, I think, but there are strings broken and it's in a bad state of repair,' Mary replied.

'Could we take it somewhere and get it fixed for you?' asked Dino.

'That harp was made by a man in Edinburgh,' she said.

'We're going there tomorrow,' said Col. 'We'll take it with us.'

Not long afterwards, Mary and her harp were topping the bill in the Royal Albert Hall, thanks, perhaps, in some small way to a blue Transit breaking down on a tour de France.

Dino, 1975

17
Dino

I had a feeling that something was wrong that morning. For a start, we had been called too early. It was a free day. Horst Tubingen knew that. He was our host and had suggested just a few hours earlier at the after-concert party that we could lie on as long as we wanted. Now he seemed troubled. 'I have made you coffee,' he said slowly. 'Please take a seat.' He paused.

I knew he wanted to tell us something important. What was wrong?

He was struggling with his English to find the right words. 'Something very bad happened last night,' he said finally.

At times like this everything seems to slow down, leaving space for a thousand wondering thoughts. I sat down and watched him as he talked to me but I wasn't taking it in.

'Something very bad happened to your family,' he was saying. 'Last night ... your family ...'

The Sands Family had played at the Logo, his Hamburg club, the previous evening, 10 November 1975. What bad thing could have happened? Had we not played well enough? Or long enough? We had built up a good following there since our first appearance in 1973. It had been a full house. Dino had pulled the place apart with his banjo. The audience sang our songs along with us. Many friends had come along to hear us and meet us afterwards. Friendships are so intense when you're on the road. There was so much to be said and such a short time to exchange all the news, the yarns, the companionship and affection. Sometimes there is only enough time for a hug and then it's time to start again, part again, maybe for good. Another one-night stand is calling and you're back on the road again, leaving behind lifelong friends you have just met, laughter, tears and passionate memories. But 11 November was free and we could stay up late and we did.

Inge Kramer had been there. She was living in Hamburg now and it was good to see her again.

Dino and I had met Inge and Susi Pitzer in Osnabrück, after a gig with the Boys of the Lough. We were on top of the world when we walked into the tavern and our eyes fell on the two beautiful young women. Soon we were sitting beside them, talking, laughing and drinking bottles of pils. Inge and I stayed good friends. Dino and Susi fell in love.

We had all been together again last night. It was like old times.

Dino and Susi had headed back to her family home in Georgemarienhutte in her pale blue Volkswagen. I can still see them clearly, smiling and shouting '*Tchüss!*' and '*Auf Wiedersehen!*' Dino's long fair hair is flying about his shoulders. He is waving his mandolin. 'See you the day after tomorrow,' he calls.

What was it that Horst was saying now? I could feel myself growing cold. He was talking about Dino.

'I wish I could change it,' he said, 'but it can't be changed … Your brother is dead … Dino is dead.'

Something about a burst tyre, a bridge, a lorry. An awful numbness was coming over me. Susi was injured, still alive, but Dino was dead. *Dino was dead.*

Horst was saying that Willy Schwenken had phoned him with the news. He hadn't wanted to wake us earlier. 'I hate to be the one to tell you this. You will remember me for the rest of your life only because of this moment,' he said, tears in his eyes.

'Do our parents know yet?' Colum was asking.

Someone had telephoned the local priest to break the news.

Anne didn't know. She had stayed over with Inge.

Suddenly they appeared. One look from Anne at our ashen faces told her something terrible had happened. Inge was struggling with tears. She already knew.

'Anne,' I said. 'It's the worst. Dino's dead. There was a crash.'

Somehow my telling it eased the unbearable heaviness that had paralysed me. Our sister was now sharing our awful burden.

Poor Anne fell back in the chair. She couldn't be consoled. We were all close to Dino, but perhaps she was closest of all. He was her big brother. He had taken her to Sheeptown school. He had helped her over the stiles and ditches down by Desert, past the old mill, over Mullan's Bridge and up through the ragged rocks of Crow Hill. How could he be dead?

We drove down the autobahn in the blue Transit towards Bremen to identify Dino's body. Colum was driving, a gentle tower of strength as always. John Keane was doing his best to comfort Anne, who sobbed quietly. She was reminding us of a dream she had had a few nights ago about Dino being shot by a blue gun. Later we would hear from Ben and Barbara, back at home, how a picture had fallen off their wall on the day he died. There were so many things we couldn't understand.

I looked around at The Sands Family. There were only three of us now. A feeling of fear came over me. Could something like this happen to another one of us? Could Anne or Colum suddenly be gone as well? My faith in the future was shaken – it could never be taken for granted again.

Anne and I flew from Bremen to Amsterdam and then on to Dublin. Col and John would follow in the van. Benny McKay of Crubeen, the folk group, met us at the airport. My parents were in bed when we got home, their eyes red and swollen.

'Is it really true?' my father said.

'Yes, Da,' I answered, taking his hand.

He burst into tears and the whole bed shook with his crying.

The wake had already started. Bridie and Eileen were in the house, and Barbara and Isobel were tidying up and making sandwiches. Neighbouring farmers with big hands and tears in their eyes were saying they couldn't believe it when they heard it on the radio. 'I'm sorry for your troubles,' they said. Liam Daly, John Murphy, Tom Wilson, Jamie O'Hara, Dominic Cunningham – they were all there. Nora Wilson had made a griddle of bread and brought it with her.

Hands reached out from everywhere for days and nights. Telegrams came from the Glenvale nuns, from the leadership of the East German Communist Party, from politicians of every hue, nationalist, unionist, loyalist and republican.

I dreaded every stage: each had a different pain, from Dino's body arriving back home to the final leaving. On the night before the funeral, I slept in the room with Dino. One last time together. I was wakened the next morning by my mother's sobbing – she hadn't known I was there. Bridie told me later that Ma didn't want to upset the rest of us by crying. What a powerful love she had, and her own heart torn to pieces.

I don't know how we could have survived that time without the neighbours and the wake. I had once been sceptical of the Irish wake with neighbours coming and going, shaking hands, telling yarns, playing music and drinking. Now I was learning how important it was. No human heart can bear the raw pain of such a parting alone. In the company of friends, remembering, remembering, remembering all the good times. Without realizing it, we were turning from death to life. We were no longer mourning death, but celebrating life. Dino's life. Laughing and crying; crying and laughing.

I dreaded most of all the day of the funeral. When we carried him out through the door for the last time and onto the front street, I thought I would fall apart. I was afraid to lift my eyes. And then the heavy silence was broken with a sound I will never forget. It was Fergal McAuliffe on the bagpipes, playing 'Donal Óg', one of the oldest and most beautiful songs ever written.

> I saw you first on a Sunday evening,
> About the Easter as I was kneeling,
> 'Twas about Christ's passion that I was reading,
> But my eyes were on you and my sad heart bleeding.

The sound seemed to fill the sky. I looked up and the whole landscape was transformed. The front street, the lane, the road, the surrounding fields, were black with hundreds of people. They had come from everywhere just to be with us and to

Dino memorial concert, 1976: Col, Paddy Clerkin, Barney Gribbin, Jimmy Burns,
Eddie McIntyre, and Willie McSherry

say goodbye to Dino. I lifted my head and proudly marched up the lane with Mary, Hugh, Ben, Col, Anne, and Dino. All of us together.

At night when I close my eyes to dream, other eyes open and he is often there. He's changed now, in a way I can't describe, but I can see him clearly, and he's alive. Of that I have no doubt.

18

Country Céilí

After Dino's death, we had no heart to go back on the road again. Nothing seemed worthwhile any more. It seemed so unthinkable, almost a betrayal, to stand onstage without him and his banjo, bouzouki, mandolin, whistle, fiddle, and all his beguiling harmonies. His dying had given us a new and painful insight into the many tragic deaths of young men and women of his age, which were happening day in and day out throughout the country. We felt the precious gift of life so keenly now that the thought of hurting or maiming, never mind killing, another human being seemed pointlessly cruel and wrong.

John Niblock's son, who lived across the fields in Croan, died in a car crash a few days after Dino's funeral. We all went to the wake and when we shook hands with the family, we knew what they were going through. We felt a deep new empathy based on mutual heartbreak.

No, we couldn't think of performing without Dino. Our friends thought differently, though, and they were right.

'Do you not think that Dino would want the music to keep going?' they asked.

Deep down we knew the answer.

Mark McLoughlin, Benny McKay, Sean Hollywood, Gerry Quinn, Fergal McAuliffe, Brian Mullen, the Ryans from Murroe, and many others began organizing concerts in Dino's memory and inviting us to play. We even had Susi join us onstage when she recovered from the accident and soon the long road to healing began.

Ben, whose own family commitments had taken him off the road, was willing to return. He was such a great all-round musician and singer that we knew The Sands Family could go on. There were many discarded invitations lying about and we began to read them again with a renewed motivation. Soon we were back visiting old friends and finding new ones with concerts in Bulgaria, Czechoslovakia, Poland, Sweden, Denmark, Luxembourg, Austria, Switzerland, Spain and Italy. In

Lisbon, Portugal, our faith in song was further restored when we joined Jose Afonso in his composition 'Grandola vila morena' before an audience of close to 100,000 people. That song, when played on Radio Renascenca, had been the secret midnight signal to herald in the Carnation Revolution just a few years earlier. The audience remembered that day of 25 April 1974, when a half century of fascism had ended. They remembered too putting the red carnations into the barrels of silent guns, being held by young soldiers no longer willing to back a dictatorship. And they remembered with tears in their eyes every word of a song that up until then had been banned throughout the land.

> Grandola, land of sun, land of brotherhood,
> Your heartbeat sings the people's dream,
> On every corner there is a friend, on every face there is equality,
> Grandola vila morena.

No wonder the word radio was in my mind when I arrived home and no wonder, too, I welcomed the phone call inviting me to join a brand-new radio station near Belfast called Downtown Radio. It was Paddy O'Flaherty, who had been presenting and producing a folk programme on the new station, and he was leaving for a job at the BBC.

'Would you be interested in taking it on?' he asked. 'You could still do your gigs.'

I thought about what all the family were doing these days, branching in various directions. Colum had already accepted some theatre work and was in the Lyric Theatre doing music for the play *We Do it for Love*. I remember being struck by the presence of a performer in that play, a tall thin youth who sang a song called 'The rights of man'. He was Liam Neeson and would later become a very successful film actor. Colum continued on his journey to stages and far-flung places. Once he rang me from a small island on the Rhine. 'I'm thinking of getting married tomorrow,' he said. His *Fräulein* was the lovely blue-eyed Barbara Wendel from Cologne, whom he had met at Ty Bedouffs in Brittany's Isle de Groix. Ben's hands were already full with projects and his time for long tours was well limited at this point. Anne had begun to do some painting and would later become involved in setting up a new integrated school in County Down for children of all religions. Meanwhile Hugh had returned from his rambles, married the charming Máirín from Rathfriland on the Hill and opened a pub in Hilltown called The Mourne Rambler, where we often gathered and sang well into the wee hours.

I had always loved the idea of radio, ever since I had hidden behind an old wireless, commentating on an All-Ireland final in a play in Sheeptown Hall. When I was a child I used to look into the back of the old wireless at home and marvel at its workings. I imagined little men talking and orchestras playing inside the shiny glass valves and wondered what it would be like to be in there.

John Rosborough, head of programmes at Downtown, and later David Sloan, were very encouraging. They assured me that it was possible, if necessary, to record programmes in advance in the event of any tour engagements. In July 1977 *Country Céilí* began, and has continued every Saturday night from six to eight ever since. I have enjoyed the opportunity it has given me to invisibly sit in the corner of so many kitchens and parlours, playing the music I love and chatting, not to strangers, but to the many friends I never knew I had. Now I'm on the inside of the radio, imagining all the people on the outside and wondering what they are doing, thinking and feeling as they listen in on a Saturday evening.

As well as playing records, I like to go out into the towns, villages and countryside to record singers, storytellers and musicians, who live in abundance all over the North of Ireland. These live events have not been without drama.

Once, just before we went 'live' from Gentle Art O'Neill's Welcome Inn, Forkhill, the British army marched in and marched out with my main guest, local poet, storyteller and national treasure John Campbell from Mullaghbawn. For nearly twenty minutes I pondered the idea of cancelling the broadcast. It was ample time to ponder many thoughts about south Armagh.

Not far away stood Moyry Castle, built by the English Lord Mountjoy in 1600 to monitor the stirrings of the local peasantry. It was now accompanied by a large British army watchtower, constructed for the same purpose. Tales of oppression loomed loud in local balladry. The notorious landlord, Johnson of the Fews, who had hunted local poets of the O'Neills, like McCooey and Ó Doirnín, and beheaded McMurphy in the eighteenth century, was still remembered in children's rhymes:

> Jesus of Nazareth, King of the Jews,
> Save us from Johnson, King of the Fews.

The Johnson name still struck terror a hundred years later when Michael Campbell, the great-great-grandfather of John Campbell, was evicted from his home in Ballsmills and sentenced to thirty years in Van Diemen's Land on trumped up charges of treason in 1846. Before his full sentence was served, however, he managed to make it back to Ireland and, like a homing pigeon, found his way into a field on his old farm. That's where his wife found him, only to discover that his mind was gone, and he would soon be laid to rest in Creggan graveyard with the O'Neills, the poets, and the Johnsons of the Fews. Now another hundred years and more had passed and we were sitting in Forkhill awaiting the return of his great-great-grandson John from the clutches of Her Majesty's soldiers.

By good fortune we hadn't long to wait and when the totally innocent bard walked in the door, a loud cheer of welcome rent the airwaves. Unshaken, unshackled and unhurried, he sat down and gave a wonderful performance to a packed house and a tenter-hooked radio audience. 'There was a misunderstanding,' he said with a mischievous grin. 'I told them I was coming from Killinaman and going to Kilmore and they thought there was murder on my mind. They should learn about Irish place-names before they come here,' he scolded.

Recorded programmes weren't always plain sailing either. At Christmas time that year I did a special family programme, and Father Hugh agreed to take part. My plan was to interview him separately, but in order to create continuity I introduced him as 'live', to prompt a round of applause from the neighbours in the parlour where the rest of the recording was taking place. The neighbours were all gathered round, well jarred with bottles of stout, laughing and talking.

'It gives me great pleasure,' I said, 'to welcome to the gathering that great man of story and song, Father Hugh Sands.'

Instead of applause, there was a shocked silence, and then a sudden scurrying for shelter. Half-full bottles were pushed into coat pockets and under sofas as half-drunk men scattered in all directions, scaling window sills and seeking doorways like they were fleeing a sinking Titanic. It was only the women and children who remained and those in the know who applauded quietly, knowing that Father Hugh was asleep in bed.

A programme well remembered in Downtown is still referred to as 'the one with the Paisley and Cardinal', although 'Sands meets the saints and scholars' was the official title. Others were featured but these two figures were the most unlikely guests to be caught swapping jokes and singing songs at the same Christmas party and so the name stuck.

Paisley phoned me later. 'You doctored the tapes, friend,' he said.

'I edited the tapes, Doctor,' I replied.

'No, you doctored the tapes, editor,' he concluded and hung up. There was some truth in what he was saying, I have to admit, but there was a good reason for it all and in the fullness of time, if not in this life then perhaps in the next, I hope he will excuse me.

It had been a bad year. By Christmas of 1978 eighty-one people had been killed, communities were growing further apart, and many of the leaders in the North were not in the mood to meet or talk. The polarization in Northern society was being amplified by political words and military deeds. I thought it might be a good idea, therefore, to invite the leaders of Northern Ireland's main churches and political groupings to have a bit of a hooley, a Christmas *Country Céilí*. This *céilí* would attempt to gather together some people who were not in the habit of spending time with each other. I would soon learn that some of these Christians didn't particularly want to be seen too close to each other, Christmas or no Christmas. Many told me there was no mission of getting them together, to sing, play music, or tell jokes.

I spoke to Éamonn Maillie and Peter Russell in the newsroom. They agreed the idea was a good one and set about helping me with telephone numbers, and soon I set out armed with hope and a tape recorder. Paisley would be most difficult, I was told. His pulpit-pounding fundamentalism didn't make him an obvious suspect for merriment and frivolity, particularly in the company of political papists and social-ist sinners. Nevertheless, he was a 'must have'. Love him or loath him, his face on television at the time demanded instant attention and his voice on the radio was compulsive listening. He would have to be there. They would all have to be there, if this was going to work.

My first visit was to a socialist sinner called Paddy Devlin. I knew Paddy of old. He was the most socialist part of the Social Democratic and Labour Party, a good friend and a good singer too. He threw back his head and sang a song, then threw back a vodka and sang another one. Paddy's two songs, Hayes and Robinson's 'Joe Hill' and Kris Kristofferson's 'Sunday morning sidewalk', reflected his working-class politics and his empathy with the disadvantaged.

'Where are you going next?' he asked, chuckling at the idea of the programme.

'Where does the Reverend Ian Paisley live?' I asked in reply.

'For a start,' said Paddy, 'I don't call him Reverend anything, I call him Ian Pais-ley. And I don't call people Doctor this or Lord that or Major my arse. They're all just people to me and they can stick their titles and their privileges where the mon-key put his nuts. And that goes for the Pope and the Queen and the whole bloody lot of them. By the way, would you like a drink or a bite to eat before you go?'

Paddy gave me directions and soon I was on my way up the Newtownards Road, regretting I hadn't taken up his offer to eat, for I realized now I was starving and I didn't want to meet my next guest on an empty stomach. I called into a Chinese carry-out near the North Road and ate my meal in the car, wondering what manner of man was awaiting me.

I drove on to Paisley's house. I was as ready as I ever would be to meet the leader of the Free Presbyterian Church.

A pair of boots stuck out from beneath a parked car on his street.

'Hello!' I said.

A young man slid out with oil on his hands.

'Is this Ian Paisley's house?' I asked.

'I am Ian Paisley,' came the reply. He looked no more than a boy. 'I suspect it's my father you want to see, though,' he said. 'I don't think he's home yet but you can knock on the door. My mother's there.'

The recognizable figure of Eileen Paisley assured me with a smile that I was wel-come and asked me to wait for her husband in the sitting room. Her daughter Rhonda sat with me. David Dunseith was talking to politicians on the television.

'Does your father sing?' I asked.

'I only heard him sing once,' she said, 'and I laughed so much I couldn't stop.' She began to laugh again at the thought of it.

Then it seemed as if the house began to shake.

'He's coming,' said Eileen, putting her head around the door.

I heard footsteps getting closer and I shivered slightly, hoping it wouldn't show. The footsteps grew louder and the house seemed to shake more. Then, standing at the door was one of the biggest men I have ever seen. He had a large head, large ears, large eyes, large nose, large mouth, large body, large everything. He seemed to fill the whole doorway. As a Catholic child, I had nervously watched the television screen as he controlled thousands with a single roar. Now he was standing right in front of me, fierce as a giant.

I explained why I'd come. I was including various leaders in a special Christmas programme. I didn't want them to talk about religion or politics, but to sing a song or tell a yarn instead. Slowly I held my microphone up to the mouth of the Reverend Doctor.

'How do you prefer to be addressed, by the way?' I asked, trying to break the ice lightly. 'Do you want me to call you Reverend, or Doctor, or Ian?'

'You can call me anything you like, providing you don't call me early in the morning,' he replied, with a loud laugh. 'Are you getting Fitt to play the mouth organ?' he asked quickly, referring to Gerry Fitt, his arch-rival and current leader of the SDLP. 'I don't know how good he is, but the more he plays it in my constituency, the more the people vote for me.'

'What about a song or a story from yourself?' I said.

He put his head in his hands and began to think.

'As you know,' he said at last, 'I'm an unreformed jailbird and the first time I went to prison, the prison doctor examined me from head to toe and said, "You're fit," and I said, "No! I'm Paisley." Then one day a prisoner swallowed a half-crown, hoping he might be let out early, and some smart fella says, "Send for Paisley, he's a doctor, he'll get the coin out." "No," came the reply, "he is a doctor of theology, not a medical doctor." "Well," says your man, "Doctor Paisley is able to get money out of a stone, so I'm sure he'll be able to get a half-crown out of this man's stomach."'

The big man was getting into his stride now, 'There was a Jewish rabbi and a Roman Catholic priest sitting in a restaurant one time and the priest said in a very loud voice, "Rabbi, when are you going to become liberal and eat the flesh of the pig?" "At your wedding," replied the rabbi.'

This was a Paisley I had never envisaged, relaxed and radiant with boyish devilment and humour. I was so surprised I could hardly laugh myself but he laughed enough for both of us. He regaled me with joke after joke, gradually drawing me into a web of companionship. He was magnetic. No wonder he has thousands of disciples, I thought. The man was powerful. Like a schoolmaster who cared for his pupils by first scaring them, he portrayed a rare mixture of charisma and awfulness. You were inclined to laugh at the joke before you got to the punchline.

'I'm going to Armagh next,' I told him, 'to see the two archbishops. I hear talk that Archbishop Ó Fiaich will be made a cardinal. And the Pope's chair is vacant. Do you think you might go for the job?' I ventured with a smile.

Paisley stopped in mid-laugh. 'I might run for Europe,' he said, 'but I don't think I'll be running for that particular office.' Then he laughed again and wished me well on my travels.

I walked away from the door with a well-filled tape and a well-shook hand, and began to consider the real contribution this man was capable of making.

Archbishop Otto Simms, head of the Anglican Church in Ireland, opened his door at eleven the following morning and I gazed upon a gentle, unassuming, and highly cultured man.

'Come in,' he said, in a plummy English accent.

I was offered tea in a delicate porcelain cup. He had remembered my phone call but with a shy smile, he told me of another call he had received just afterwards.

'It was one of my ministers, actually,' said Dr Simms, 'but he didn't realize it was I who answered the phone. "Is his nibs in?" asked the junior clergyman rather gruffly. "I'm afraid," I said, "this *is* his nibs speaking." The poor man, of course, was very embarrassed, but I couldn't help having a little laugh to myself. It's so important to have a little laugh sometimes.'

I liked this man. Despite his apparent aristocratic affectations, I felt very relaxed in his home. An authority on the Book of Kells and medieval Irish literature, he delicately fingered through some old papers to find the poem he wanted to contribute.

'When the monks were working on those heavenly intricate letterings,' he said, 'one wrote a little poem, perhaps by way of recreation, on the margins of a page and it has been preserved in the old manuscripts to this day. It was inspired by his little white cat Pangur Bán:

> I and Pangur Bán my cat
> 'Tis a like task we are at:
> Hunting mice is his delight,
> Hunting words I sit all night.
>
> Practice every day has made
> Pangur perfect in his trade;
> I get wisdom day and night
> Turning darkness into light.

Dr Simms read this deceptively simple little poem with a respect due to Shakespeare.

'We have all got our own little tasks,' he said with a smile, 'haven't we? And speaking of such tasks, I don't want you to leave Armagh without roping in the other archbishop. He's a wonderful singer, you know.'

We stood at the door and viewed the heavenly reachings of both cathedrals, built on sites where, it is said, the sun and moon were once worshipped.

'I'm not sure which is highest,' he remarked, 'but I do know they point in the same direction.'

I bid him goodbye and headed in the direction of the Catholic spire.

I had met Archbishop Tomás Ó Fiaich twice before. In my college days I had attended a masterly lecture he gave on Irish history and social justice and recently I had met him at a reconciliation party, which he had organized in the archbishop's

Archbishop Tomás Ó Fiaich
(photo *Belfast Telegraph*)

palace, Ara Coeli. Quite unknown to the media, he had Willie John McBride, the rugby player, sitting beside Scán Ó Síocháin, the general secretary of the GAA, and various other commonly perceived political rivals eating and drinking together. When his guests left, he had invited me to stay for a few songs and a 'wee brandy', for he hadn't had the 'chance of a drink all night'. I knew he was not only a fine singer but an authority on the Irish song tradition, and I was looking forward to this return visit.

'What sort of a character is Paisley?' he asked straightaway with a mischievous smile. 'What did he do for you?'

'He told jokes,' I said.

'Isn't it good to laugh at the seriousness of it all sometimes?' He leaned towards me. 'Did you hear the one,' he began, 'about the young priest hearing confessions for the first time and this man walked in and confessed, "Bless me, Father, for I have sinned and I have been making *poitín*"? The priest gave him absolution but wasn't too sure of how much penance to give him as there was no mention of *poitín* in the canon law books he had read. "Hold on a moment," he said to the penitent, and nipped into the other confessional where the old parish priest was hearing and whispered, "There's a man in here that's making *poitín*. How much will I give him?" The old priest thought a while and then said, "If I was you, I'd give him no more than a half a crown a bottle."' He sat back and chuckled. 'What about yourself?' he said. 'Would you like a sup of something?'

I declined his offer just as the phone rang and Mamie, his housekeeper, came in. 'Another explosion, your Lordship,' she said. 'Two killed, I'm afraid.'

The archbishop excused himself and I heard him give a statement to the press.

He returned, his face sad and pained. 'I'll need a little while alone,' he said. 'Mamie will bring you a cup of tea. You'll have to excuse me for a few minutes.'

I turned off the tape recorder and tried to imagine the pressure he was under, that they were all under. There was word that British Intelligence had made representations to the Vatican to stop him being made cardinal. He was 'too Irish', they were saying.

He came into the room again as I was sipping a cup of tea. 'I'll sing you a lament,' he said. 'It was written by Art Mac Cumhaigh, the eighteenth-century poet who is buried just out the road, in the graveyard of Creggan. It's called "Úirchill a' Chreagáin".' He closed his eyes and an ancient longing for the land he lived in was poignantly conveyed in the words of the poet:

> Ag úirchill a' chreagáin sea chodail mise 'réir faoi bhrón
> Is le héirí na maid'ne tháinig ainnir fa mo dhéin le póig
> bhi gríosghrua garth' aici 'gus loinhir ina céibh mar ór
> 's ba e fochshláinte 'n domhain a bheith 'g amharc ar a' ríoghan óig.

In the sean-nós way, he spoke the last few words of the song, as if to return both singer and listener to earth again.

'What about "The oul' Orange flute"?' I said, trying to lighten his mood.

'I'll give it to you,' he said, 'although I don't know what sort of a fist I'll make of it. Will you give us a wee vamp on the guitar?'

And so began his famous version of the well-known Protestant parody.

> In the County Tyrone near the town of Dungannon
> Where many's a ruction myself had a hand in
> Bob Williamson lived there, a weaver by trade
> And all of us thought him a stout Orange blade …

That recording would be broadcast during a BBC News bulletin when the much-loved cardinal died suddenly in Lourdes a short time later.

Ulster Unionist Party leader Harry West had a different view of the land. He was a hard-nosed, practical Protestant farmer who had just returned from the fair in Enniskillen with five cows and three calves.

'What's the scheme?' he asked, with a unionist suspicion and an Ulster affection for intrigue.

Being reasonably satisfied with my reply that I had no particular agenda in mind for the programme, he sat back in an armchair and viewed his large farm through the window. Gradually a broad grin spread across his face as if he were mentally fast-forwarding the story that had come to mind. Having arrived safely at the punchline, he looked at me triumphantly.

'Switch that thing on,' he said.

Mrs West, who had politely brought me a comfortable mug of tea and biscuits, looked up at the ceiling as if to say, What's this man going to come out with now?

'I had reason to visit an old pair out in the country, as part of my constituency work,' he began, 'and sat down at the table for a welcome cup of tea and a slice of baked bread with the old couple. Suddenly the old man eased himself up on one hip and let out this rather loud noise. I passed no remarks but the dog, which had been lying under the table, immediately jumped up and over the half-door as if running for his life. "Why did he do that?" I asked the old man. "Well," says he, "the oul' lassie there is stone deaf and the dog knows he'll get a beetling, for she'll blame the dog."'

Mrs West looked up at the ceiling again, her worst fears confirmed, and Harry laughed uncontrollably. But he was a seasoned storyteller and there was more where that came from, plenty more.

Each place I visited had a warm welcome and an enthusiastic performance. In Belfast City Hall, the Lord Mayor, David Cook of the Alliance Party, gave a strong recital of Seamus Heaney's 'Digging' and his wife Fionnuala sang 'She moved through the fair'. Wry political cartoonist Rowell Friers did a radio tap dance, his party piece with clicking teeth, before giving directions to Gerry Fitt's house in west Belfast, where the future Lord Fitt welcomed me into the house that he would soon be burned out of.

'Some people call this a tin sandwich,' he said, putting the harmonica to his lips.

He was like a stand-up comedian, firing out one-liners like spits of tobacco, aimed at myself and Alan Murray, a journalist who had arrived to take photographs. Some of Fitt's jokes were black, others blue, but few would not have raised a chuckle on that cold night in the bleak Ulster winter of 1978, when a bit of laughter was a rare and sacred thing.

All these politicians were entertainers. Maybe that's why they were in the public arena in the first place. Sometimes their stories tore strips off their opponents, but deep down I had the feeling there wasn't much distance between any of them. Weren't most of them fellow workers anyway? They were doing the same job, drawing the same pay, and running for seats in the same parliament. They were walking together along the corridors of power, talking together in aeroplanes and laughing together in quiet rooms. Yet at the first click of a camera they felt a duty to snarl and swipe like well-paid prizefighters. Perhaps they felt that the voters, baying for their money's worth, deserved nothing less and would feel short-changed if the fault lines of friendship suddenly appeared in Ulster's fundamental rock face. Since the two communities were being driven further apart by such artificial media wars, it seemed only right to use the same media devices to redress the balance and show that these leaders were human, just like the rest of us.

The response to the programme was immediate and positive. Calls came from everywhere and everybody. A statement from the Ulster Special Constabulary Association was issued on 30 December:

> The Association feels that after tonight's get together with Tommy Sands and the Ulster politicians, Northern Ireland can never be the same again. Tommy's presentation has done more to foster good will and understanding than all the Westminster and so-called peace initiatives put together.

I was delighted to hear the programme repeated many times and transmitted by many stations, including RTÉ, BBC World Service, and the National Public Radio in the US, and my biggest thrill would always be that for an hour or two at least we felt just that little bit more neighbourly towards each other.

Another twenty-two years would pass before I would turn my programme into another political 'party', and for good reason, I felt. That would be after the Good Friday Agreement, when the guns had fallen silent but the Northern Ireland Assembly had ceased to operate and civil conversation on the media between opposing factions was a rare event. It would feature a new wave of politicians still battering on the same shore.

I was having a pre-concert nap in a Swiss hotel, when suddenly angry voices with Northern accents began shouting out of the corner of my bedroom. It was David Trimble and Martin McGuinness. They were arguing on television about who was responsible for the collapse of the Assembly but speaking from separate CNN studios. Unfriendly conflict was still media friendly. When I arrived home, I went up to Stormont and into the only open office I could see. It belonged to Lord Alderdice. He was the Speaker of the House, but there was no one left in the House to speak to. They had all gone home.

I put an idea to his secretary Georgie Campbell and events manager Dermot McGreevey – how about inviting everyone back for another Christmas party? They were very supportive. Downtown Radio agreed to record the concert and the invitations were sent out.

I rang some faithful musical friends like Mary Black, Steve Cooney, Laoise Kelly, Roy Arbuckle and others. They formed the backbone of the gig; the politicians did the rest. Songs of beauty, compassion and humour came from Minister of Agriculture Bríd Rodgers, PUP leader David Ervine, and Ulster Unionist David McLagherty. Deputy Speaker Jane Morrice of the Northern Ireland Women's Coalition recited a poem of great tenderness and then laughed about the time she had danced with Omar Sharif. There were tears shed too and the night was unforgettable. There was also a love song from Sinn Féin's serious Minister for Health, Bairbre de Brún. It was the first time I had heard her sing for over twenty years and she brought me back to the late seventies and memories of a summer's evening when politics seemed far from her mind and she was laughing, young and free at a party with a French girl. That was the girl who taught me 'Plaisir d'amour'.

19

Plaisir d'Amour

There was a session in the Hermitage in Newry. The proprietor knew how to look after musicians – a pint or two and a smile. That was all, but any less and the music-makers would not have come. I decided to drop in for a tune. I knew John Watterson would be there, Benny McKay, Paddy Clerkin, Tommy Fegan, Donal O'Hanlon, Manus O'Boyle, Eddie Ruddy – the usual crowd. At the end of the night I noticed a dark girl stand up to put on her coat. She was a stranger and no one seemed to know her. I could see her clearly now despite the haze of smoke for she shone through like a star on a stormy night. She had long dark hair, bronzed skin, high cheekbones and a sensuous mouth.

Eddie Ruddy followed my gaze. 'She's a Hightalian, I houl' ye, or a Spaniard. One of those foreign weemin,' he said, not wanting to appear impressed. 'I wonder what brings her to this godforsaken country?'

Then she was gone.

I searched for her at other sessions in different places. Days passed, and then weeks, but I didn't see her anywhere. I began to think it had been a dream.

Then one evening Ann McCracken and Tommy Fegan said, 'We're throwing a party, would you like to come?'

'Is the pontiff a papist?' I replied.

'Be there at nine then, your holiness,' said Fegan, 'and don't come with both arms the same length.'

I brought some of Arthur Guinness's best stout.

It was near the end of the night when suddenly the vision reappeared. I was coming back from the kitchen with a refilled glass and there she was, sitting on a cushion on the floor, like a yoga mistress. Two young women sat at each side of her. I knew one of the women – Mary Wall was a singer and a treasure and the life and soul of every party. The other, I would learn, was Barbara Brown, or in Irish, Bairbre de Brún. She was the girl's roommate. They were laughing hilariously at some joke. I hoped it wasn't at me, for as well as the Guinness, a bottle of Power's whiskey had been produced at this stage and, as I would later be told, it had made an impression on me.

'Cat'reen is her name,' whispered Ann McCracken in a French accent, amused at my curiosity. 'She's the new French *assistante* working in Armagh. Would you like to meet her?'

'Ach, I don't know, Ann! Not now,' I said. 'Neither English nor French are capable of furnishing me with sufficient vocabulary at this moment.' I held up my glass as proof, but in truth it was the beauty of her darkness that had frightened me. It would be several weeks before our paths would cross again.

Gerry McAlinden and his French wife Christine had invited me to a fondue supper. 'Bring whomever you like,' said Christine that afternoon with a mischievous Gallic smile, 'but that French girl Catherine is coming. She and Bairbre are expecting you to pick them up at eight. And that's eight o'clock sharp,' she added with a Continental swagger, 'not eight Irish time.'

Catherine Bescond in Brittany, 1976
(photo Francois Gazagne)

'Understood,' I said to Christine. I was determined there and then to be strictly punctual on this occasion and began to carefully ponder the possible hurdles. There were just a few small things to be sorted out before I could collect the girls. One was to pick up my father from the pub and deposit him safely at home. That wouldn't be easy for that was the last place he would want to go if the slightest sniff of a party was in the air. I also needed a quick shower and change, and I was driving a red Hillman Estate bought from Noel Kehoe many miles ago, which owed nothing to anyone anymore. In recent months she had developed a bad habit of overheating and breathing out hot steam through the dashboard. The old cure of cow dung in the radiator seemed to be less effective these days in keeping her cool. She also had an insatiable thirst for motor oil. Her constant red light never even blinked in gratitude. The more she got, the more she wanted.

When she came to a trembling rest outside Eileen Grant's pub, the Chief had just launched into 'The races at the Bridge of Mayo', a long song by any standards.

He was in company with a dozen or so Bridge men, including Liam Daly, and I knew I would have to bring him home as well. Things weren't looking good. Liam's legs were long and awkward, even when he was sober, and to get that man into a car and then coax him out of it again could even transgress the boundaries of Irish time. He would also want to stop somewhere on the way home for bacon.

The Chief's song, which extols the victory of 'the Camlough grey mare', has a spoken part in the middle. When the mare eventually clears the last lyrical hurdles of innumerable double verses, you might think that the song was over. You would be wrong. A dispute is lodged by some blackguard or other, for some reason or other, and the whole race has to be run again. However, if the Chief felt there was insufficient respect for the song and order for the singer, he was liable to have the race run several times. This had to be handled very carefully. The big clock on Eileen Grant's wall was saying seven fifteen and the race wasn't even finished the first time round.

I slipped out and sped down the road for Liam's bacon, in advance, and a carry-out of whiskey and beer, for I knew he'd want that too. When I got back to the pub at seven-thirty, the Chief was just starting the re-run.

> It's now my intention a few words to mention to draw your attention a
>   few lines I implore
> Of how it was stated and well meditated and n'er celebrated in verses before
> 'Tis surely a folly to be melancholy but to drink and be jolly's the best fun
>   I know
> How seven fine cattle the best of good mettle to run for a saddle at the
>   Bridge of Mayo

Eventually we got the Mayo races safely finished and I left Liam and the Chief at home. I quickly showered, circumvented a sow lying in the middle of the Ryan Road and headed for Newry. The French race had begun.

I would have arrived at eight o'clock, too, had divine intervention not decided to take the wind out of my sails at the foot of Cooper's hill with a puncture in my left back tyre. That held me up somewhat but with bated breath and blackened knuckles I was knocking on Catherine's door at eight-thirty, a mere half-hour late. I dared not offer my oil-stained hand, so I kissed her cheek instead.

'You're fairly Francofied,' remarked Barbara, offering me her cheek in turn.

And eight kisses later, as the Breton tradition demanded, we were on our way, young and excited and wondering what the night might bring.

That night would bring many delights – a lovely meal, a *chanson d'amour* or two and a step closer to Catherine. But it was not close enough. Catherine was leaving Ireland in a few days, perhaps forever. She was going to Mexico. It was all planned. She had already followed her love of adventure to many lands. She had taught French in Spain, taught Spanish in Sweden, had trekked several paths through North Africa with a rucksack and donkey. She was ready for the road again.

'What about tonight?' I said hopefully the following day.

'Where are you taking me?' she asked.

'To a wake,' I said.

'A wake!' she cried. 'Who's dead?'

'As a matter of fact,' I said, 'there's nobody dead, but there's a friend of mine who has always wanted to hear what people will say about him when he dies, and he's going to lie in a coffin tonight and pretend to be dead.'

Catherine looked puzzled but agreed to come. In all her travels she hadn't come across this tradition. 'You have strange friends,' she said.

Bobbie Hanvey, admittedly, was no ordinary man. When we arrived at the Oak Grill in Castlewellan, he was safely shrouded in a fine oak coffin in the lounge and Hilda, his better half, was graciously collecting an admission fee at the door.

'It's for a good cause,' she said with a wink, 'but if you sing a song, I won't charge you.'

'It's a deal,' I replied.

A doubtful-looking clergyman was swaying by the side of the coffin, sucking at a whiskey bottle, and occasionally sneaking a sup to the corpse. Éamon McMullan and the Poachers had struck up a tune in the corner and the place was filling up nicely.

I went up to the coffin. Hanvey opened one eye. 'What are they saying about me?' he whispered.

'Not a bad oul' divil,' said one.

'There's worse,' said another, 'but they're nearly all hanged.'

'Who said that?' hissed Hanvey, eyes closed.

'I'm not too sure,' I whispered cautiously.

Hanvey had become something of a legend in his own lifetime, a one-time psychiatric nurse in 'The Mental' in Downpatrick, a full-time photographer, a part-time radio presenter, and an all-time eccentric. He liked to challenge life, and had given us all many a good laugh. Now he was lying in his coffin, still as death.

'Mind you, he was a bit of a twisty bugger,' someone said.

Hanvey gave a twitch in the coffin.

'The time has come for the emptying of the bladder ceremony,' announced the clergyman quickly, joining several others in carrying the corpse to the toilet.

Catherine looked at me in disbelief. 'Is this a normal Saturday night in your life?' she asked, in a tone that straddled suspicion and sympathy. But without waiting for an answer, she said, 'What happens next?'

'I have no idea,' I confessed.

It was when a pinch of snuff landed in the corpse's eye, possibly by accident, possibly not, that the night really came to life. Hanvey jumped up in the coffin with nothing on him but a white shroud and a pair of blue underpants. 'Where's the bastard that tried to blind me?' he shouted.

In no time there were tables in the air and drinks flying.

In the wake tradition the occasional row was not out of place – a case documented in County Clare tells of the cousin of a corpse being heard to say, 'Lord, wouldn't it be it a poor thing if a good man was lowered into his grave without a blow being struck?' Whereupon he turned round with his fist and pasted the man beside him and a row started that spread all over the graveyard.

The fact that in this case the dead man was still alive and kicking (literally) did-n't seem to dampen the spirit of the fight. Eventually, however, with the help of the fake priest, we managed to get him settled back into his coffin and there he remained curiously quiet for the duration of the wake. A sobering old rhyme leapt to my mind with a new life.

> Here lie the remains of dearest Bob,
> Not dead but drunk. By God.

It was another thought that came to Catherine's mind. She said later that she should have run away, at that moment, then and there, when she still had the chance. She was only joking, of course. I think.

We left hand in hand and kissed goodbye.

'Would you wait a while and I might go to Mexico with you?' I ventured sincerely.

'How long is a while?' she asked with a smile.

She was going back to France first 'to tie up some loose strings', she had said in her newly discovered idiomatic English. She had tied up my heart-strings as well, if she only knew. The future seemed vague and we wondered when, or if, we would ever meet again.

I was going to Austria for some concerts in November. I decided to write her a let-ter suggesting we meet somewhere, a long letter. A faint heart never won a fair maid, they say. There was no reply, and I thought maybe she hadn't received it. She had said she might be picking grapes to earn some money before leaving but she didn't know where exactly. Perhaps Perpignon. Then one day, out of the blue, a sun-kissed postcard arrived. The postman had shoved it under the door in Ryan and it had been well kissed by the rain too before my eyes saw it. Water in Ireland doesn't only run downhill, it runs up as well and sideways. I could make out the word Perpignon at the top and *bises* at the bottom. *Bises* was French for kisses. *Peut-être, peut-être, si pos-sible* – she might come! *Ça dépend.* What it depended upon she did not say.

I arrived in Vienna railway station, where she had mentioned meeting, but she wasn't there. I met Herr Walter instead. He was my promoter, producer, translator and director. He soon became my bodyguard and torturer to boot, for even though he meant well he never let me out of his sight. He had a large pair of red-rimmed glasses that kept misting up and that he wiped from time to time with a white hand-kerchief. Instead of hair he had a black hard hat, which was adjusted constantly to save his bare head from the winter winds.

There was a warm feeling in the hall I was to play in. Outside it was dark and the snow was falling softly. Vienna was beautiful and romantic, but it would have been much more beautiful and romantic had Catherine been there. At the end of the concert Walter handed me albums to autograph and then handed them back to the buyer.

'I know you need your peace,' he said. 'You have troubles enough in Ireland.' He was a Catholic and it seemed like he wanted me to make a good impression on Austrian Catholics. There was no beer to be seen. I was under the spotlight.

'You stay with me tonight,' he said. 'Come, we must go. We start early in the morning.' He was like a military commander. He didn't enjoy music much, he admitted, nor did he laugh at any of my jokes, come to think of it. He did confess though that he 'found it hard to keep in a few times'. That, coming from him, I accepted as a whopping compliment. And so it continued throughout the week until Innsbruck. That was the last night, the last concert. It was then that I saw her. I couldn't believe it. Catherine had arrived. She was in the third row on the left. She squeezed my hand at the interval. She looked more beautiful than ever in a white blouse and light summer skirt with red and dark burgundy flowers. Her eyes shone brightly, lightening the darkness of the winter.

'I've booked you a single in the Goldener Adler tonight,' cut in Herr Walter, ignoring Catherine and looking into my eyes as if sensing an occasion of sin. 'It's my favourite hotel. It's all arranged. An early night would suit us both. Your train leaves early in the morning for Dusseldorf. Doesn't it?'

Earlier Catherine had told me she had booked a double in a small hotel near the river. I should have said, 'Have a swim in the Inns, Herr Walter.' But I didn't, I couldn't and I don't know why. He was like a bishop of the worst kind standing between earth and heaven, using his power not to provide a door but to stand sentry at the entrance. Perhaps I didn't want this bishop to know my intentions – once a Catholic always a Catholic. That's when I told him the lie.

'Actually I can't stay in the Goldener Adler,' I said. 'In fact I'm not staying in Austria at all. I must go back to Düsseldorf tonight. Something has come up.'

'Is that so,' he said. 'And how do you propose to go?'

'On a late night train,' I lied again.

'There's only one train,' he said, wiping his glasses and looking at his watch furiously, 'and that goes at eleven. I will take you to the station but we must go immediately after the concert, no encores, no talking, and no autographs.'

'That's putting you to too much trouble,' I said. 'Sure I can get a taxi.'

'It's my responsibility to get you to the train and get you to the train I will,' said Herr Walter.

My God, I thought, how did I let this happen?

Like some class of sheep being led to the slaughter I climbed into the back of his black Mercedes 2000, somehow not believing what I was doing. Catherine got in beside me, believing it less.

'What's going on?' she asked.

'Let the hare sit,' I whispered.

'Let what hare sit?' she shouted. 'Whose hair?'

I should have known she wouldn't be familiar with that expression but I didn't feel that now was the best time to explain so I kissed her instead, long and longing, for all sorts of good reasons.

'Waken up!' shouted Walter, screaming to a halt. 'Give me that guitar quickly.'

'No! Not at all, Herr Walter,' I pleaded. 'Goodbye now, you have already done enough.'

'And much more than enough,' he said, 'but I will see you to the train, for you don't know the language and only then can I relax for, believe me, I need a good holiday after all this stress.'

I visualized having to get onto that train and go to Düsseldorf. He had already shaken my hand and was waiting for me to do just that. He began to smile dryly and wave wildly, even though we were standing facing each other, just a few yards apart. I smiled and waved back. It was now or never. I jumped onto the train and looked out the window. He was still waving and staring vaguely through red-rimmed, double-glazed and hopefully unwiped glasses. I ran down the corridor and jumped out again like a bird from a cage, panting and falling over my luggage, calling Catherine, calling a taxi. I didn't feel too smart. We fell asleep almost immediately in the small hotel by the river. The excitement had worn us out. This had been worse than Hanvey's wake. I hoped she wouldn't think it was always like this. Next morning we would start anew.

The sun was shining through the breakfast window of the small hotel and the sparkling Alps seemed to dwarf the entire sky, but I was reluctant to go outside. I feared we would meet Herr Walter – he seemed to be all over Austria.

'Why don't we go to Italy?' I suggested. I wasn't actually needed in Düsseldorf for a week. She didn't answer and seemed deep in thought. Perhaps she had had enough. A sudden dismay came over me.

'Catherine,' I said nervously, 'would you like to come to Italy?'

Slowly she lifted her head and looked into my eyes. 'Do you have to ask?' she whispered. There were tears on her cheeks and on mine too and soon we were kissing and hugging and cappuccino got spilt into raspberry jam at the breakfast table.

'Where would you like to go?' asked the woman at the railway station. She didn't seem to recognize me from the night before, thank God.

'A small village in Italy,' I replied.

She suggested several but we thought they sounded too crowded.

'Perhaps a quieter place with few tourists,' said Catherine.

The woman delicately scratched the bridge of her nose with the point of her little finger. 'It has to be Vipeteno,' she said.

We found that it was quiet; the streets were empty and no wonder. It was bitterly cold and big chunks of ice battered us as we made our way across the street and through the double doors of a stately tavern. At the front of the bar there sat a bald man with red glasses. I recognized him instantly. It was Herr Walter and he looked like a man who had just been surprised on the toilet by a nun.

'It's a nice day,' I stammered.

'Do you think so?' he replied.

We burst back into the blizzard gallantly in search of some place where he wasn't. The sound of an old man playing a mandolin called to us from the door of a small hotel with no name on it. We sat down and ordered a bottle of red wine.

The old man playing the mandolin had a friendly face. A young girl, perhaps his granddaughter, came over with two glasses. We realized we had found heaven. It was a week that would change our lives and even though we would soon be parting at Torbo station we knew we had found something that would never be lost.

Our wedding, 1979 (photo Bobbie Hanvey)

And Mexico? Well, the 'while' would be longer than we envisaged. It would be eight years later and with two magic children, a fair-haired Fionán and a dark haired Moya, that we would make it to Mexico. When we married, the official photographer would be Bobbie Hanvey and the photos would be taken from the highest ridge on the roof of Sheeptown chapel – where else? There would be food and music aplenty and a love song reared on a week of white lies and red wine.

> Remember Vipeteno in the high Italian snow
> Cold the night but warm the love just you and I alone
> An old man played a mandolin and a young girl poured the wine
> And your eyes said all I longed to hear
> When you held your glass to mine

20

Humpty Dumpty

'It's windy,' says he.

'It's Thursday,' says I.

'So am I,' says he. 'Let's have a drink.'

The Belfast banter brightened me. I knew little about this drinking den but perhaps it was the place I needed. I had been heading for a toilet with a pub attached but I had got no further than the pub and the first man in it. In Belfast when you don't know the hostelry, you go to the toilet first, not for the usual mundane reasons, but to read the graffiti. It gives you a good idea of where you stand.

'Would you be the man that I met in Honolulu?' he said, looking at me with a pair of red eyes.

'I've never been to Honolulu in my life,' I replied soberly.

'Neither have I,' he said. 'It must have been two other fellas.'

He let a roar of a laugh out of him and threw back the last dregs of his Guinness. 'I'll have a drink from you now,' he said, 'and whatever you're having yourself for you do look thirsty.'

'I feel Friday,' I said.

'Pure zanity,' he said. 'If you didn't laugh you would cry.'

That night I would consume more alcohol through my ear than through my mouth but the strange humour of my new-found philosophical friend was exactly what I needed at that moment. Words had made us fools in the past. It was time to get our own back and make a fool of them for a change. His name was Willie, he told me, but people usually called him 'Paddy's Willie' because Paddy was his father's name.

No wonder he was the way he was: if his father was Paddy that probably meant his father was Catholic but his own name being William suggested a strong Protestant connection somewhere in there. Maybe his mother was a Protestant and he was the product of a mixed marriage.

'Still thirsty,' he said, 'and by the way, it's not Friday, it's Saturday.'

He was right about that if nothing else. It was Saturday all right, the day *Country Céilí* is broadcast. Tonight it had driven me towards the drink.

It was one of those hot summer evenings in July 1980. Political tension was hanging in the air like a gorilla on a child's swing, fuming to be pushed. It was chancy to push any more.

It would be better after the Twelfth; we all knew that. My father used to say that he loved to hear the thunder of the Lambeg drums and the lighting of the sticks. It would clear the air and exorcise the fears. But now wood and tyres were being piled high on the Newtownards Road to burn the Pope and a turncoat called Lundy, who had let the side down as recently as 1689. That night some anonymous callers had suggested that the presenter of *Country Céilí* should be flung on the bonfire as well.

It wasn't the first sectarian threat I had received since the beginning of the programme, nor was I the first presenter to be promised the fires of hell by earthy listeners from both sides of the Northern divide. There were times when it was advisable to take a different road home. And times when it was better just to forget about it all. Tonight I did neither, for the phone calls had struck a chord somewhere within that revealed the twist we had all got ourselves in. Such twists need to be untwisted – to make sense out of nonsense and make nonsense out of sense. Perhaps that's what pubs are for.

'You're looking very serious altogether,' said Paddy's Willie. 'Don't neglect humour, ye boy ye, for hilarity is about all we've got left ye know and what are you thinking about anyway, with a face on you as long as a Lurgan spade?'

'I have to go to the toilet,' I said. I felt like putting up my hand for permission. I still hadn't checked the grafitti.

'Wait till you hear this one first,' he said, landing a frothy spit of Guinness in my left ear as a half verse of home-brewed poetry poured forth.

'Speak your mind,' says he.

'Speak me what?' says I. 'And "Mind what you say", you mean?'

'No mind, that most manipulative of editors, will doctor my words,' I said. 'I'll speak the truth instead, silently.'

He was so close now I could hardly make him out and besides my ears were still ringing with phone calls.

A unionist had complained about all 'that effing Fenian diddly-dee music' I had played just before the news and a nationalist had given out about an instrumental version I had played of that 'feckin' sectarian Orange sash'. The diddly-dee music in question, I remembered was a pair of reels, 'Rakish Paddy' and 'McLeod's reel', well known in every Irish music session, and the 'Sectarian sash' was an instrumental version of the Orange marching anthem 'The sash my father wore'.

I had tried to explain that the music belonged to all of us, like the smell of a flower or the foam of a wave, but I didn't get too far. The music had already been grabbed in handfuls and made into fists to be flung, and songs to be sung in both defence and attack. In the fury of it all the facts had been well warped and history had tumbled head over heels.

The diddly-dee man solemnly swore that traditional music played in Ireland had nothing to do with Protestants. It was 'the music of Catholic republicans', he maintained. Loyalist paramilitaries had actually threatened to bomb pubs where such reels were played. They didn't realize that many such tunes belonged to their own 'Planter' tradition, and perhaps such threats were acts not of patriotism but of ignorance and betrayal. 'There is no evidence to suggest that the reel in its present form existed in Ireland until 1790,' I explained, 'when sheet music containing the well-known Scottish reels – yes, you've guessed it – "Rakish Paddy" and "Miss McCleod" first appeared in Dublin. Similarly the modern hornpipe was probably imported from England, perish the thought, around the same period. And as for republicanism, it was the mainly Presbyterian leaders of the Northern United Irish-men, influenced by the anti-Catholic ideals of the French Revolution, who intro-duced republicanism into Ireland in the first place.'

My flow of learning silenced the bonfire gatherer on line two for the full space of a quarter second. 'A load o' shite,' he concluded.

'The sash' was a different kettle of fish.

'He's on line three,' said Maurice Hawkins, the duty editor in the newsroom, 'are you in or out?' Maurice was a straight-talker from up round Larne somewhere. I took the call, beginning with the history of the song.

True enough, a few lines of that tune were enough to start a row in an empty room, but its earlier days would have brought a different reaction. 'The sash', which now had the reputation of creating division, had actually been written to lament divi-sion. I came across the original version whilst poking through old manuscripts with my good friend and folklorist Mick Moloney in the snowy Poconos of Pennsylvania.

The original version, 'Irish Molly', although published in New York in 1830, had been around much earlier and was one of the most popular ballads of its day. (This 'Irish Molly' is not to be confused with the one composed by a Tin Pan Alley duo called Harper and Newton and recorded by The Flanagan Brothers in the 1920s, and later by De Danann and Maura O'Connell.) The song I had discovered with Mick had lain dormant for many years. It was known throughout the concert halls of Europe and attracted the ear of Beethoven, who happened to be looking around for some good tunes to form a basis for new creations. He wanted to be different from Mozart so instead of looking towards French and German folklore he picked twenty-one Scots and Irish melodies. His love for 'Irish Molly' would leak through in the first movement of a piece that would become known as his Piano Concerto Number One.

The song comes from that great well of Scots-Irish folk tradition, a song of unre-quited love. Young McDonald from Scotland falls in love with Irish Molly but a marriage can never take place because her father refuses to accept a foreigner as a husband for his daughter. Young McDonald goes to America broken-hearted but carries his love for Molly in a song.

I was now in full flight and sang the chorus down the phone:

> She is young and she is beautiful
> Her likes I've never known
> The lily of old Ireland and the primrose of Tyrone
> She's the Lily of old Ireland and if you would like to know
> My heart will always hunger for my Irish Molly O.

'Well there didn't seem to be too much love in it when it was played outside my house last night,' said the caller on line three.

Maybe he was right. Time waits for no man; it just turns his head around.

'Are you listening to me or are you not?' said Paddy's Willie.

'I'll be back in a minute,' I said, stepping round him and squeezing my way up a corridor of sucked-in beer bellies, en route to the house of silent revelations.

At first I could see nothing written on the walls. Is this some sort of undercover joint? I thought. Slowly, however, the work of the local sages became manifest as my eyes adjusted to the light of a lone bald bulb dangling from the toilet ceiling.

'Paisley for Pope.'

'Help the police … Beat yourself up.'

'Be alert … Ulster needs lerts.'

And underneath, 'Be aloof, we have enough lerts.'

Yes, there was a sense of humour here of a sort, but I was still unsure of the pub's persuasion.

Before I went back to the bar I came across one lone line of graffiti.

'Humpty Dumpty was pushed.'

I liked that. We had always accepted that he had just fallen off the wall. Maybe there were many more 'truths' used as reasons for keeping us apart that needed to be questioned. This was revolution.

Paddy's Willie was still holding up the bar when I got back.

'What's that song you're humming to yourself?' he said.

'Humpty Dumpty was pushed,' I replied absently.

He took a fit of laughing. 'Wouldn't it drive you to the drink!' he said. 'I think I'll have another one to clear the head.'

The following morning I got a call from Jackie Dixon, organizer of the Belfast Folk Festival.

'Would you like to put on a show this year?' he asked.

'Yes, Jackie,' I said. 'It will be a musical called "Humpty Dumpty was pushed" and I would like its world première to be in Belfast, that's if Belfast is still in the world by then.'

It was and the show, based on the song 'Humpty Dumpty was pushed', featuring Colum and I, was performed at the festival four months later, November 1980, at a time of great tension in Belfast.

It was a rather challenging experience. The show looked back to current times from some far-off point in the future. After politely thanking our audience for wearing the period costume we asked them to help us try and understand our wacky forefathers who lived way back then, around 1980. It allowed for much musical imagining, risqué lyrics and the logic of Paddy's Willie.

Me: It seems they were killing each other back then.

Colum: Not at all! How could they be killing each other if they were Christians?

Me: But they weren't Christians.

Colum: Oh, they were Christians. It's written in the Royal Ulster Vocabulary.

Me: But if they were Christians how could they be killing each other, you answer me that.

By turning upside down that which was already downside up we hoped to somehow land back on our feet again. By turning the present into the past we could ask ourselves in the dreamy light of hindsight questions like, Why?

> Whatever you say, say nothing when you speak about you-know-what
> For if you-know-who could hear you, you know what you'll get
> They'll take you off to you-know-where for you wouldn't know how long
> So for you-know-who's sake don't let anyone hear you sing this song

We finished that night with 'Daughters and Sons', a song dedicated to all the people who would make that peaceful future possible and in some eyes we could see far off tears of longing. Elated by the success of the show we stepped outside into the night. It was November, it was cold and it was Belfast. The present was still. It had not moved anywhere and the night was tense.

Seán McKenna, a republican prisoner, had refused food in the H-Blocks of Long Kesh. The first hunger strike had begun.

I remembered seeing Seán McKenna as a young lad on my way to St Colman's, helping his father, John, who was caretaker in those days. John was one of the few known republicans and when he died as a result of an alleged beating by soldiers, it was somehow inevitable that young Seán would join up.

He was near to death in the Kesh when he was taken off that hunger strike by his superior, Bobby Sands, in exchange for promises by British officials that political status would be granted to republican prisoners. When the government reneged on those promises, Sands himself went on hunger strike and would not be coming off. On 5 May 1981 he was the first hunger-striker to die.

'You are either with us or against us,' said both the British government and the republican movement. The British equated support for the hunger-strikers with support for IRA killings. The IRA likened the non-support of hunger-strikers with a willingness to let them die. Most people would have said that they were against all killings but questions were seldom framed to cater for such views.

Belonging to the clan of Sands was reason enough to be stopped, searched and harassed by the security forces at every opportunity, to the extent that we avoided English airports and harbours altogether. This was a very minor annoyance, however, compared to the procession of coffins adding up. The cycle was becoming constant and unbearable. The daily news would tell the repeated tale of a hunger-striker becoming weaker, going into hospital, then into a coma, then he would die and be replaced by another, and so it would continue. Negotiations were attempted but collapsed time and again, often with but a single word dividing the sides. 'The noble art of losing face may one day save the human race,' said poet Piet Hein, but neither Margaret Thatcher nor the republicans had the strength to give way to save life.

In Irish history the hunger strike was traditionally the last weapon in the armoury of the weak against the strong. It was never entered into lightly. The ritual fast or *Troscadh* dating from the old Brehon laws was a legal form of redressing a balance just like the ancient Hindu custom of *Dharna*. In fact it was said that the hunger strike that led to the death of Terence McSwiney, Lord Mayor of Cork, in an English prison in 1920 had inspired Gandhi to revive the *Dharna* tradition as a moral political weapon against the British Raj in India. In the *Troscadh* tradition the hunger strike could be ended only by the accused and ostracization and bad tidings would be visited upon the wrongdoer in the event of the accuser's death. This translated into twentieth-century Northern Ireland meant that new recruits would be joining the IRA in their thousands to redress the balance.

On Saturday, 26 September 1981, I opened an envelope addressed to me at Downtown Radio. It was a request to play a song for Liam McCloskey. I knew that name from the newspapers. Liam McCloskey from Dungiven was at that stage the longest-fasting republican on the hunger strike. He was now in hospital and had lost his sight. He was near to death but could hear the programme. The request was from his sister. 'Please play "No man's land",' she said.

I sat alone in the studio and a cold chill ran up my spine as I heard Eric Bogle's words sing out into the sad hills around Dungiven and back into the hospital ward of the young dying patriot.

> Did you really believe them when they told you 'the cause'?
> Did you really believe that this war would end wars?
> Well the suffering, the sorrow, the glory, the shame,
> The killing, the dying, it was all done in vain,
> For Willie McBride it's all happened again
> And again, and again, and again, and again.

On Monday morning another chill ran up my back as I read the newspaper headlines. McCloskey had ended his hunger strike.

For many months I wondered if that song had affected his decision and how he had survived fifty-five days of fasting. Had he regained his eyesight? Was he in hospital or prison? I had never met him, but he was often on my mind.

One winter's night a few years later during the interval of a concert with The Sands Family in a small theatre in Stuttgart, Germany, there was a gentle knock on the dressing-room door. A young man stood in the corridor. 'I'm Liam McCloskey,' he said. 'Thanks for playing that request.' I could hardly believe he was standing before me.

We went for a drink after the concert. Yes, he told me, he had a vague recollection of hearing the music; he had been very ill. His mother had been begging him for hours. Begging for his life. If he wouldn't, perhaps couldn't, save his own life, his family would save it for him when he went into a coma. He was dying for his comrades. They were dying for each other. His cousin Séamus O'Kane, the bodhrán maker, went round the beds of all those waiting to die. He asked them each individually, 'Do you want to die?' No, they didn't want to die but they wouldn't let each other down. 'Right,' said O'Kane. 'That's it!' It was the families who ended the hunger strike after ten of them had died. He was glad to be alive. Now he was a living patriot, serving as a community worker. He was making others glad to be alive and I was glad to be alive in his company. People like that are good for the soul.

Later I would spend time with another community worker gladdening people's lives. His name was Ronnie Crutchley. I had met him first in Maghaberry Prison when I was doing a concert there. He was a prison officer. Several of his friends had been killed during those terrible times but now he was out of the service, singing songs of being free and playing a Spanish guitar. His passion for making the best of where life landed him was well summed up in his relationship with the key of C.

It came from the time he had his wee finger accidentally cut off by a saw but he managed to retrieve it and put it in a bag of ice. In the Ulster Hospital at Dundonald, surgeon Nick Harte told him he could save it and sew it back on again.

'Tell me,' said the surgeon, eyeing the callus on the tip of the dismembered pinkie. 'Do you play the guitar?'

'I do,' said Ronnie.

'So do I,' said the surgeon. 'And tell me, have you any problems at all with the C chord?'

'Well, actually, I do,' said Ronnie. 'I find it difficult twisting my wee finger onto the bottom E string.'

'So do I,' said the surgeon, 'and since every crisis is also an opportunity, I would suggest that as I sew this finger on again, I will give it a little kink to make it easier to reach the bottom E. It will be no cheaper and no dearer. It's up to you.'

'A good idea,' said Ronnie. 'We'll make the best of the future, for we can't improve the past.' The past would leave its mark on all of us.

During chemotherapy many years later, shortly before he died of cancer, Ronnie would find relief in his songs and this one in particular, which he sent me, written in the key of C.

When winter's cold and darkened days
Turn to spring and summer shade
And fields of corn in sunlight sway,
It's time that men let down the blade.

We grew our crops and raised our boys
That they in turn could use the spade
To till the soil and reap the joys
In fertile earth let down the blade.

We also taught our boys to kill
For reasons none of them had made,
We left them with a legacy
A ditch of blood and death to wade.

The harvest ripe, the time is now,
Let's reap this chance that peace has made
And put our hands back on the plough
And never more take up the blade.

When conflict's done, lay down your shields
And swords and guns, the scythe remade,
It's time that men returned to fields
And in peaceful work let down the blade.

21

On the Run

The bother began in Munich. A choir was singing to open the concert. Ben would later maintain that among their otherwise perfect pitch, there seemed to be some small sense of discord, like a voice somewhere that was off-key. It caused him unease. On that evening, though, we had no way of knowing that someone would emerge from a place in the choir who would wreak havoc on our lives and nearly cause us to give up touring altogether.

After our concerts we always made a point of meeting our audience to sign albums, CDs, books, admission tickets, or just simply to say hello. In our tours, covering hundreds of cities and thousands of miles, we meet a great many people, and most are a pleasure to know. Rarely have I met someone I didn't like or in whose company I felt uneasy. We were soon to discover, however, that Frau Gundula Grissler would be an exception to the rule.

At first she appeared quite normal, lining up with everyone else waiting to meet us. She wanted the lyrics of 'Nicaragua', a song we had written. It wasn't until we were saying our goodnights and goodbyes that we realized she had taken the keys to our hotel rooms. We wouldn't be going anywhere without Frau Grissler.

'Follow me,' she said.

We thought that perhaps she was on the staff of the concert organizers.

She let us into our rooms but stayed to ask more questions about the songs, what they meant and why they were written. She showed no signs of leaving, even though we were clearly tired and wanted to turn in for the night.

'We can meet at breakfast,' I said eventually, 'and answer any further queries you might have then.'

And the next morning, there she was, waiting to watch us eat our sausages and drink our coffee. No answer to her questions seemed to satisfy her appetite.

'Where are you playing tonight?' she asked.

We showed her our itinerary. It was public knowledge anyway.

'Will you give me a lift to Salzburg?' she said quickly.

'There's no room in the bus,' Ben answered with equal swiftness.

'I'll lie in the back with the double bass,' she suggested.

'You wouldn't be insured,' Colum said with a frown.

In the end she wore us down.

'We'll take you part of the way then, to get you on the road,' I said.

She told us that she was used to travelling in uncomfortable conditions. She had once been a Munich football supporter and travelled for free under the floors of railway carriages. She liked the excitement, she said. Then she let slip a strange remark, which should have sent the alarm bells ringing.

'Football fans who take knives with them to fight at matches are stupid,' she said. 'Blades are better. They're easier to hide.'

In hindsight we should have put her off at the next town; it's hard to credit now that we could have been so trusting.

She showed up at the first two concerts in Austria, and all was well. Even the third and fourth, too – sometimes friends liked to join us on the road for a while. But as time wore on it became clear that this woman was different. There was a strange look in her eyes difficult to read. We had no way of predicting where it would all end.

The first obvious sign of trouble, I suppose, was her increasing impatience over insufficient attention paid her at after-concert parties.

'You look at that girl in a different way than you look at me,' she complained. 'Why is that?' Then the smile, which began angelically enough, would run aground on some invisible iceberg far from the shores of satisfaction and sink into a curious darkness.

Unknown to us, she was telling concert organizers that she was our roadie and would need accommodation. She was everywhere now, showing up at every concert, every party and every breakfast the following morning.

'What do you actually want?' demanded Ben one night, after she had tracked us down once again at some small pub in the north of Würzburg.

She looked at him with that strange smile. 'Perhaps a Sands baby,' she replied, as cool as you please.

This was getting too much.

'If you don't mind, Gundula,' Col said one morning, 'we want to go for a walk alone, to discuss private things.'

'I understand,' she said accommodatingly. But then she added, 'You don't mind if I walk ten metres behind, do you?'

How can you stop someone walking behind you on a public street? It got to the point where we were running round corners and darting up back alleys, but she would always find us in some restaurant and would sit at a table nearby. The weeks passed and she changed from being a nuisance to a menace. Things turned sour. She hated us now.

Two thousand Deutschmarks mysteriously disappeared from my dressing room during a Bavarian solo tour and brake pipes were cut in the tour car, driven by our road manager, Herman the German. We contacted the police but they didn't seem interested. Concern for long-haired musicians with leftist leanings was not at the top of their agenda. 'You have no proof,' they said.

They were right, we had no proof, but we also had no doubt about who took the money and who cut the brake pipes.

We would soon learn what this dangerous woman needed the money for. She was right behind us on the autobahn in a big dark blue van. It was difficult to keep your mind on positive things like music or performing. All our thoughts were being filled with Gundula. That was what she had wanted all along, of course.

'Can't we talk about something else?' sighed Col. 'Apart from Gundula, this has been a wonderful tour.'

'Apart from that, Mrs Lincoln, how did you enjoy the play?' said Ben from the side of his mouth.

But Col was right, it had been an amazing tour.

I recalled the surprised look on the lovely face of Polish feminist Hélène Letoile when I suddenly embraced her and asked her be my girlfriend for an hour in the crowded room of the Communist Party headquarters in Elizabeth Strasse in Salzburg. She had no English and my German was almost non-existent.

'There's a strange woman on the warpath,' I tried to tell her in French.

She helped to dress the bruised finger I had caught in a restaurant door earlier that evening trying to escape '*la femme bizarre*'.

'Weren't Friedl Bahner's musings interesting?' said Col, steering elsewhere the conversation but keeping his eye on the rear mirror at the same time.

'Plenty to chew upon,' said Ben.

We had met Friedl some weeks back in the salt mines of Hallein, near Salzburg, the site of the largest Celtic museum in the world. He organized the big Inter Celtic Festival there.

'Isn't it very strange to have The Sands Family playing at a Celtic festival in Hallein?' he had remarked.

'What's so strange about that?' I replied.

'You come from Ireland, for God's sake,' he said. 'You are just like returned Yanks, coming back here, you know?'

'What would you be meaning by that now?' said Ben, narrowing his eyes suspiciously.

And as we crossed the border between Austria and Germany, 500 feet underground in the salt mine of Hallein, undisturbed by customs or emigration, Friedl's story of the Salt People slowly unfolded. The Celts on their journey westward settled in the area of Hallein many many years ago. They weren't called Celts then, of course, and no one took much notice of them. Then salt was discovered in these hills in 800 BC.

'We would like some of your salt,' said the Germanic tribes who were arriving from the north.

'That may well be,' came the reply, 'but we have grown fond of the stuff and we'd rather hold on to it ourselves, if you don't mind.'

'Are the Germans after your salt?' whispered the Romans, who had overheard the conversation.

'They are indeed,' said the people of Hallein, who were becoming known as the Selle or Salt people.

'We'll help you fight them,' said the Romans.

The Romans helped the Selle people and helped themselves to their salt as well. The Selle people, the Celts, were banished from this lovely place, and they travelled all over Europe and beyond, taking their culture with them, some going as far as Ireland.

'Now, centuries later,' Friedl said, 'you Irish have come back here with the music all changed around and jizzed up and you call it Celtic music. That's why I say that you are just like returned Yanks.'

'That's a good story,' I said, 'and there's a ring of truth in it, but tell me this, where is all the old music today? I'd love to hear some traditional music from this area.'

Friedl smiled up at the ceiling of the mine. We could still see the strains of salt, along with perfectly preserved, petrified human excrement, more than a thousand years old.

'It's all gone,' he said. 'Not a trace of the music remains.' He laughed. 'That's why we have you here, of course, isn't it?' he said. 'Keep on playing. We need you.'

It got me thinking about the real returned Yanks and how important Irish-America had been for the preservation of Irish music. At a time when the music was ignored or even despised at home, the Irish-Americans had held on to it, treasured it and kept it safe until better times came along. The recordings in the twenties from Michael Coleman and the Flanagan Brothers, through to The Clancy Brothers and Tommy Makem in the sixties, had rekindled a pride in a sleeping culture. Even now, people like Mick Moloney and his group the Green Fields of America were bringing the music, song and dance of Ireland to stages right across the States. He had musicians like Séamus Egan and Eileen Ivers, and dancers called Michael Flatley and Jean Butler. Soon they would be known in Ireland too and would reignite a new wave of Celtic excitement across the world.

'I wonder did the Celts come to Ireland at all?' asked Colum as we whistled along the autobahn. 'Is there anyway of knowing for sure?'

'Take off your socks!' said Ben. 'If the second toe is as long as your big toe you're a Celt.' He was bringing us back to the early days of agriculture when hunter gatherers had discovered that food could be grown on the spot rather than having to be sought after. When some had settled down to heavy farming and their toes spread out with the weight of it all the Celts had kept on running and their feet developed differently. 'I'll have you know', laughed Anne, 'we're more Celtic than the Celts themselves.' All our second toes were longer than our big toes.

We knew less, though, about the one who was thundering behind us just now in a big blue van.

Suddenly Gundula was speeding up to pass. She was screaming alongside us, staring across in an unnerving kind of way. Then she swerved towards us across the crowded road.

'Jesus Christ, she's trying to run us off the road,' shouted Ben.

'Look out!' I yelled.

Col jammed on the brakes and steered for the hard shoulder. We came to a halt, van trembling and tyres smoking.

'Why the hell did she do that?' I panted.

Gundula was nowhere to be seen.

Nerves shattered, we made our way cautiously to an autobahn stop. We needed coffee or something stronger.

When we got to the next gig, Gundula was sitting in the front row.

'Do you realize you could have killed us all and yourself too?' I snapped at her.

'I know,' she said calmly, 'but perhaps that is the solution.'

We were scared now. How were we to get rid of this woman? It seemed there was no place we could go that would be safe from her. She even managed to circumvent the tight security of the Deutschland Halle in West Berlin. We arrived to find her sitting in our dressing room with a bottle of whiskey as a peace offering. We were in no mood for her games and suggested she get psychiatric help, which only sent her into a fury.

So it was with a great sigh of relief that we passed through the gates of Checkpoint Charlie and into East Berlin, where we were well known and had many friends. We would be safe there at least. We were playing in the Palast der Republik with Harry Belafonte, Inti Illimani and Udo Lindenburg, in a concert against the deployment of cruise missiles in West Germany by NATO.

Next was Bulgaria. We were preparing for a live national television programme with musicians from Syria, Lebanon, Afghanistan, Russia and Ireland. Dolores Keane and John Faulkner were the other Irish representatives. It looked like rain. When it rains there, it rains! They set up studios both inside and outside. Some of the Syrians and Palestinians had been in the war. They had missing arms and broken legs. I had a sore knee, an old cartilage injury from playing for Saval against the Bridge in the Down County Championship. I had crutches under my auxters.

The Bulgarian President Todo Chicov came and shook hands with us all. One of his party pointed at my leg.

'Were you in the war too?' he asked.

'Not as such,' I said. It wasn't the time to go into detail. Suddenly there was a brattle of thunder and the sky opened. I threw away the sticks, hopped to the nearest tree and fell beneath it. I fell on top of a Russian woman called Tanya Vladimirsky, who in turn fell on top of her husband, Sergei. They played in a Muscovite group called Granada.

'Sorry,' I said.

'We'll excuse you, if you come and play in Moscow,' said Sergei.

'I'd love to,' I said, 'and I will.'

I did.

He had a good sense of humour. He also had a balalaika and we played a tune under the tree until the shower passed.

> May there always be sunshine,
> May there always be blue skies,
> May there always be Mama,
> May there always be me.

> *Pust' vsegda budyet sontse,*
> *Pust' vsegda budyet nyeba,*
> *Pust' vsegda budyet mama,*
> *Pust' vsegda budu ya.*

I had learned that Russian children's song from Pete Seeger many years ago.

From Sofia we flew back to Munich and were met at the airport by Herman the German. He looked worried.

'She's on the warpath again,' he said simply. 'This time she's says she's got Semtex.'

'We're back in the Free World,' muttered Col, heaving the double bass off the carousel.

'And the police say they can do nothing until she does something they can prove,' said Herman.

The gig was in Dehnburg, a typical old Bavarian town. Many of the beautiful *Fachwerk* buildings had been restored and the theatre was wooded and charming. We were just beginning our last song when the manager whispered something to Colum.

'Don't panic,' he said, 'but there's a car on fire outside the door. Make this the last one.' There was a fear the fire might spread to the theatre.

As we launched into 'The winds are singing freedom' we could smell the tyres burning. The audience called *Zugabe!* but there was no time. I looked over at Ben.

'That's our car,' he said.

And he was right.

The police came and the fire brigade too, but the car was a burnt-out shell before we had struck the last note.

'We know who is responsible,' we told the police.

'Perhaps it was a cigarette,' an officer said, examining the car.

'We never smoke in the car,' we said impatiently.

'Then perhaps it was an electric fault,' another proposed, before they disappeared with the breakdown truck towing the remains of Herman's car.

The next morning Herman began wistfully poking through the ashes with the toe of his shoe. 'What's that?' he said, pointing at a small object.

It looked like the shell of a bullet. Then we found another and another.

'Mein Gott!' said Herman. 'Es ist eine Bombe!'

It was a crude device made from bullets and gunpowder. We went back to my hotel room, where some friends had gathered, and rang the police.

'It was not a cigarette,' I said angrily down the phone. 'It was a bomb!'

The policeman's answer astounded us. 'Yes, we know,' he said. 'We are making enquiries.'

Maybe they were and maybe they weren't. All sorts of conspiracy theories began to whistle around the room. Was it part of a plot to stop our touring? Were our politics too left wing for the powers that be? Were our songs too peaceful at a time when a Cold War wanted to rage? Was Gundula acting alone? The more we discussed it, the more sinister the events appeared to be turning. Was she part of a neo-Nazi group in Nuremberg?

Herman had had enough. He was going home. His car was destroyed and Gundula had been pressurizing him to give her money for work she said she had done to promote the tour. He had a wife and family. We knew how he felt.

We considered what action we could take, and made two phone calls. The first was to Nan Sands, the local SDLP councillor at home. She called John Hume and asked him to contact his Bavarian counterpart in the European Parliament. The second call was to Andrea Altenhovel. Andrea was a singer and teacher from Hanau, but she was also a fencer and had recently defeated the German Olympic champion. I had met her six months earlier during my solo tour. Her friend Anna Stübing was coach of the German hockey team, and her father was a judge. Within two hours the three of them were sitting in the foyer of our hotel.

'How can we help?' they asked.

They drove us to our next concert, an open-air event in Saarbrücken organized by Hassa and Wolfgang Schmidt of the Communist Party. There were Special Branch detectives in the green room and sniffer dogs under the stage. We had asked for protection and we were getting it – the judge and the politicians were on the case and if life had seemed crazy before, it was even crazier now. We couldn't go anywhere, and I mean *anywhere*, without an armed detective on each side of us.

'What's going on?' whispered Wolfgang. 'Usually the police come here to make trouble for our festival. Now they come to protect us. Why?'

'That's why,' I said, pointing at a solemn figure seated in the front pew like she was waiting for Holy Communion. Gundula had a ghetto-blaster under her arm, presumably to record the evening for posterity.

'Can you have her removed?' asked Ben nervously.

'She has paid for her ticket,' said Hassa. 'We can't remove her.'

'What about the police? Can they do nothing?' I asked.

'Not until Frau Grissler does something,' said one of the detectives. 'Then we can arrest her.' He patted his gun, concealed in his pocket.

'We are working on an injunction against her,' said Anna Stübing, 'but that will take time.'

Nothing happened that night or the next, but the suspense of it all was draining. We knew she was biding her time.

On the way to the airport and home someone asked Colum if he wasn't crazy going back to Northern Ireland with all the terrorism there. He just smiled and said something about everything being relative.

Despite the Troubles of Northern Ireland all around us, the village where we now lived was relatively tranquil and unconditionally beautiful. Colum and Barbara, Catherine and myself had always wanted a place with enough space for two families, a recording studio, a language school and a multitude of visitors. We found it in Rostrevor between the mountains and the sea in an area we had long admired, just a few miles from Ryan and already with many friends involved in artistic and musical meanderings. We had performed one of our first concerts there as children and had been moved by the music and friendship of the Farrell family, Siubhán and Eibhlis as well as the Morgans, McQuaids, McGraths, Murphys, Sherrys, Sloans and Tinnellys. The village, because of its setting, had long held an attraction for those with an eye for beauty. Miss Douce in Joyce's *Ulysses* had told Stephen Dedalus that her holiday in Rostrevor had been 'Tiptop … gorgeous'.

Generals, majors and soldiers of fortune had been well rewarded down the years by the Crown with plots for their labours, as did lords and ladies of varying degree. Major General Ross, for example, who in 1812 set fire to the Presidential Mansion in Washington and was indirectly responsible for it being named 'The White House' when it was subsequently whitewashed, had once owned our abode. More recently it had been the property of the Queen Mother's people, the Bowes-Lyons family. The grounds had grazed Siberian Yaks and the stables had housed sleek, velvet-eyed Arabian steeds. That's where we lived, in the stables, but we had made some alterations and there was room enough for all of us.

We couldn't avoid a quiet titter as we read a codicil connected to the deeds of the property added during World War 1. 'No portion of these assets should benefit a German, Austro-Hungarian or Turk without the express sanction of the Crown.' Barbara grinned, she was German. Catherine was French, 'Not much better than a Turk, my dear,' she quipped. Thankfully that war was long gone and the current Troubles were out of earshot, but then again, as Colum said 'everything is relative'.

One morning our milkman mentioned the presence of a stranger sleeping in the woods behind our house. 'It was a woman and a hardy one too,' he said. 'I think she might be foreign.'

A few evenings later Colum's little girl Niamh offered us a sweet.

'Where did you get the bag of sweets?' asked Colum.

'I got them from the nice woman in the forest,' she answered.

'What does the nice woman look like?' I asked.

'She has brown hair and a round face and she said she was from Germany.'

'Did she say anything else to you?' asked Colum, trying to sound calm.

'Not very much,' Niamh said, 'except that she thought our house would be easy to set on fire. Would you like a sweet, Uncle Tommy?'

'No, Niamh,' I said, 'my tummy's feeling funny.'

Any doubts we may have had about who the nice woman was were banished a few hours later. That night a stone came through Colum's window and a knife sliced my car tyre. Gundula had come to Ireland.

We called the police, but she was nowhere to be seen.

Our next gig was the Ballyshannon Folk Festival. It was one of the friendliest festivals in the country and for its first two decades we had played there every year without a break. Big Phonsie and Anthony Travers, Carmel and all the gang had been organizing the event for weeks in advance. It was a great chance to spend some time with other musicians. De Danann, Christy Moore, Danny Kyle, Andy Irvine, Dolores Keane, Máirtín O'Connor, Séamus Begley and Steve Cooney, Sheevon, Mary Black, Kieran Goss, Frances Black, Ian Campbell, Cran, Joe Burke, Na Casadigh, Dervish, Déanta, Heritage, Crawford Howard, Clannad – they were all there. There were friends from all over Ireland, Europe and America – Neil Johnson from the *Belfast Telegraph*, Geoff Harden, Noel Devlin, Big Nace from North Carolina, Carola Preuss from a German radio station, Karen and Matthias Koehler from Rodgau, Harold Jüngst from Duisburg, Carsten Panduro from Denmark, Big John McMahon and Briege and many others we knew from the long road.

Martina, the little masseuse from Stuttgart who occasionally travelled with us in Europe, was also there. She was sleeping in a tent under the stars. In the middle of the night she opened her eyes. She wondered at the clarity of the stars, hundreds of them, perhaps millions. She had never seen so many stars. No wonder. There was no tent, that's why, just ribbons. A silent knife had been at work in the dark. Little Martina was judged to be guilty by association. Gundula was 'on the tear'.

During that weekend, a member of the Garda Síochána was assigned to look after me. Tom was 6'2" and stayed up all hours of the night while we sang, played and drank pints of stout. I don't think he ever had a weekend like it.

'That woman must be crazy,' he said.

Perhaps she was, but Gundula was smart enough to cover her tracks and never be caught at her grisly work. It was ironic really. Here we were going around the world trying to get people to talk and make peace with each other, yet a vendetta was being directed against us, and people associated with us, and no amount of talking would get us anywhere. It all seemed so unbelievable, like the plot of a bad whodunnit, that we stopped telling people about it. When Gundula was out of sight, I tried to put her out of my mind. What else can you do?

22

The Man from God Knows Where

I was sitting in the Liverpool bar in Belfast with playwright Martin Lynch and his brother Brian, waiting to board the boat. We were due to perform at a musical event at the British Labour Party conference in Bournemouth. I was interrogating Martin about his controversial but highly successful autobiographical play *The Interrogation of Ambrose Fogarty*.

'Did that Branch man actually walk across your back, the way it was portrayed in the play?' I asked.

'He did,' said Martin. 'More an attempt to humiliate than to hurt, though. His job was to break people like me. My job was not to be broken by people like him.'

Lynch's links, in his younger days, with the Official IRA had led to his arrest and questioning in the infamous Castlereagh interrogation centre in the seventies. The treatment he received was not untypical. That's why so many could identify with Ambrose Fogarty.

'At the end of the day, I was the stronger one,' he said, 'for I had total belief in the cause of uniting the working-class people. His only motivation was a pay cheque at the end of the month. I don't bear any ill will towards him and I'll tell him that if I ever meet him again. His name was Michael Malone. It takes its toll on you, though,' he added.

Boarding the boat, we were confronted by a Special Branch man. Nothing unusual about that in those days.

'What's your name, sir?' he said to Martin.

'Martin Lynch,' he replied.

'Are you sure it's not Ambrose Fogarty?' asked the plain-clothes cop.

Martin's eyes opened wide. 'I don't believe this,' he said.

He called me over. It was his interrogator in Castlereagh, the man we had just been talking about.

'What the hell are you doing here?' asked Martin.

'Just biding my time,' said Malone. 'I'm waiting to get out of this work. Just the matter of a short while now. I'm going into community policing.'

In a year he would be dead, shot by the Provisional IRA in a Liverpool bar in August 1987. He had walked over too many backs.

But now we were on our way to Liverpool. We were met at the other side by a contingent of politicians and musicians. Among them were Glasgow man Hugh Jordan, guitar in hand, and the legendary Dominic Behan, with a half-filled bottle of whiskey. Dommo was hell on wheels when he was drunk, but he was a scholar and a gentleman when he was only half jarred. It was all about timing – getting him before he shifted into belligerent gear. When his big brother Brendan was 'indisposed' and unavailable to speak at the London opening of *The Hostage*, Dominic had been called in to say a few words. He was well beyond the halfway stage to insobriety and before he was done, he had lambasted the audience, the theatre and the British Empire with mouthfuls of unprintable curses. The audience was shocked and disgusted, except one man in the balcony who had been dozing throughout Dominic's tirade. He rose unsteadily to his feet and roared, 'Good man, Dommo. Give it to the bastards!' It was Brendan, of course.

No doubt overshadowed by Brendan, Dominic was a wonderful writer, singer and entertainer in his own right. He wrote many great songs and his earthy, vernacular style guaranteed that they slid seamlessly into the folk traditions of both Ireland and Britain. 'Liverpool Lou', 'The sea around us', 'Come out you Black and Tans' and 'The patriot game' can still be heard in any Irish pub around the world.

In the aftermath of a great night's music in Bournemouth that year, he was rasping out an old United Irishman poem written by Florence Wilson from Groomsport, County Down, 'The man from God knows where'. It is about Thomas Russell, who, with 'Young Warwick' (Presbyterian minister Archibald Warwick), was hanged in Downpatrick gaol after the cause was lost again in 1803.

It is a dramatic poem and Dominic flung off his coat and rolled up his sleeves. There was a rare mix in his audience. Activists from all parties and groupings in the North had come to make their case at the conference and were now making contacts in the half dark. There was no shortage of unease. The two wings of republicanism were drinking quietly and separately. There were loyalists in the room, and Tories, as well as the inevitable Special Branch men and others no one seemed to know. Big Mick Mulcahy, the coal miners' union leader, fresh from battle with Margaret Thatcher, had just given a tender rendition of 'I gave my love a cherry', with Brian on the whistle and myself on guitar. Vincent Hanna, current BBC political commentator and former singer with the Glen Folk Four, called for order. The barman had served the last drinks and the lights were further dimmed. Dominic began in a low voice.

> Into our townlan', on a night of snow,
> Rode a man from God knows where;
> None of us bade him stay or go,

Nor deemed him friend, nor damned him foe,
But we stabled his big roan mare:
For in our townlan' we're a decent folk,
And if he didn't speak, why none of us spoke,
And we sat till the fire burned low.

Dominic stopped. I've never been sure if he intended a dramatic pause, or if he forgot the words, but a voice from behind took up the poem from where he left off. It was an accent from home. Dominic joined in and, like two actors on a world stage, he and the stranger shared the story to its tragic conclusion.

Amid a great round of applause, Dominic called me over to the bar, which had opened again. This was like home. 'There's a poet here wants to meet you,' he said. 'He's the man from God knows where.'

I saw the stranger who had helped out with the ballad. There was something familiar about him. 'Which part are you from?' I asked.

'Belfast,' he said. 'My name's Spence ... Gusty Spence.'

It couldn't be *the* Gusty Spence, I thought, the man who had started all the trouble back in the sixties. Hadn't he got life? Gusty Spence, the very devil incarnate. It couldn't be him. This man looked human, even friendly.

'I like your song "There were roses",' he said softly. 'What are you having?'

Before the pint arrived, I had learned that he was indeed the UVF man, and before the pint was downed, my appetite would be whetted for more insight into the strange life and times of the legendary loyalist.

'Anyone who would regard me as a hero,' began Gusty, 'I would be worried about them.' He looked down at his hands. 'But at least I have learned something from life,' he added. 'When I went into Crumlin Road prison, the republican prisoners shouted across the wire at us "traitors" and "planters". We shouted back, "Remember 1690" and "No surrender". In time, and there was plenty of it, the shouts turned to arguments and eventually arguments turned to discussions.

'I started to read something about my own history and listened to the republican's reading of theirs. Our origins had made us adversaries; our experience had made us victims. Republicans went on hunger strike for political status and so did I. We found that by coming together on issues that concerned us both we could be stronger, more effective. When we finally agreed upon a version of history that accommodated us all, we concluded that ordinary working people, both Catholic and Protestant, had been used and abused by the powers that be down the years and that firing guns at each other was not the way to improve life for anybody.'

Two weeks later I got a phone call.

'Andy Tyrie would like to talk to you,' a voice said.

I had often seen Tyrie's tough, uncompromising face on television. Leader of the Ulster Defence Association, he was prominent in the Ulster Workers' Council strike, which brought down the power-sharing Executive in 1974. Frequently for the UDA, just to be a Catholic was to be a legitimate target. His headquarters in east Belfast was not an obvious place of hospitality for anyone from my tradition. But after a few moments on the phone with him, any fears I had were quickly swept aside. We were talking about songs, Ulster songs.

Bobbie Hanvey had played 'Down the river' on his Downtown programme, a song I had written and recorded with The Sands Family on a German album called *The Winds are Singing Freedom* about the betrayal by Britain of the Ulster working-class Protestant.

> You promised that you'd stand by me from the very start
> And you told our sons and daughters to be loyal,
> You have no further use for me, you've gone and broke my heart
> And you sold us down the river in the end.

Tyrie had liked the song and wanted to hear more of what I had to say.

'We're up here in Gawn Street,' he said. I knew the street on the Newtownards Road.

I asked Catherine to come with me. She's a Norman, born and bred, and a true, fearless daughter of Calvados. Her background might have some relevance in a conversation that would range from the native Irish to the Anglo-Normans and beyond. She was also very well informed in politics, both Irish and European, and was interested in knowing more of the local situation. Through her eyes I had already seen so many sights my own had missed.

The graffiti along the Newtownards Road, however, were signs for Ulster eyes.

'What does KAT mean?' asked Catherine, viewing the white paint marks on the red bricks of Dee Street.

'Kill All Taigs,' I said, wondering if this trip was a good idea after all.

'The people must be very fearful,' she said simply. 'Both the writer and the reader.'

'Why is the red hand painted on the walls?' she asked. I told her stories remembered from years back about two brothers racing in boats to claim the land. The owner of the first hand to touch the land would become the owner of the land. One brother falling behind somewhat, cut off his hand and flung it to the shore and so became the owner. The O'Neills of Ulster who came from Munster in the fifth century claimed the story, but the Protestants of Ulster opened their Bibles at Genesis 38:28 at the birth of Zarah and Pharez, the twin sons of Judah. The firstborn would be the rightful heir and when the hand of Zarah appeared first the midwife tied a red ribbon round it. Lo and behold, however, in the excitement of birth, the red hand disappeared and Pharez was the first whole child to come tumbling body and soul into the world and so the trouble started. Now both sides claim the story, the hand and the land.

'We're talking chosen people here,' said Catherine with a shudder, 'or is it the perfect race?'

We turned into Gawn Street and parked the car some distance from the door of the UDA headquarters. Broken-down vehicles were parked near the building as a shield against car bombs. We knocked on the door and waited. We were scrutinized through the peephole for several seconds and then slowly bolts unbolted and locks unlocked.

'Mr Tyrie is expecting you,' said a well-preserved middle-aged woman with light brown hair. 'He's just finishing his meeting. Come on up.'

We climbed a well-trod, rickety staircase and came face to face with the instantly recognizable black moustache of the supreme commander of the UDA.

'You're welcome,' Tyrie said. 'This is John McMichael.'

McMichael was writing some final notes on a page. He looked up and smiled. 'Just a moment,' he said.

I looked round the room. Near the doorway in a small bookcase I noticed a large book entitled *The Life of Mahatma Gandhi*. Resting on top of the bookcase was a statue of the dying Cú Chulainn, complete with a crow on his shoulder. On the walls there were several paintings based on the *Lebor Gabála* (The Book of Invasions), a medieval chronicle of the legendary history of Ireland.

'Is that Jim Fitzpatrick's work?' I asked. Planxty had recently brought out an album with a Fitzpatrick cover and I recognized the intricate detail of his work.

'You're right,' said Tyrie. 'It's fine stuff.' He sat down behind the table and motioned us to take a seat. McMichael, finished his writing, gave a friendly nod and left.

'You seemed surprised at the Cú Chullain statue,' Tyrie said with a smile. 'Cú Chullain defended Ulster against the men of Erin, you know. We are carrying on that work today.'

I was familiar with Ian Adamson's book *The Cruithin*. I had interviewed him on *Country Céilí*. The Cruithin (the Irish word for Picts) were the original inhabitants of Ulster, until they were banished by the Gaels to Scotland. Now they had come back and reclaimed the land that was rightfully theirs. Adamson's theory had given a fresh sense of identity to the loyalist men of Ulster and strengthened the cause of the UDA.

'We had a festival here a few years ago,' said Tyrie, 'to promote British culture. The organizers brought over Morris dancers from England, who danced around the streets with bells on their heels. The local people laughed their heads off. That's not the culture of east Belfast. It belongs to some part of England. We must explore our own Ulster culture. That's where our identity lies. Your song "Down the river" is interesting. I'd like to hear more of these ideas.'

'Where are your own poets and writers?' I asked. 'They could tell that story much better than me.'

Tyrie took a long pull of his cigarette. 'I'll give you two reasons why that tradition for us is thin on the ground,' he said. 'For a start, the Calvinists regarded it as unholy to dip into the arts.'

I was aware of the competition between villages in Wales, organized by

Methodists in 1904, as to which would have the biggest bonfire of fiddles. Catholic priests in Ireland viewed dances at crossroads with similar disapproval, hence parochial halls were built. Dancing can lead to unmarried sex and mixed marriages, God save us. A loss of control not only for the lovers but equally and perhaps more so for the religious leaders whose job it was to control the flock. Wasn't there a joke going round about that? 'Why are Presbyterians not allowed to have sex standing up? Because it might lead to dancing.'

'Secondly,' said Tyrie in a serious tone, 'even though we knew we were no better off than the people on the Falls Road – well, maybe further up the dole queue – for us to write songs of protest against our conditions was to somehow rock the very boat we were sailing in. It would be disloyal.'

'Songs have often been necessary to give a voice to the voiceless,' I suggested, 'Perhaps you already had a voice in the establishment.'

'That's the very point,' said Tyrie. 'We thought we had but the voice of ordinary working-class Protestants was not being represented. We were taken for granted by the British Empire and betrayed by well-heeled Unionist politicians. We want to improve living conditions for everybody. There should be a place for everyone in Ulster, Catholic and Protestant, unionist and nationalist. But it must be within an Ulster framework, the majority want it that way. It's common sense. We are in touch with the Workers' Party about these things, but we can't move too quickly.'

The following week I found myself in the headquarters of Sinn Féin on the Falls Road. I had gone there with Billy Graham, political correspondent with the *Irish News*, who had arranged to interview Danny Morrison about talks between Hume and Adams, which had broken down. We were welcomed by the unlocking and unbolting of stout doors, a familiar sound. From inside, I looked through the window and saw a picture that was also familiar. I had seen it in Gawn Street – the same redbrick houses, the same unemployment, the same problems, the same people – and at that moment I realized that there would be a solution. It would not be easy to achieve and it would largely depend on the commitment and staying power of people in both those headquarters. They represented what we were all capable of, both good and bad. They had the power to do the worst, but also the potential to do the best. It was only a matter of time before they would sit down together, for everyone's sake, and talk.

I wrote a song and sang it for the first time at the Belfast Folk Festival of 1986. I called it '1999'.

> Oh IRA and UVF this song is just for you
> As you sit down at the table now to see what you can do,
> At last you've come together after all the tears and time
> It's sad you didn't do it back in 1969.
>
> I remember well your little girl, she had ribbons in her hair
> When she came to play that summer's day with the children in the square,

With Gary McMichael (photo Robyn Diamond)

To think they could be here today still laughing and alive
If strong men had been wise men in 1979.

It was always all or nothing, there was nothing in-between,
Compromise was treachery, that's the way it seemed.
But now we're left with nothing but a future we must find
And count the cost of the chances lost in 1989.

Oh IRA and UVF this song is just for you,
As you sit down at the table to see what you can do,
At last you've come together after all the tears and time
It's sad you didn't do it in 1999.

In January 1987, as the UDA continued to kill and to be killed, John McMichael presented the document *Common Sense* as a way forward towards peace. Its title was inspired by the eighteenth-century visionary Thomas Paine and received a relatively favourable response across the board. In December of the same year an IRA bomb exploded under his car. He died instantly. His son Gary told me that the reason his father went into politics was to try to create a better society for his children. Gary McMichael would soon follow his father into politics, for the same reason.

23

14,000 Miles

Catherine and I were blessed with two treasures, a son and daughter. Fionán was first and, as his name in Irish would suggest, he was the fair-haired one. His skin was fair too and his eyes were clear, inquisitive, humorous and blue. His little sister Moya was different, like Catherine. She had black hair, beautiful brown eyes and sallow silken skin. Despite my Uncle Patrick's comment that nobody walks nowadays, Moya was learning to do just that and Fionán was learning to run. They were growing fast and I was relearning the wonders of daisy chains, rowan bangles and singing leaves as well as finding the magic of fairy trees, hazelnuts and Brigit's crosses, all over again. We learned to swing and climb trees and sometimes I'd show off by hanging upside down from a branch by my knees. Fionán smiled as if to humour me and told me to be careful. Moya tried to pull me down to earth again, perhaps on the assumption that when you're on the ground you can fall no further.

Night-time was story time and sleep would be strenuously withheld until stories in both English and French would satisfactorily unfold. Although all efforts were appreciated I learned that stories, songs or poems without happy endings were somewhat frowned upon by Moya and Fionán. This came to me quietly in the midst of a long sad poem about a blind piper called Caoich O'Leary, when I thought I overheard Fionán conspiring quietly with his baby sister. 'If you pretend you're asleep he will stop,' he whispered. Moya let out a less than subtle snore and I burst out laughing.

The children united had strong bargaining power – one would ask for a story and the other would ask for a song, knowing that if each were to be satisfied I would have to give them both. That's how I developed the song/story combination idea. The story of the song of Willie Brennan was a big hit and it was requested over and over again.

> It's of a brave young highwayman this story I will tell
> His name was Willie Brennan and in Ireland he did dwell
> 'Twas on the Kilworth mountains he commenced his wild career
> And many a wealthy nobleman before him shook with fear

With Catherine, Fionán and Moya (photo Bobbie Hanvey)

And it's Brennan on the Moor, Brennan on the Moor
Bold brave and undaunted is young Brennan on the Moor

This was followed by the rather roguish tale of Willie Brennan, first supplying a poor family with rent money to pay off a greedy landlord, then stealing it back from the landlord when the payment was safely recorded and duly passing it on to another family in similar straits. My children were both half asleep three-quarters way through. They already knew the ending and were reasonably content with it. Moya opened one eye. 'What will we do when you are away?' she said. 'We'll have none of your stories for two weeks.'

It was true I was going on tour again. 'Maybe you could put them on a tape,' said Fionán, 'and we can hear them while you're on tour.' So that's what we did. Later when Wendy Newton from Green Linnet Records visited our house and listened with Fionán and Moya she suggested we put it out on an album for more children to hear. We named the album after a meeting place where I had once played many years before, *Down by Bendy's Lane,* and soon I would get the chance to bring them on tour with me.

'There were roses' was becoming popular in the US thanks to Mick Moloney, Robbie O'Connell and Jimmy Keane, who had recorded it on an album of the same name.

'It's time you came back here,' said Robbie.

Tucson concert with Mick Moloney and Eileen Ivers (photo Mike Wolke)

I had known him for years. A nephew of The Clancy Brothers, a great song-writer and a wit to boot, he had run a legendary gig in the family's Tinvane Hotel in Carrick-on-Suir. The Clancys, the Mooney sisters, Roxanne O'Connell, and the likes of Paul Grant, Martin Murray, Ned the Fiddler, and Dermot Morgan were all willing partners in many a crazy night we had there.

Robbie had returned to the US and hooked up with Mick and Jimmy. They were part of the Green Fields of America, which Mick had gathered together like the Magnificent Seven of Irish music in the States. Michael Flatley, Jean Butler, Donny Golden, Séamus Egan and Eileen Ivers all had played and ploughed their early fur-rows in The Green Fields and I regarded it as a great honour to be asked to join up when Robbie left to join his uncles in The Clancy Brothers. Robbie introduced me to Mike Dinsmore from Delaware and Caroline Quandt from Washington DC, who agreed to set up some gigs for our tour of America.

'Where do you want to go?' asked Mike on the phone.

'Everywhere!' shouted Catherine over my shoulder. 'Including Mexico.' And to me she whispered, 'I think it's time, don't you?' It had been eight years since the night I had asked her to postpone her trip to Mexico so that I could accompany her.

We bought an old Dodge camper van in Wilmington for $1600 and began a 14,000-mile journey of a lifetime. Six-year-old Fionán wanted to see deserts and five-year-old Moya wanted to see bears. They would both be more than satisfied.

We started in Philadelphia at the Irish Céilí Festival. I was performing but also recording chats in dressing rooms to send back to my weekly radio programme in Belfast. I interviewed Mick Moloney first and could have filled ten programmes with him alone. His own music experiences and the musicians' lives he had touched and been touched by were like a potted history of Irish music itself.

After starting a group during his university days in Dublin with Donal Lunny and having 'hits' with Paul Brady and the Johnstons, Mick took to the road, first England, then Norway and eventually the place where he set up home, Germantown, Philadelphia. There he discovered many wonderful Irish musicians but the only available venues were in pubs, with audiences more interested in drink than in music. Moloney set about creating a new platform for their talents. He went to the National Arts Council of America and demanded that traditional music be afforded the same respect as classical or other forms. He helped to open the doors of performing art spaces, city halls and theatres all over the country, giving the musicians and their growing audience a new sense of worth. His labours had already begun to bear fruit when Catherine and I arrived. Coming from the homeland, I was inclined to regard Irish music in America with some scepticism. It just wasn't the real thing, I thought. But I was coming to realize that the music being played by these Yanks, both young and old, was second to none and better than most anywhere. Mick introduced me to brilliant youngsters like The Egan Family, Joannie Madden and Eileen Ivers, who had listened to and been inspired by the older generation, like Ed Reavey, Martin Wynne and Eugene O'Donnell. I asked Eugene if he ever missed Derry and the home he had left behind many years earlier.

'Every single day,' he said sadly. 'Every single day.'

At the folk festival in Philly I met up with Mark Moss and Jim Musselman. Mark was the new editor of the legendary *Sing Out* magazine. Jim was a lawyer and comrade of Ralph Nader and had taken care of Paul Robeson's affairs in the last years of his life. Jim gave me Pete Seeger's address. 'Go up and see him,' he said. 'He'd love to meet you.'

Driving in upstate New York I couldn't hold back my enthusiasm and the 55 mph speed limit was, I fear, sometimes forgotten as I pressed the old Dodge onwards to the small town of Cold Springs. I had the wonderful feeling that a hero would soon become a friend.

I remembered listening to Pete's voice on the radio as a child and had later read of his travels, riding freight trains with Woody Guthrie in the forties, collecting folksongs with Alan Lomax in the fifties, and marching by the side of Martin Luther King in the sixties, singing the civil-rights anthem 'We shall overcome'. Pete Seeger wasn't just a popular singer who had had hit records for a few years. This man was a real star, whose light continued to shine through the dark days of McCarthyism, when he was dragged in front of the Un-American Activities Committee, right up to the present day. He was at the forefront of many human-rights initiatives striving for a more progressive and humane America. Throughout the time he had been banned from radio and television because of his leftist views, he had kept on singing and campaigning for a more just and peaceful world. Perhaps the best proof of his stardom was the fact that he was able to carry this mantle of greatness with such ease, remaining down to earth and friendly.

'You'd need a four-wheel-drive to get up the laneway,' said Pete on the telephone.

Pete Seeger with Moya and Fionán

'I'll meet you at the foot of the lane.'

He was much taller than I had imagined, maybe 6'2", and his long arms hugged us all as the snow fell thick and fast around the forested slopes of Bear Mountain.

'Are there bears here?' asked Moya.

'Arlo Guthrie had one come up to the window of his car the last time he was up here,' said Pete's wife, Toshi. 'But don't worry,' she said with a smile, 'you'll be sleeping in the barn where it's safe and cosy.'

Soon Pete had the banjo on his knee – the instrument sported the words 'This banjo destroys hatred' – and he sang 'No Irish need apply'. The song told of the Famine and how the Irish survivors who had the crossed the Atlantic found they had another struggle to overcome – racial prejudice.

'My great-grandmother came from Belfast,' he told me. 'Her name was Neilson. She had a sixth sense. She told her husband that she dreamt he shouldn't go to work in the mill in Poughkeepsie. But he went anyway, and was killed that day by a saw.'

Pete had countless stories and wise words for all of us. Toshi had only one lesson and it was for me. 'Don't let your kids grow up without you,' she said. Fionán was interested in everything. It was so good to have him on tour. Sometimes he went off to quiet places all alone and came back with treasures unknown to the rest of us. 'Has that young man Buddhistic tendencies?' Uncle Hugh had asked. Fionán would just sit back and smile. Now he was laughing and enjoying every moment and Moya was celebrating her fifth birthday. She blew out the candles and made a wish, which became a poem.

> When I grow up, she said, I want to be magic …
> So little realising, so much
> She warmed the cold, softened the road,
> Lit a star, cured the head.
> You are already magic, I said.

Pete and Toshi, along with their kids, had toured the US thirty years before. He gave me some addresses of people they had met. 'I don't know whether they're living or dead,' he said. We thanked him for the contacts and headed off in the green camper to discover America.

During the next two months we travelled through thirty states and played at forty concerts. I did radio programmes from the bluegrass hills of Kentucky, the Bluebird Café of Nashville, Lake Pontchartrain, the Everglades of Florida, the Red River Valley of Texas, the Appalachian Mountains, Route 66, San Francisco Bay, and Old Faithful of Yellowstone Park. We had a swim in Florida, a flat tyre in Baton Rouge, a broken window in Seattle, and when we arrived in El Paso, we went south of the border down Mexico way and swore we would return for a longer visit.

Several weeks later we were rattling up a dirt road in the Mariposa Hills of north California with one of Pete's addresses in our fist. We were visiting the ranch of Bob Di Witt. Bob was a 75-year-old hippie who wore a big hat and no shoes. He had sold some land to Woody Guthrie and introduced him to his third wife, 'Pete and Woody were good ole friends of mine,' he drawled. 'I used to go to all the folk concerts but now I'm too old and they come to me.' On his ranch were three makeshift theatres, each built without a back wall to allow the music to escape and echo down the valley, so that his neighbours could enjoy it too. Bob had a drum kit that he played with everyone, whether they needed percussion or not. My audience that night was a huddle of Native Americans lying on blankets in front of me and a man from County Armagh. I have no idea how he had got there, but he said he wouldn't be returning home until Armagh won the All-Ireland.

Bob was an amazing character, wild and free, and I asked him for an interview the next morning. 'Before I talk on the radio,' he said, 'there are two conditions to be met.'

If he's looking for money, I thought, I don't have it. I was just getting enough from each concert to get us to the next one. 'What's the first condition, Bob?' I asked warily.

'The first condition, is' – Bob raised his fist in the air and brought it down with a thump on the wooden breakfast table, sending muesli and his wife Dori's home-made plum jam up in the air – 'I must be in the nude.'

'And what's the second one?' I asked, trying to imagine him without his large hat.

'The second condition is,' he said, 'you must be in the nude too.'

It was Friday and I needed this interview badly. It would be too late to broadcast if I waited to nab someone in San Francisco, our next stop. Moreover, I knew I would never meet a man like this again. The next thing I knew there we were in the altogether having a great yarn in the American Wild West:

Me: I'm sitting here with Bob Di Witt in the hills of Mariposa and not a sock between the four of us. Why must it be like this, Bob?

Bob: Because I'm a straight-talking man, and if I talk with anyone, there must be no barriers, no pretence, just you and me, man to man.

Me: You always walk around in your bare feet. What about all the thorns?

Bob: Buddy, it's just like life, some you take out and some you leave in, and you just walk on ...

As we hit the road, we knew we wouldn't meet him or his likes again.

During my concert in Bethlehem, Pennsylvania, Patty Mohr handed me a paper crane that she had made and asked me to write a song about Sadako Sasaki. Sadako was just a baby when the USA dropped an atom bomb on the city of Hiroshima in the same year that I was born in the town of Newry, 1945. Ten years later the little girl developed leukaemia as a result of the deadly radiation. There is an old tradition in Japan that if you can make a thousand paper cranes (the bird associated with good health and long life) then you can have whatever wish that you want. Sadako made a wish that she would be well once more and that such bombs would never be allowed to fall again. With great hope in her heart she began to make the paper cranes but she could only make 644. A tale of truth and beauty was beginning to breathe a sense of great sadness and yet great hope into a new song.

> Her hands are growing slower but her hopeful heart is racing
> She has made six hundred cranes and forty-four
> But the headaches keep returning
> Her fingers they are burning
> She whispered I just can't make anymore
> *Sadako, let me make a paper crane for you*
> *Sadako, let me help to make your dreams come true*
> The children leave the classroom they are crowding round her bedside
> They're making paper cranes with loving speed
> Soon there'll be a thousand and your wishes will come true
> *Sadako, are you smiling in your sleep?*
> But the pains of life are leaving and the only dream she's dreaming
> Is a dream that bombs will never fall again
> And that's the dream they carry as they gather at her graveside
> And gently place a thousand paper cranes
> *Sadako, let me make a paper crane for you*
> *Sadako, let me help to make your dreams come true*

Travelling within the great extremes of mighty America this little song would move many to tearful expressions of both compassion and concern. In Little Rock, Arkansas, a big man with a suntanned face asked me angrily if I had ever heard about the people who bombed Pearl Harbour. I didn't know what to say. My song was just about a little girl who hurt no one. Soon I would hear an extraordinary story of another little girl.

I was playing back in Philadelphia's Tin Angel with Manhattan fiddler Lisa Gutkin. 'I want to introduce you,' she said, 'to an old friend who lives here in Philly. She writes poetry.' The next morning we knocked on the door of an elderly lady called Itka Frajman Zygmuntowicz. She was glad to see us and soon was preparing a welcome salad. She was cutting tomatoes with her sleeves rolled up and I noticed something written on her left arm. It was a number, 25673. I thought at first it was a telephone number but then another possibility dawned.

'Is that what I think it is?' I whispered to Lisa. 'Yes, she was in Auschwitz,' said Lisa, reading my thoughts.

Auschwitz was now a museum of human horror and I had been there on a visit once, which I would never forget. Perhaps what had chilled me most of all was one room in that terrible place full of human hair.

'I was only thirteen when they took me to Auschwitz and nineteen when I was rescued,' she said.

'How did you manage to survive all those years?' I asked.

'I have often thought of that since,' said Itka, 'and now I firmly believe that my survival and my reason for being able to speak to you today is due perhaps to one sentence that my lips managed to utter to a German officer shortly after my capture.

'The first day I arrived in Auschwitz all my family were killed. I was numbed and terrified. I didn't want to live anymore. I had no tears left to cry. I just wanted to die. But I didn't die and gradually amidst all the terror I felt something inside telling me to live. When I was called by my number 25673, I whispered to myself, I am not a number, I am Itkola. That's what my father used call me, Itkola.

'One day a German officer came and beat me so badly I couldn't move. I was lying in my blood on the ground. He looked down at me and I heard him say, "I will finish you off later."

'I looked into his eyes. "You can't," I said.

'He was shocked. "What do you mean?" he said. "I can kill you very easily, with this gun, with my bare hands."

'"No!" I said. "You can't kill me."

'"Why can't I? he asked, suddenly puzzled.

'"Because you are a good man," I said, "for I see the kindness in your eyes. You can't kill me."

'He gave a kind of grunt and went away. When he came back he didn't hit me again. Perhaps it was the first time he had ever been told that he had kindness. Perhaps he had been treated like dirt by superior officers. Perhaps it was a miracle. I don't know. Any time afterwards when the lorry came round gathering people to be taken away he would say. "Stay with me Itka, you'll be all right." Instead of becoming my executioner he became my protector.'

In January 1945 Itka was moved in a forced six-day march from Auschwitz to Ravensbruck and later to Malchow, where she was liberated and brought to Sweden. I bid her goodbye with the words of a beautiful song echoing the fate of her countless compatriots.

> On a wagon bound for market sits a calf with a mournful stare
> High above him there's a swallow winging swiftly through the air

If her protector warranted a song it could have been drawn in part perhaps from the ominous words of Gestapo founder Hermann Goering: '... the people can always be brought to do the bidding of the leaders. That is easy. All you have to do is tell them they are being attacked and denounce the pacifists for lack of patriotism and exposing the country to danger. It works the same way in any country.'

When we reached Washington DC, at the end of our tour, we peered through the gates of the White House but there was no sign of Ronald Reagan. He was in Berlin making a speech about the Evil Empire of the East. Soon it would be time to go and gird the loins for the 'evil' East. Before that, however, Catherine, Fionán and Moya returned to Ireland and I had promises to keep with The Sands Family on the near side of what the West called the Iron Curtain and what the East called the 'anti-fascist dam'.

I rang Catherine at home from a phone box in Bamberg, Bavaria.

'Are you all right?' she asked.

'Yes,' I assured her. 'I'm grand.'

'Are you *sure* you're all right?' she repeated. Then she said in a sob, 'Tell me you're safe.'

'What is it? What's wrong?' I asked, worried now. This wasn't like Catherine and I was a thousand miles away.

'I'm not supposed to tell you this,' she said, 'but I must tell you. I got another phone call last night.' Disturbing calls in the middle of the night had become an all-too-frequent occurrence in recent weeks. No voice, just background noises, perhaps of a pub somewhere.

'Did anyone speak?' I asked.

Her voice was trembling. 'You will be shot tomorrow in Kaufbeuren,' she cried.

I knew Gundula had a hand in this and I also knew I couldn't regard it as an empty threat. Outside it was raining steadily. The others were waiting for me, along with our two new 'roadies', Andrea and Anna.

'We have an appointment with the commander of the *Polizei* in Bamberg,' said Anna. 'We will see him as soon as we enter the city.'

The commander was seated at a large wooden desk when we walked into his office. Around the walls were mug shots and area maps. He told us that Bamberg was a respectable city and he wanted to keep it that way.

We answered his questions as best as we could: when and how we had met this woman, what her motives were and where she was last seen, what her job was and where she found the money to buy a gun. The last question was easy. In my pocket, was the answer.

The commander believed that if she was serious, then she might be as liable to strike in Bamberg as Kaufbeuren. He opened a drawer and pulled out a small black handgun. It made a low, ominous thud as it fell on the desk. This man meant business. There were now other police officers in the room and he was giving them orders.

But the concert came and went with no sighting of Gundula. Perhaps it would be Kaufbeuren after all. The local police were already in place when we arrived for our sound check. A big Alsatian dog was sniffing around for Semtex.

'You have a full house tonight,' said the concert organizer, trying to cheer us up as we sat locked in the dressing room.

'Are there any civilians?' asked Col sardonically.

'Just the one,' joked the organizer, 'and she's armed.'

It was good at least that we could laugh. The dressing-room table was full of goodies but I had little appetite. Amongst the sumptuous food and drink I noticed the usual two kiwis. I liked kiwis. That is the wonderful advantage of German organization – if you want something special, it will be written into the contract and every single item will be delivered religiously. I laughed to think of the reaction you'd get from some promoters back home if you asked for a kiwi. 'Try the cobbler's shop for that stuff,' or, 'I'm not your mammy, you know.'

I will always remember the police unlocking the door and letting us onto the stage. I will always remember the burst of applause from our audience, oblivious to our worries, willing us on with their warmth.

That was a strange night. To stand on a stage and perform properly it is necessary to be completely at ease with oneself and at one with the audience. You must be ready to mentally fling your arms open wide and embrace every single person in that room. Otherwise you have neither power nor purpose nor any good reason to perform. We looked out into the blackness. Was there someone out there, either Gundula or an ally, ready to do us wrong? We dared not let the thought cross our minds. Few faces were visible in the wake of the stage-lights but the people were singing with us, feeling the pain and passion of the music.

We returned to the dressing room, locked the door, unlocked it and took an encore and took another and another. The man with the key was fed up turning and twisting. He left the door open. The feeling in the auditorium was electric.

Someone said they saw a woman who fit Gundula's description, walking out with a satisfied smile. Some thought that she had gained all the attention she was seeking, which had been her main motivation in the first place. Others said that she hadn't dared to make a move for fear of instant arrest. Gundula never went to jail and never troubled us again. I have seen her from time to time, at a distance, but we've never spoken. Maybe it's best to keep it that way. According to all accounts, she has settled down now in London, living a more stable life, without feeling the urge to chase the likes of us around the world.

24

Lessons in Moscow

On 7 December 1988 at 11.41 am there was an earthquake in Armenia. 25,000 people were killed and 31,000 were injured. Tremors were felt over a wide area and hearts were touched all over the world. I knew it would not be difficult to get local help in organizing a concert to raise some money for the relief fund.

Geoff Harden was running a weekly folk club in the Parador Hotel on Belfast's Ormeau Road. He had recently moved from the long-standing Sunflower Club in Corporation Street. I rang my good friends David Hammond, Tony McAuley, Kieran Goss, Crawford Howard, Martin Lynch, and the rest of The Sands Family. They would all be happy to perform. I decided that a name like Paul Brady would give it an extra boost. 'Yes!' said Paul on the telephone. 'What do you want me to do?'

Neil Johnston, always supportive of such events, wrote an article for the *Belfast Telegraph* and when the night of the concert arrived, there were three times as many outside the Parador as could be held inside. We put on a separate performance in each function room of the hotel, and the street concert was the biggest one of all. The singers rotated round each group of musicians and soon more arrived to join in the cause. After a magical night of music, we were able to hand over a goodly sum to the Irish-Soviet Friendship Society for the aid effort in Armenia.

The Society was made up of an interesting group of people, mainly from east Belfast, long involved in trade-union politics. They told me of a major fund-raising concert planned for Moscow in a few weeks' time and asked if I would be willing to go and represent Ireland in a gesture of solidarity. I thought of the wonderful city of Moscow and of a promise I had made to a Muscovite musician called Tanya under a tree in a Bulgarian thunderstorm. British Airways generously donated a first-class ticket for the flight, with all the luxury that entailed. I was not unaware of the irony as we moved into Soviet air space, 30,000 feet above the heads of the proletariat.

I was soon brought down to earth, though. 'Passport!' barked the immigration official in the Moscow airport.

'No problem, officer,' I said, buoyed up with friendly champagne and licking my lips in anticipation of fresh glasnost and perestroika cocktails from the new Kremlin cabinet of Mikhail Gorbachev.

'Visa!' continued the peaked-cap official.

Visa? I had no visa! With all the excitement I had forgotten about a visa. The policeman laughed at the very idea, and so did the second-class passengers piling up behind me. 'I've come to play at the big concert tomorrow. You've got to let me through,' I pleaded.

'Wait a moment,' said the man.

His superior arrived and laughed even louder when he heard my tale. Russian airport police had a great sense of humour that day. 'Sit in that room,' he said.

I sat down with a sigh and looked around. A few police officers stood at the door; otherwise I was alone. I settled myself for a long wait and reached for a book in my bag. My tin whistle caught my eye. I closed my eyes and began a tune called 'Jackson's last instructions' that I had learned from my father's fiddle. Several tunes later, I opened my eyes again to discover I was surrounded by a crowd of airport police. I went to put the whistle away.

'No, don't stop,' said one. 'I like that music. It's Arabic, isn't it?'

'Well, no,' I said, 'not really. It would be Irish, more or less.'

'Are you sure it's not Arabic?' he insisted.

'There might be Arabic influences all right,' I said truthfully, 'but essentially it's Irish.'

'There's an Irish guy playing tomorrow at the big concert in the Olympic stadium,' he said then.

'That's me,' I said. 'Or it will be me if I ever get out of this room.'

He left quickly and came back with a man in civilian clothes.

'Who is due to meet you here?' asked the newcomer.

'A representative from Friendship House,' I answered. 'And possibly a young woman called Tanya.'

'They are here,' he said, handing me my passport. 'You are free to enter.' Then, as an afterthought, he remarked, 'There is a gentleman with a beard and a bicycle. He is knitting socks. He awaits you also.'

Puzzled by this odd description, I followed the official up corridors and through doorways. Moscow was magnificently cold. Serious faces shuffled past wrapped in woolly *shlyapkas*, like actors in an old black-and-white spy movie.

'You will soon be warm,' said Tanya. 'A reception is waiting in Friendship House after your visit to Red Square and tomorrow night after the concert you will come to our house. Sergei is cooking a special meal.' She kissed me and disappeared into the night.

The large black Volga slid into gear. I was in the back seat all alone and surrounded by brown leather. Sitting up front in the passenger seat was Anatoli Kusmyenko, head of Moscow's International Friendship House. 'We are running late,' he said. 'It's a pity your friend could wait no longer, the man with the bicycle. I'm afraid our visit to Red Square will be just a fleeting one, but there will be more time later.'

'Yes,' I said, 'but who is the man with the bicycle?'

Anatoli didn't hear. He was showing the driver a good place to park. It was dark, but well-placed spotlights lit the splendour of Moscow's famous landmarks. I would enjoy further visits to this city, but my first glimpse was magical.

'Moscow is the heart of Russia,' Anatoli was saying. 'But the heart of Moscow is Red Square.'

'Does the "red" refer to the colour or politics?' I asked.

'Neither,' he laughed. 'It comes from the Russian word for "beautiful". *Krasivaya* sounds like *krasnaya*, meaning 'red' and this led to the incorrect translation.'

'It *is* beautiful,' I marvelled.

There were many questions I wanted to ask but one in particular was nibbling away at my curiosity. Who was the bearded, sock-knitting bicyclist? I knew of only one person who could fit that description, but he wasn't in Russia.

The last I heard of Peter J. Emerson, he had travelled across the central part of the African continent on a bicycle and published a remarkable account of his journey called *What an Unusual Title for a Travel Book*. He spent a considerable amount of time with various tribes, enjoying their company, learning their ways, and experiencing their hardships too – he had caught malaria.

Born to an English Catholic mother and an Irish Protestant father, he had joined the Royal Navy and worked on board an A-class submarine, keeping the world 'safe and well'. One day in Mombassa he found hungry street-children picking grains of corn from cobblestones just to stay alive, and he began to realize that the world powers were doing anything but keeping the world safe and well. Half of humanity was in a state of starvation and the weak were being exploited, rather then protected, to maintain the status quo.

He restarted a branch of CND in Northern Ireland in September 1980 and the Green Party in May 1982. It was at a strange time when some journalists, more naïve than patronizing, considered everything to be fine the way it was and regarded anyone who tried to change it as a bit eccentric. With Reagan in the White House and Brezhnev in the Kremlin the arms race was spiralling out of control. More money was being spent in the art of killing than in the art of keeping people alive. Meanwhile, the nuclear-power industry was installing power stations without regard to, or knowledge of, their long-term safety. Emerson, a nuclear physicist as well as a naval officer, had a good knowledge of the dangers of both the nuclear industry and the defence business and this was apparent when I first met him at a CND rally in Botanic Gardens Belfast in 1981. He lived by his beliefs, practised what he preached and his awareness of and care for the planet we live on was as consistent as the bicycle under him.

'What was the name of the man with the bicycle?' I asked Anatoli Kusmyenko. He handed back a copy of *Pravda*. 'Do you recognize him?' he said.

I looked at the photograph in the newspaper. 'That's Peter Emerson,' I said. 'How in the name of tires and tubes did he get here?'

'You'll soon know,' said Anatoli. 'He is your interpreter at the concert tomorrow night.'

That concert was one I will always remember. The atmosphere was breathtaking, the emotion unforgettable. The song I had written for the occasion would strike a chord in a way I could not have envisaged. I was aware that the majority would not understand one word of what I was singing about. But there was only one word that needed to be understood – Armenia.

Peter Emerson, sporting a new pair of woollen socks, introduced me in fluent Belfast, tinged with Russian, to the packed arena of Moscow's Olympic stadium. It was like playing to Hill Sixteen in Croke Park at an All-Ireland final, with the spectators all cheering for the same team.

Most of the audience was made up of Armenians. Rather like the Irish diaspora, Armenia had more of its natives living outside of the country than in it. Their history was one of terrible oppression and bloodshed and a surging desire for independence, nationhood, and freedom from ties with Moscow was climaxing at that time. I sang the chorus and they nearly tore the roof off with their response.

Armenia, Armenia, in every land there's a helping hand
Armenia, Armenia, the whole world sings for you …

I walked off stage to the deafening sound of the chorus still ringing round the stadium. Their desire for autonomy at that moment had overshadowed the horrors of the earthquake. I felt elated, but some faces backstage seemed less enthusiastic.

Tanya smiled knowingly. 'You were great,' she said. 'I'll tell you the rest later.'

'We begin with a toast,' Sergei said over the meal he had cooked for us, stretching across the table with a bottle of vodka to fill our glasses. 'May the peoples of our countries be forever friends and may the cold walls that divide us melt in the warmth of good music.' A toast is always a serious proclamation, and we happily joined in – communist, Christian and Muslim.

Boris Lansky, who explained that he was 'a lifelong Party man', asked slyly, 'Where are you from? Is it Ireland or the United Kingdom?'

'There are various opinions on that,' I answered, closing one eye.

He nearly spilled his spoonful of soup on the tablecloth with an over-generous laugh. 'I like that,' he said. 'I like that.'

Soon we were talking about the big concert and the wonderfully unified audience.

'There was more on their minds than an earthquake,' said Tanya. The people of Armenia had just experienced the first ethnic conflict in the Soviet Union. She showed me a cutting from *Pravda*. The headline read: 'Nash Olster'.

'What does it mean?' I asked.

Peter, who had been speaking in Russian, switched back to English for my benefit. 'It means "Our Ulster",' he said. 'It refers to the troubles in Nagorno-Karabakh.'

Soon they were all talking excitedly and discussing the similarities between Belfast and a place that I could not even pronounce – Nagorno-Karabakh. For years these people had lived peacefully side by side. Now they were burning houses and shooting each other in the dead of night.

Sergei explained: 'In the 1920s when the Soviets were drawing up boundary maps for the Caucasus, they observed that the Armenians, who were almost exclusively Gregorian Christian, were going to the church, and the Azeris, who were mainly Muslim, were going to the mosque. They are different, they concluded, so they drew a circle round one group and another circle around the other. At once a small group of Azeris found themselves to be a minority in the Armenian circle, and a small group of Armenians found themselves to be a minority in the Azeri circle. Each group shouted, "We don't belong here; we belong over there." Out came the maps again and more circles were drawn, until the whole area was carved up into little islands, each owing allegiance to another island some distance away.'

'It's like,' said Peter, 'if west Belfast, an Irish nationalist area in British Northern Ireland, was made part of the Irish Republic, and some Protestant part of County Cork, say, in the Republic, was joined politically to Northern Ireland.'

'One of the biggest of these islands in the Caucasus is Nagorno-Karabakh,' Sergei continued, 'where no one wants to be in the minority, so it is a question of, literally, where to draw the line.'

'I'm beginning to understand,' I said. 'But if this is the beginning of democracy in the Soviet Union, things don't look too promising, do they?'

'That's why it's so important to get it right,' said Peter. 'Otherwise there will be constant ethnic conflict all over the Soviet Union and Eastern Europe. There are already tensions in Afghanistan and even Yugoslavia. Tribes with bitter memories of past history will not want to be in the minority where the enemy is in the majority in any new state. We must seek a decision-making system that will promote people coming together, rather than one which forces them to be torn apart.'

'Without the loving boot of communism to stamp authority on our base instincts, anything is liable to happen,' said Boris, refilling our glasses. I could feel another toast coming on.

I was wrong. It was a joke. Boris, like many others, enjoyed the humour directed against the hierarchy of his own party.

'What has forty teeth and four legs?' he asked.

Nobody seemed to know.

'A crocodile!' he answered.

'What has forty legs and four teeth?' No one knew that either, it seemed. 'It's the Central Committee of the Communist Party.'

Peter took a sip of vodka and then a bite of lemon.

'Tell me about your article in *Pravda*,' I said to Peter.

'"*Da illi Neyht*", "Yes or No". It seemed to provoke a lot of interest,' Peter began. 'With coming democratization here, people are looking for alternatives to the one-party system of government. Many look towards the West for new political and democratic templates and structures. My article preaches caution. Coming from Northern Ireland we should be able to tell them at least what not to do.

'Take Great Britain, for example. Even if Maggie Thatcher gets 51 per cent of the vote that means 49 per cent of the voters (and probably a much higher percentage of the entire population) have no say in the running of their country for four years. The party whip system, which takes its name from the hounds in a hunt being whipped into line, ensures that by virtue of its majority, however slim, the ruling party can pass whatever laws it likes. This is not democracy, which should serve all the people; it's majoritarianism, which serves only the interests of the majority.

'In a place like Northern Ireland, majoritarianism has caused trouble. The boundary line was drawn to ensure a built-in unionist majority and a nationalist minority. It's like two wolves and a sheep holding a "democratic" vote on what they should have for dinner.'

With Tanya Vladimirsky in Moscow

I could see his point.

'The fault is not in the people,' he went on. 'It's not even in the politicians. The problem lies in the voting system that is forced upon us at election time. This method of election – first past the post – magnifies the differences between people and ignores the similarities. A referendum in Northern Ireland, for example, that demands simple yes or no answers to 'Are you Irish?' or 'Are you British?' ensures that the majority will vote yes to the British option and the minority … They will not vote at all because they know there is no point. They are already beaten before it starts. Instead of demanding a referendum, we should be thinking about a "preferendum".'

'What's a preferendum?' asked Tanya, whose knowledge of the English language didn't stretch that far.

But it was time for another toast – this time from a striking woman called Irina. 'May the coming elections bring peace, justice and prosperity to the Soviet Union.'

We all drank more vodka.

'We all have various ideas on any given topic.' Peter smiled seriously, responding to Tanya's pre-toast question. 'Not only the two extreme positions that are presented on our ballot sheet, which may split the allegiance of the population, but the many more reasonable views in-between. Instead of limiting a Northern Ireland electorate to contentious choices like "Brits out" or "Dublin out", we could consider options like joint sovereignty, or an independent Northern Ireland in a new Europe, or an independent state within Ireland, and so on. Voters could award points to the various options listed. In a ballot paper with ten options, say, ten points would be allocated to their most preferred option, nine points to their next favourite, eight points to their third choice, and so on. The option with the most points overall would win. It may not be the first choice of any one group, but it would be the first choice of the whole group. Every view would be respected and every vote would be counted. That is democracy.'

'Is that not similar to proportional representation?' I asked.

'No!' said Peter. 'PR is a big improvement on first-past-the-post elections but it's still adversarial. Given that we are in an already divided society, the almost inevitable consequence is that both "halves" then themselves divide into two. If an extremist gets his quota, he's in, maybe satisfying some but scaring others. In the preferendum everyone finds his or her best possible compromise and the one who succeeds will be generally acceptable to all.'

'How did you think of such an advanced idea?' asked Tanya.

'It's not my idea,' said Peter. 'I learned it from the African *baraza* tradition, where the elders sit in a circle and search for consensus. This group of old men are chosen to look after the needs of the tribe. The more contentious the issue, the more anxious they are to achieve an agreed consensus. If they can't reach agreement the first day, they come back the second and the third, for however long it takes. They always find a way. I'd love to try the idea back home,' he said.

'Why not?' I said. 'I'll help you organize it.'

It was late now. Sergei took down his balalaika. 'Do you remember this one?' he said to me as he began to play.

> May there always be sunshine,
> May there always be blue skies,
> May there always be Mama,
> May there always be me.

He handed me the balalaika. 'It's yours,' he said. 'A gift from Moscow.' I haven't seen him since, but I often think of Tanya and him and the first time we met, under a tree in a thunderstorm in Bulgaria.

25
Long Live the Chief

On 11 July 1989 I got a phone call from Ben. He was in Ryan and I knew immediately from the tone of his voice that something was wrong.

'The Chief's gone,' he said. 'He's dead.'

The words seemed incongruous that beautiful summer's morning. The birds were singing in the bushes at the front window and the children were playing in the garden.

As I drove down the narrow Ryan Road, I met the ambulance coming up, and we had to slow down to pass.

'A heart attack,' the driver told me.

My father had been at the Booley Fair in Hilltown the night before, singing and telling yarns. The fair celebrated a very real sense of belonging and place in music-making, dancing and traditional sports. My father had been refereeing the grass-rope-twisting competition and the winner would receive the Mick Sands Cup. He had come home from a singing session in the The Mourne Rambler, a pub belonging to my brother Hugh and his wife, Máirín. It was when preparing to return that he died, as if in mid-song.

It was hard to believe the Chief was dead.

I recalled a party in Newry when he fell down the stairs with a bottle of Guinness in his hand and a song called 'Nell Flaherty's drake' on his lips. He had landed on the last step in a sitting position, with his eyes closed and the bottle upright in his hand. But there was blood on the stairs and we feared the worst. Gabriel Scally, a young doctor, opened my father's eye. He was greeted with an indomitable glint and the words, 'We will rise again.'

'Please do,' said Gabriel, 'because we have to take you to hospital to put some stitches in that head of yours.'

'I will rise up surely, young fella,' answered the Chief, 'but not until I finish the song that I started at the top of the stairs.'

He finished the song and then off to Daisy Hill Hospital we all went. My song 'We will rise again' recalls that evening:

> I have heard the springtime singing
> And I've seen the young girls laughing
> And I heard an old man sing this song,
> There's light in the eye, never say die,
> We will rise again.

My father was tough and he had to be. His life had been a hard one, from ploughing rocks in Ireland to building blocks in England. He had regrets and often said he had great sorrows. But life goes on and he went on with it and against it.

I remembered the nights he came rolling home penniless from the fairs. Once he brought home Seán McGuire, on an old 78 rpm record. 'Put that on the gramophone quick,' he said, 'and it will lift the hearts of the whole townland.' McGuire, fiddle player extraordinaire, was never the most modest of men. He even scolded me in a live broadcast from the Ulster Hall when I introduced him as a great fiddle player. 'What are you talking about?' he snapped. 'I'm an effing brilliant fiddler player!' And so he was.

Years later when the Chief was very ill in bed, he said. 'It's too late to send for the doctor. Send for McGuire.'

McGuire didn't have to be asked twice. He landed at my father's bedside and played all night, reels and jigs, slow airs and hornpipes. The next morning the Chief jumped up out of bed and maintained he was better than ever he was.

> Up to the bridge and down to the wire,
> Over the top, he's a saint, he's a liar,
> You can take your fiddle down,
> You can throw it in the fire,
> For you never heard the likes of Seán McGuire.
> The years went by and my da grew older,
> Lying in the bed like a dying soldier,
> 'One last wish I would require,
> Don't mind the doctor.
> Send for McGuire.'
> Well he came that night and he played to morning,
> Music magic, cheerful, charming,
> My father cried, 'I feel no pain,' and in no time at all
> He was back on his feet again.

But now he was dead. People would be arriving soon. I knew I had to cry but I couldn't.

Before the wake began, I went for a walk down the fields. I went into the Wee Field, where he had played football with us when we were children. I walked into

The Chief, in Gorman's, one for the road (photo Bobbie Hanvey)

the Long Field, where we had gathered spuds behind his spade. I walked into the Field Above the Dams, where he had found the stray sod that my mother had walked on. I walked into the Low Field, where we had snared rabbits and he told us stories of Fionn Mac Cumhaill. I walked into the School Field, where we had dragged a thorn bush to cover the grass seed after the dolly mare had died. Then I walked into the wee loanin, and under the hedge, lying in the nettles and dockens, I saw an old rusty bucket sticking out of the grass. That was once the shiny bucket in which I carried corn to his red sowing fiddle in the Field in Front of the Door. And then it all came out. I began to cry, the tears pouring out until the pain and sorrow were released and I was ready to face the world and my father's wake.

26

The Fall of the Wall

I was in Derry at the time, in a bed-and-breakfast; out of bed, in fact, and just into my breakfast. Suddenly there was cheering from the corner and I knew some strange thing had happened. It was coming from the transistor radio. Early morning murmurs promptly grew mute, knives and forks fell silent and harmless upon fried eggs and bacon.

'The Wall's coming down. The Wall's coming down!' someone was shouting. It was an on-the-spot reporter trying to be heard above the crowd. He was at the Brandenburg Gate in Berlin. 'It's historic; it's monumental; it's unbelievable.'

I had begun to write a song called 'Dresden' about the inevitable possibility of the Wall coming down, but just now I was stunned.

'Herr Krenz, the former head of Culture who has taken over from Chairman Honecker, has bowed to the will of the people and instructed that the gates be opened,' shouted the reporter.

Our middle-aged hostess was pouring me a cup of tea out of a big silver teapot. The hem of her white and red spotted apron was wrapped around the handle to stop it from burning her hand. 'Would that be a good thing or a bad thing?' she asked, breaking the silence in the room. She was the kind of Derry woman who gave the impression of knowing little, but I surmised otherwise.

'It might be both,' I said.

'Indeed and it might,' she said and walked away repeating, 'indeed and it might, be dad, indeed and it might …' like something in a musical.

'Will that affect our performances there?' said Shivaun O'Casey.

Shivaun liked my songs and felt that I dipped into the same well of thinking as her late playwright father, Sean O'Casey. She was only half awake. There had been many late night rehearsals and just the previous evening Brian Friel had cooked us a wonderful meal at his house and we sang and talked till morning. He had just written a new play called *Dancing at Lughnasa* and had offered a part to one of our com-

With Eileen O'Casey and Catherine (photo Shivaun O'Casey)

pany, the talented Gerard McSorley. That had extended the celebrations further. Our performance of *The Shadow of O'Casey*, a new show written by Shivaun, with music from myself, was due to open in Derry's Guildhall shortly and was destined for East Berlin in February of the new year. Shivaun's mother, Eileen, an old show-girl herself, enjoyed looking in on the rehearsals. Her own life had many facets. Harold Macmillan, the British prime minister, had asked her to marry him after Sean died. Was it odd, I put to her, being wooed by both an Irish communist and a British Conservative? They were both great human beings, she told me. O'Casey's work had a huge following in the German Democratic Republic. Would the fall of the Wall affect our visit?

'Indeed and it might,' I said to Shivaun. The lady with the teapot smiled but didn't look up or otherwise acknowledge the echo.

In February 1990 Berlin was buzzing with a strange excitement. A new day was dawning, but few were forecasting the weather ahead. Old friends like Manfred Wagenbreth, Scarlett Seabolt, Wacholder, Jörg Walter, Marianna Oppel, Wolfgang Stein, Big Olli, Whiskey, and many festival acquaintances, had been voices of a quiet revolutionary movement within the old system. Thousands had demonstrated on the streets. They called for the freedom to travel where they wanted; they called for free elections and democratic reform. Now the mighty powers of the Western world would determine what those reforms should be and, perhaps, it would be the

Deutschmark that would decide who would travel and who would not. Our play about O'Casey was still relevant, maybe more than ever.

We sat downstairs under the tree in the Haus der Jungen Talente and drank a Cuba Libre. That's where we had so often gathered down through the years to sing songs of hope and freedom with Inti Illimani, Quilapayun, Carlos Mejía-Godoy, Isabel and Angel Parra, Sergio Ortega and so many others. Those songs had been voices for a voiceless people made silent by unjust regimes in other places backed by multinationals. Now the multinationals would be scrambling, chequebook in hand, over what was left of the Berlin Wall. There were just a few of us now and we knew it would be for the last time. The mood had an odd mixture of a wake, a wedding and a birth.

'Places like this will be closing down,' said Jack Mitchell. 'The new government won't be putting much money towards the arts any more.' Soon Jack would leave his adopted Berlin home and move to Galway.

One young woman called Ilona who had been studying art history had been advised to change subject and go into computers instead.

'You might get a job painting computers,' teased translator Jörg Walter.

Ilona was worried for the future. 'Will we become like America,' she wondered, 'with slums, drugs and guns and hospitals and health care only for the rich?' No one really knew the answer.

Manfred Wagenbreth, a highly respected musician and broadcaster with Radio Leipzig, had been told by his new boss from the West that his programmes must change.

'Have you ever heard my programme?' asked Manfred.

'No,' said the new boss.

'Then how do you know?' asked Manfred.

'Because I know,' said the new boss.

Elke Bitterhof was no longer anchor of the television news. In an interview with Communist leader Herr Krenz, she had addressed him in the familiar form of you, *du*, rather than the formal, noncommittal *Sie*. It was now the wrong political grammar and she lost her job on the spot. It seemed a far cry from singing songs together in the Hotel Stadt Berlin.

'But there'll be so many new places to go in the West,' said Scarlett Seabolt, 'and friends to visit too.'

There would be great new days to come. We drank to the future.

For us there were many new places to see in the East. One was Saalfeld, the one-time capital of the extinct duchy of Saxe-Saalfeld and one of the most ancient towns of Thüringia. That's where I met Marlene Shoener. Her long blond hair hung loosely around her shoulders and she looked like she could begin laughing at any moment.

'I like your songs,' she said seriously, 'particularly that one about the "Children of the dole". I know it from your record *Singing of the Times* on the Amiga label. It sold very well over here. Everyone has a copy.'

Festival in East Berlin (photo Gabriele Senft)

I knew it had sold well in excess of 200,000 copies in the GDR and I knew I was due quite a generous royalty fee too, but when the Wall came down, the company was swallowed up by a Western one and refused to pay back royalties to anyone.

'I actually recorded that track live in East Berlin ten years ago,' I said.

Back then they had difficulty in understanding what 'dole' meant. I tried to explain that in the West if you don't have a job, you get paid a subsistence fee each week by the government, but when you get that money, you're not allowed to work. The East Germans thought that was a strange concept, since they had no experience of unemployment in their country.

'We know all about it now,' said Marlene Shoener.

'What do you do yourself?' I asked.

'I'm a minister,' she said, taking a farewell sip of pils. '*Evangelisch!* Would you like to see my church?'

'Better than etchings any day,' I said.

She had a black bicycle with a basket on the front and off she went, I walking as smartly as possible, through the half-lit streets of Saalfeld, surrounded by ancient walls and bastions of the past. Sometimes we parted company to pass on either side of large piles of unwanted household goods left on the footpath.

'Tomorrow is *Sperrmüll* day,' she said. 'The lorry comes around in the morning.'

'There may not be much left by the morning,' I said, noticing people gathered around some of the piles. One had a Mercedes with a trailer hooked behind.

'They're from the West,' she said. 'Isn't it ironic, we are buying plastic kitchen furniture and throwing out antiques?'

'Like the baby with the bath water,' I suggested.

'Yes,' she said. 'And with all our faults, we had so many good social policies and dreams. Now perhaps they will be discarded too.'

Finally she stopped and took a large iron key from a pocket in her jeans. Looking up, I saw the ancient Gothic church of St John's of Saalfeld. 'This church has been here since the beginning of the thirteenth century,' she said. 'It has witnessed much history.' She told me that in recent times the church had been a place of refuge for those opposed to the government, but since the fall of the Wall, the congregation had fallen.

I looked up at the magnificent stained-glass windows, some broken and others dilapidated. 'I suppose you will be getting new money from the church in the West to renovate this place?' I ventured.

'No!' she said. 'They refuse to give me money until I stop preaching that capitalism is anti-Christian.'

I thought that was odd. 'What do you mean?' I asked.

'A large percentage of this city has been left jobless by the new powers,' she said, 'including my husband. Formerly we had prosperous industries and we knew no unemployment. Now they buy our factories for a pittance and then immediately close them down. This is not Christian. Our young people are broken. They have lost their sense of morality.'

I remembered a contention in Dostoevsky's *Brothers Karamazov.* If God doesn't exist, then everything is permitted. Now it seemed that if communism didn't exist, everything was permitted.

In Dresden I met with Birgit Kühn near the ruins of the Frauenkirche, the Cathedral of Our Lady. Close by, a picture of Comrade Lenin from Russia had been replaced by a picture of Colonel Sanders from Kentucky. A new menu was on offer. We walked a walk of former days and slowly a song I had begun before the Wall came down was finding its closure. It made its debut in the Concert Cellar of the famed Dresden Bärenzwinger.

'It's closing down as a venue,' she said. 'The church owned it originally and now they want it back again. All those houses on the other side of the street, where people have lived and shared together for years, will be returned to the descendants of their original owners. Many are "Wessies". There will be a new rent, which these old people cannot afford. Where can they go?'

'Socialism was such an ideal,' I said. 'Unfortunately humanity was not able to live up to it.'

'Then it should have been designed with humans in mind,' she said with a trace of bitterness. 'But we will go on. We have done so before. There are better days ahead.'

'Birgit,' I said, 'what about America? You are able to go now.'

'Does the invitation still stand?' she smiled.

'Will we meet in Michael's Restaurant in Manhattan on Monday week and listen to Woody Allen play the clarinet?' I suggested.

'*Ja wohl!*' she said.

Ten days later some New Yorkers who had seen everything there was to be seen would gaze on a real East German perhaps for the first time. She would look quite normal actually for a woman from behind the Iron Curtain. In fact she would look well nourished too, highly intelligent, quite beautiful and could discuss any topic raised relating to affairs of either the East or West. Later in Kerrville, Texas, I would sing the song of Dresden and locals would wonder what it was like to live there. The blonde beneath the 'ballad tree' with a light beer and a faraway look would know better than anyone.

> Lenin Square in Dresden is lonelier today
> For Hans and Ingrid's only son has just moved away,
> He's gone to the West side, the land they call the free,
> Searching for a better way to raise a family.
> And Hans and Ingrid are silent, they can't believe their eyes
> As memories of other times come flooding to their minds.
> They gave the Party everything, that was their proudest boast,
> And the leaders of the nation were the ones they trusted most.
> Where have all the dreams gone?
> *Wo sind all die Träume hin?*

27

Twinkle Twinkle Little Star

It all began at an after-concert party in St Louis, Missouri, when I met Jill Berry-man, assistant director of the Sierra Arts Foundation of Reno, Nevada. Her boss, Patricia Smith, later told her that there was no point in trying to bring an Irish artist-in-residence to Reno, because there wasn't even funding available to bring one from Winnemucca in the same state. Jill Berryman, however, wasn't the type to give up easily. She had shed tears when she heard 'There were roses', and she felt that songs that sprang from the conflict in Northern Ireland could have an impact on the gang-land prisoner community of Reno.

'Will you come and sing for them?' she asked, but said first she would have to arrange the financing.

'I'll come,' I decided, 'and we'll sort out the rest later.'

When I arrived at Wittenburg Hall and walked past guards and through strong, locked doors, I had been given no instructions and no agenda. I was, as they say, as nervous as a long-tailed cat in a room full of rocking chairs.

'What am I supposed to do here?' I asked Jill, as she finished her introductions.

'Just be yourself,' she said.

And what is that supposed to mean? I thought, slowly strapping on my Louden Belfast guitar. I hoped that Jill knew what she was doing.

I sang about my childhood and told stories of friends, the ordinary people of the North, who had been bitterly divided in the conflict. The hatred has been caused by complex historical events, I explained: a person could be hated because he or she was born on the wrong side of the street. There were those who gained a lot from these divisions, but more often it was the poor and oppressed who suffered most and ended up in jails and graveyards.

The young people gave me a fair hearing. Perhaps such a captive audience has little choice, but as the concert went on I could feel the barriers lifting and a strange bond developing. Perhaps they were coming to regard me as some weird type of kindred spirit from a far-off land, rather than part of an establishment that had confined them. They sat around me in a large semi-circle, with guards separating the girls from the boys like parish priests at a Legion of Mary *céilí*. They were very young, almost children, but some of these kids had already witnessed and participated in terrible crimes. Others had been convicted on drug charges. Most had no family. That's why many had joined gangs, and then they'd ended up in this place, where prisoner categories were determined by behaviour. A purple uniform depicted a better attitude and saffron indicated an improvement in behaviour, but those dressed in white had not yet proven themselves.

'Would the shackled ladies move to the front?' said a guard, and a new section of my audience walked falteringly towards the front. Three lovely young women with silky black hair and large brown eyes sat down and looked up.

'Once upon a time', I began, 'there was a wee boy called Paddy Magee. He was a great wee lad altogether. He could tie his own boots, go to bed at night when he was told, get up in the morning and eat his breakfast, or anyone else's he could get his hands on, if the truth were told. Good and all as he was, though, he had one problem. He had no story to tell. And when people sat round the fire on a cold winter's night and everyone was doing their best to help shorten the winter, whenever it came to Paddy Magee's turn to tell a story, down would go his head, big red face, no story to tell.

'Well, it wasn't too long till the word got round about Paddy Magee, and any time he walked into a house, people would stand up and walk out, for if you don't say anything, you won't be asked to repeat it too often and it wasn't long until he became known as Paddy Magee, the boy with no story.

'Paddy was very sad and lonely because nobody would talk to him and one morning he got up, put a small bundle on his back and headed off down the road, all on his own, the poor wee fella. He walked and walked and didn't realize it was getting late, because he kept his head down for fear of meeting someone who would recognize him as the boy with no story. And still he walked until the night overtook him on the road and he saw that it was dark, and the wind began to blow and every bush along the side of the road was going backwards and forwards, like an old man's face laughing at him. Eventually he found that he was lost and he was very sorry he ever left home. He was sleepy but there was no place to lie down and he became very afraid and a shiver ran up his back. Then in the distance he saw a light. There, in the middle of the darkness, was a large house with a big oak door. He dreaded knocking on the door. But what could he do? Eventually he gathered enough courage up inside him to close his cold hand into a small fist and knock half-heartedly on the door.

'From away at the back of the house, he could hear big heavy steps getting closer and closer. He had no idea of who or what would confront him. Then slowly the big oak door creaked open.'

There was silence. I gazed around the inmates of Wittenburg Hall's tough detention centre and I saw the wide eyes of children, just little children, hypnotized by an old story.

'Is it getting too scary?' I asked, attempting mischievous innocence. 'Will I stop?'

'No! No! Keep going!' they answered.

For another twenty minutes the story continued about all the incredible and dramatic events that befell the boy with no story until the end came and he realized that because he had no story in the first place he now had the best story in all of Ireland.

'And from that day on there wasn't a house in Ireland that wouldn't take him in and that wasn't happy to see him coming and sad to see him going away. And now you have a story too and you won't have to be running through graveyards in the middle of the night to get one.

'Bee bow bended, my story's ended, put on the kettle and make the tay and if they weren't happy that you and I may.'

I looked around at the faces in front of me as they gave me a cheer. They seemed content to stay longer but a shrill whistle blew and they were all on their feet like robots. Watching them walk in single file towards the door, I was conscious that whatever their failings, they could never be accused of having no story to tell. Their tales would be sad, even pathetic, but gripping and interesting nevertheless. But what could I do about it? I left the building feeling helpless and inadequate.

I was exhausted that evening as I went down to the casino of the El Dorado Hotel and changed $10 into nickels. I pulled a lever and watched the fruit machines spin.

Suddenly Jill was at my side with a Jack Daniels in her hand. 'Do you expect to win?' she said with a smile.

'I don't know,' I said, 'but I haven't much to lose either.'

'They liked your songs and stories,' she said. 'What will you tell them tomorrow?'

'I don't have a clue,' I said wearily. 'I appreciate your faith in me, Jill, but I don't think I can go on with this. The feeling of hopelessness in that room is getting to me. I can sing and make them happy for a few hours but then what? They just go back to their cells. What happens when I leave?'

'They'll think about your stories,' she said.

'It's their stories I'm thinking about,' I said.

'Then get them to tell their stories,' answered Jill.

It would take a long time, I thought. That's if they would talk at all. How can you put a whole lifetime into a few minutes?

'Isn't that what you do in your songs?' said Jill.

She was right. Songs can do that. That's what a song is for.

I sat on my huge bed that night on the fifth floor of the El Dorado with a refilled Jack Daniels in my hand. It would help me sleep. Tomorrow morning and Wittenburg Hall would come soon enough. I looked out the window and wondered what the world was sniffing up its nose tonight and sucking down its gullet to gain inspiration. If we only knew how best to breathe the air, already freely given, and feel the stimulation hidden in-between then it would be really inspiring. Between inspiring and expiring. Breathe in, breathe out, breathe in again. I switched off the TV, which I'd forgotten I had switched on, and opened my eyes again. Every gaze had a story to tell. The guitar lay at the bottom of the bed and unwritten songs from the streets below filled the room. I gazed on until the light left my eyes and entered my head.

'A song can be what you want it to be. It can have just one word repeated a hundred times, or have words enough to fill a hundred verses. It can be deep with love and longing for people, place or time, or flighty, as the baby-ownership type, like, I'm your baby, you're my baby and baby don't you forget that, baby. It's still a song, baby. Songs are about everybody and nobody and nothing and everything and about as many other things as can be talked about in-between. Perhaps it is when talk alone has run aground that songs begin to rise and come into their own. While words may well make their way unaccompanied to the ends of the earth, when borne on wings of song they can fly higher and seep deeper beyond those ends. Perhaps the first song sung by man was to reach to the beyond before him and search the beyond within him.'

'If you say so,' said Jill, yawning round a right-hand bend the following morning and straightening into Virginia Street in 'the Biggest Little City in the world'. 'But go on,' she said with a smile. 'I'm just tired that's all.'

Jill gave a lot of her time and energy to helping others, people on the point of despair and people in despair. She took inspiration from her special friends, her children and especially her partner, Steve. 'He has a strong shoulder,' she said. 'I don't know what I would do without him.' There were other friends too, like Shaun Griffin, the great Nevadan poet, and Stacey Spain, an exceptional teacher and Buddhist playwright. There was also Ray Valdez, the 6'7" Aztec Indian who had been released after a long jail sentence for a minor drug offence and was now teaching art to the prisoners with great success.

'The story is not only what has happened but what can happen, if we find it,' I went on.

'Have you found a story for them today?' asked Jill.

'Yes,' I said. 'But it's not a little story from me, it's a big story from each of them.'

'Sounds profound,' said Jill, 'but do they know it, and if they do, will they tell it?'

'They might sing it,' I ventured. 'Music reaches deeper. Who is the most important person for them in the whole world? Is it a parent, a friend, God, who?'

'The judge,' said Jill. 'It is the judge who will decide their future.'

'Could we find a judge willing to listen to their song, if they wrote one about their lives?'

'We can ask,' said Jill, warming to the idea.

Jill was right. The judge was the most important person for all the inmates of Wittenburg Hall.

When I told them what I had in mind, they questioned me in disbelief.

'You mean, there's a possibility we can sing a song to the judge?' they said.

'A possibility,' I said. 'I will meet the judge tomorrow night.'

'What's the use of writing a song if the judge won't listen to it?' said Migo, a kid from New Mexico, slamming pencil and paper on the desk. Like so many others, his life was full of broken promises.

'I promise I will do my very best to make it happen,' I said.

I don't know if it was blind faith or because my beard and accent reminded him of some class of leprechaun that could do the impossible, but Migo sat up straight, grabbed his pencil and shouted to the others, 'All right, let's do it.'

I have been writing songs all my life but I had never attempted to teach others how to write. It's amazing, however, what a mixture of adrenalin and terror can do when you're standing alone in front of ninety young offenders. Adrenalin was working on the floor also and suggestions came flying up until a detailed plan emerged.

It was extraordinarily simple. There were to be three verses, with four lines in each verse. The first verse would be about the past, the second about the present and the third about the future.

'The first line of the first verse will be a sentence about the place you were born,' I said to the eager faces. 'Second line, describe what it was like; third line, a sentence about your family; fourth line, a sentence about whether you would like to return to that place. Don't worry about rhyming, we can do that later.'

Some started to jot things down.

'Don't write yet,' I said.

Migo looked up suspiciously. 'Why not?' he asked.

'We need an air,' I said. 'A melody. You all have different words but we need a melody that you can all use.'

I thought of popular American melodies and singers.

'What about an Elvis Presley song?' I suggested naïvely.

Many of them didn't know Elvis Presley or else didn't want to know.

After much deliberation, we discovered that the only tune everyone knew was 'Twinkle twinkle little star'. Cultural life, for many, had ended about the age of five.

'We'll have a chorus too,' I suggested, and added, 'One thing before you begin. We're going to need some hope in these songs. If the judge feels you have no hope or vision for your own future, you'll worry him and he'll put you in a place where he won't have to worry about you. If you don't have a vision, then create one now and repeat it like a rosary until you believe in it.'

'What do you mean *hope*?' shouted a pale gaunt youth called Broom. 'There *is* no hope.'

'Well,' I said, 'if you complain and whinge all the time, people get fed up and turned off and they'll stop listening to you.'

I told them a story I heard once of a fisherman sitting on a pier smoking his pipe when suddenly an arrogant tourist fell into the water beside him and began to shout. 'Hi you, I can't swim, I can't swim. Are you deaf or stupid or something? I can't swim.'

The old man went on smoking his pipe and paid no attention.

The tourist came up for the second time with the salt water coming down his nose.

'Hi you, are you blind as well as deaf, you baldy bastard, can't you see, I can't swim, I can't swim!'

The old man just went on smoking his pipe.

The tourist came up for the third time with a fish looking out of his ear. 'Hi you, you baldy oul' huer, may you be afflicted with the itch and have no nails to scratch yourself with. Can't you see I can't swim, I can't swim!'

The old man slowly took the pipe out of his mouth and quietly replied, 'I can't swim either sir, but I don't keep shouting about it all the time.'

'Will you help me then?' cried the tourist.

'Of course I'll help you,' said the old man, reaching out his hand. 'Why didn't you ask me in the first place. Come on out of there now before you get your death of cold.'

They liked the yarn and a busy silence descended. Soon some were ready to search for rhymes and others were finished except for the odd line. Hands would go up from time to time, looking for gentle words to explain horrific deeds. The freedom of verse was giving them leave to expel a darkness from within, which could never have been released by prose.

One young woman called Annie was in tears. 'I can't write,' she said. 'I just want to cry.'

I told her that her words were beautiful. 'Just write down what you said to me. That's a wonderful opening for any song,' I encouraged.

'I'm stuck,' said José.

'Read what you have,' I whispered.

'My youngest brother he got killed right beside our favourite hill / They came and took my dad away…'

'What did they do with him?' I asked.

'They locked him up in Reno jail,' he said.

'You have it, José,' I said. 'Just write that down.'

Counsellors would later say that they were not aware of the details of José's young life.

'So you wanted to meet me,' Judge Frances Doherty said to me with a smile.

Her father was from Donegal and her mother was from Belfast. Yes, she was fond of music too and very aware of its powers. She was familiar with the old Irish

Receiving a Doctor of Letters with Jill and Catherine

keening traditions and the soulful lamentations when songs reach deep inside and free the buried passions of fear, hurt and longing.

'If I taught them to write a song about their life,' I ventured, 'would the court accept it as a plea in their defence?'

She looked interested. 'Let me consult on this one,' she said.

I met Reno Judges Brent Adams and Chuck Magee and heard their caring counsel and progressive attitudes and found them willing to listen. Adams, a cello player, invited me to speak in his court during a lunchtime break. I took the guitar and sang my case. In the jury were lawyers, barristers, clerks and judges singing in chorus and clapping in unison towards an apparent unspoken verdict of 'innocent but sane'.

The song I sang was written by a young prisoner called Danielle.

> I was born in Stanford on the bay,
> It seems so long now so far away,
> There were pretty flowers all around,
> They grew up but I grew down,
> Will you hear me, will you hear me?
>
> When I was only very young,
> My dad left home before my life begun,
> He only wanted pushing drugs,
> My mama cried and she gave me hugs,
> Will you hear me, will you hear me?

When I was eight we moved to Dayton,
That's where I learned that word called hating,
When I was ten I ran away,
My ma and grandma cried all day,
Will you hear me, will you hear me?

I sold my body to buy my food,
I was beaten, bullied and abused,
Now I want to turn the page,
I'm a girl of seventeen years of age,
Will you hear me, will you hear me?

'It is difficult sometimes to know what feelings lie inside,' said one judge. 'Sometimes in court the accused arrives with a lawyer who tells his client to say nothing and let him do the talking. To send these young people to an adult prison will get them off the streets, but often if they are not criminals going in, they will be coming out. Our responsibility is to do what is best. Some are addicts before they are even born; they need help, not more hurt. The more we know about their path to this point, the better we can plot their journey onwards.'

A few days later Frances came to me. 'We'll do it!' she said. 'If a song helps to express their truth, or their story, as you say, it will better the human condition for all of us.'

Everyone was delighted. Barney Brady, the ex-Donegal footballer and current honorary Irish consul to Nevada, and his wife, Marge, always supportive to progressive thinking, threw a great party. We couldn't wait to go back to Wittenburg with the news. 'It's so good,' said Jill. 'We all need help. We are all so vulnerable.'

At that moment, however, on the verge of great comfort, we had no idea of the sorrow that would strike at the heart of Jill Berryman.

Steve, who had been such a 'strong shoulder' to Jill as she strove to bring relief to the less fortunate, was himself secretly fighting his own demons within. I couldn't begin to imagine her pain and shock the morning she found him. He was still seated by his desk. The pistol he had put in his mouth was lying on the floor.

Soon we met in that troubled room. Jill had called her artist friends around her, to try to release Steve's spirit, to ease her pain and that of her children. She wanted each of us to call on the healing powers of our own traditions to help Steve's spirit fly free.

Ray Valdez was no stranger to such gatherings, being raised in the Aztec traditions of the spiritual Temazcalli. From the initial ritual of gathering fire twigs, to a prayer to the four directions accompanied by an ancient drum, the emphasis was on the mortality of human existence and freeing of the spirit from the fetters of the body. Shaun's rich poetry and my penny whistle were followed by words from Stacey Spain. She ended by the touching of two small bells. A tinkling tone sounded throughout the room and slowly faded.

Uncannily, as if on cue, there was a loud flutter at the window and a large mountain hawk was floating there. Then, just as swiftly, it was gone, its large muscular wings prising its lithe body skywards. After the initial chill of surprise a great peace descended on the room. Jill was weeping. Then we were all smiling with new relief and drinking a toast to the one who was Steve, the one who was gone.

Maybe Steve would have never found peace here. Perhaps he didn't want to be helped. We were certain, though, that many young eyes who greeted our arrival in Wittenburg were crying out for help and smiling with excitement about singing for a judge. There seemed even more urgency now than ever before and Jill remained at the forefront.

'We must never give up on these kids,' she said, even though it seemed that society had already given up.

'There is more money being put into the building of prisons than the building of schools,' said Ray Valdez. 'Is that the mark of a civilized society?'

The songs were now mining rich and deep, freeing complicated souls to the strains of a simple tune. For some, the song would affirm their hopes; for others, it would confirm their chains; but for all, a new liberty of inner truth was being sought and they were performing like shining stars. Later I would receive letters from both inside Wittenburg and outside, and when I learnt that Danielle, who was 'born in Stanford on the bay', had been released and had given birth to a beautiful baby, I could almost hear again a lullaby being sung, perhaps to a well-known children's melody called 'Twinkle twinkle little star'.

28

Unsung Heroes and Unwritten Songs

It was eleven o'clock at night and I was about to go to bed. I had been in the studio all day long, for several days, and I was tired. The dark November rain had joined forces with a strong east wind from Carlingford Lough. They began to pound and pummel our old huddle of Bangor Blue slates, which were now rattling on the roof like the chattering of frightened teeth. The rusting leaves from the two oak trees at the back of the house were racing each other frantically into the four corners of the courtyard as the storm rose and fell and then rose again. The noise it made was loud and alarming. That's why I didn't hear the knocking on the door. The young man could have been there for some time. I discovered him only when I went to lock up for the night.

The presence of a stranger standing on my doorstep startled me. I was struck by the calmness of his posture, as if he had always been there. He had a small wooden box tucked under his arm.

'Who is it at this hour of the night?' I asked.

'My name is Rob Scott,' he said quietly. 'I'd like to play you a reel on the flute. I want to hear what you think of my playing.'

'Come in, Rob,' I said, 'but it's a bit late.'

We sat in the kitchen.

'Where did you learn the flute?' I asked.

'I'm from the Shankill,' he said.

This was unusual. What was a Protestant doing wandering about south Down at this hour of the night in these troubled times? If he was a Shankill man, was 'The sash' not a more likely tune to head his repertoire than an Irish reel? I put it to him.

'It's a long story,' he said, piecing together the three sections of his flute.

'There couldn't have been much call for reels and jigs on the Shankill.' I said.

'Not much Bach or Beethoven either,' he said flatly and lifted the flute, licked his lips, and blew a low throaty note.

'I grew up on the Shankill Road, running around and getting in trouble and all that stuff,' he said then. 'My mate Sammy and me, we were stealing the odd car now and again, doing a bit of joy-riding. Sammy was into other things as well. We were wild. We were doing things the local paramilitaries didn't like, and not doing things they did like. One evening Sammy called to our house. I knew there was something wrong. He looked pale and terrified. He asked me to go down to the pub with him. He said he'd got the orders to go. "I'm going to get kneecapped," he said. "I have to go tonight."'

Rob grimaced and paused. 'He had to go. Whenever you get the word, then you have to go. Otherwise you get nutted,' he said, pointing at his head with the flute. 'I went with him. At ten o'clock the men came and told him to come out to the carpark. Sammy asked me to go with him and hold him.'

Rob told me how he held his best friend as tightly as he could while a gun was put behind each kneecap. 'They said the damage wouldn't be permanent this time. There are different ways of doing knees. They warned me to say I had seen nothing.'

'I borrowed money and cleared out after that, went to London, got into drugs, then one night music was coming from a pub I was passing. It was the most beautiful sound I ever heard. When I went inside, I saw that they were all Irish. I hadn't heard this music before, but I felt it was my music. I got a job and saved some money. I bought a flute and learned to play it. It give me a reason to live. You're a musician and you make radio programmes of Irish music. I want you to tell me what you think of my playing. I need to know.'

He put the flute to his lips and began to play.

The sounds that came were disciplined but had a certain wildness.

'I have never heard the likes of it,' I said with admiration.

He smiled. 'Do you know what my name means? The meaning of Scott?'

When I didn't answer, he said, 'It means "Irish man".'

He had studied folklore in search of himself, and had learned how Míl had married Scota, the daughter of the Egyptian king. How they came to Ireland and then sailed to Alba and called it Scotland. He wasn't sure how much truth there was in the story, but he had found a new identity for himself in it.

He was happy to have discovered his music and furious that his state education had led to an ignorance of his own culture. 'This is my music,' he said again. 'I'm a loyal Prod from the Shankill, but this Irish music is part of me and I'm a part of it.'

I thought of a remark by the Belfast poet John Hewitt, made when he was very old and I was very young, at a debate I was chairing in Newry Arts Centre.

'Are you British or Irish?' I had asked.

He smiled and said: 'I was born in Belfast; I'm a Belfast man. Belfast is in Ulster; I'm an Ulster man. Ulster is in Ireland; I'm an Irish man. Ireland is in the British Isles; I'm British. The British Isles is in Europe; I'm a European. Do you want me to go on?'

Hewitt had exposed not only the shallowness of my question but also the crude point-scoring the politicians had been pushing at us for years. Are we this or are we that? We are all these things, Hewitt was saying, but we are much more.

Rob was putting away the flute now.

'What happened to Sammy?' I asked.

'They left me holding him. He was screaming. A car stopped. It was a nurse. She knew what had happened. Belfast people are very kind.' There was no trace of irony in his voice as he said the words. 'She took us to the Royal Victoria Hospital. It's the best in the world for knees. They have had plenty of practice.'

There is a saying in Ireland that beside every nettle grows a docken. Perhaps like many other sayings, it has a grain of truth. Every illness has its remedy, if only we know where to look. Belfast, for example, has its problem with shattered kneecaps, so a knee-treatment hospital was established that was the envy of the world. Events forced the medical profession to focus upon, and find a treatment for, this horrific injury. Perhaps a solution to our political plight could be nurtured also and, in turn, provide a template to help solve similar problems in other countries.

When Rob left that night, I thought of a verse I had co-written:

> Once there was a chicken, through a wire fence was picking
> For a grain of corn so near and yet so far
> And as he lay there dying, he never thought of trying
> The open gateway just a yard away.
> There's another way,
> There's another way,
> For to climb this hill together,
> There's another way.

I had written the song in Pennsylvania with a group of children from the Bruderhof Community. We were holding a protest against Capital Punishment outside Death Row at Penn State Penitentiary at the time. Rubin Hurricane Carter was with us too. I had remembered him on the wireless in Ryan from a lifetime ago. He was the leading contender for the world middleweight boxing championship. He had served life for two murders in-between, two murders which he hadn't committed. He told me about coming out of 'the hole' and looking into a mirror that someone had stuck up on a prison wall with Elastoplast. He could see nothing but hatred staring back at him. At that moment he knew he would never survive the sentence, for hatred would destroy him first. To survive he had to rid himself of hatred. Keeping it was like taking poison and hoping your enemy would die. He had to forgive, not for his enemy's sake but for his own survival. His life began to change after that. Even when he was released he was already a free man.

Were there open gates staring us in the face and we couldn't see? Was our problem made worse because of how we viewed it?

Over the long, bitter years, peace marches had come from all sides but often disappeared in opposite directions. We all wanted peace but, at the end of the day, what

With Rubin Hurricane Carter

kind of peace? The peace of an IRA surrender, or the peace of a British withdrawal? That was the question and that was the problem. After the death in 1976 of the three little Maguire children in Belfast, killed by a runaway car driven by an IRA volunteer who had been shot by the British army, the tragedy cried out for all sides to lay down their arms. Their deaths inspired a peace movement led by Mairéad Corrigan and Betty Williams. There was an outpouring of grief, but when the movement could not find a common basis for supporters to unite, it lost its power. Yet it provided inspiration for many, and Mairead, the aunt who later became the stepmother of the surviving Maguire children, would travel the world with her message of peace and justice for every child.

We had to find a peace for all and a freedom that threatened no one's peace.

> Oh Freedom,
> Everybody wants it, everybody needs it,
> Freedom – but no one wants to give it away.
>
> Sometimes me and you, we're like an Arab and a Jew,
> We can't live together, we can't live apart,
> The butterfly of freedom is fragile and fleeting
> If we pull it from each other
> We will tear it apart.

For years there were countless unsung heroes. Politicians and ordinary citizens, community groups and churches, communists and trade unionists, all urging their own sense of hope.

My good friend, writer and broadcaster Sam McAughtry, who often travelled on the train from Belfast to Dublin, found that the service was frequently disrupted by IRA bombs on the line. Sam, a Protestant ex-army man, thought it ironic that an organization dedicated to the unification of Ireland was creating a barrier to travel between the two states. It was Sam who founded the Peace Train movement. When he asked me to sing on the train, I joined the train at Newry station and had to pass a picket of very vocal IRA supporters, many of whom I knew. They viewed the Peace Train statements as loud on IRA violence but mute on British army violations. Meanwhile, a strong unionist element, which wanted the border built higher, was angry that a Protestant like Sam should want an open line between Belfast and Dublin in the first place.

Clonard Monastery on the Falls Road had long been a quiet space for lively debate. In November 1987 Father Alex Reid had drawn up a discussion paper outlining a way towards a settlement if the IRA called a ceasefire. He accepted the republican position that Ireland's future should be determined by all its people, but argued that this would only be possible with the consent of both nationalists and unionists in the North, which in turn could only be achieved through dialogue and agreement. And he held the view that Britain wouldn't stand in the way if both communities in Northern Ireland decided to opt for a united Ireland. In the past Britain had always stated that Northern Ireland must remain within the United Kingdom as long as the majority so desired, but there was never much talk of what would happen if the majority desired a united Ireland. Would Britain abandon the unionists? Would Britain (or America, for that matter) agree to a unified, and neutral, independent Ireland?

There was little chance of an IRA ceasefire as long as Thatcher was in power. She would be sure to regard such a move as an acceptance of defeat, and the IRA had not been defeated. She had breathed new life into the republican cause in 1981, when she allowed ten hunger strikers to die in the H-Blocks. Bobby Sands's election win that year also taught the republicans that the ballot box could prove as useful as the Armalite to further their cause, and as time went by the value of mainstream politics was becoming more apparent. When John Major replaced Thatcher in 1990, there was a growing realization by all parties that no one could win this war. They could keep on fighting forever, but everyone was losing. In 1991 Secretary of State Peter Brooke announced that Britain had no 'selfish strategic or economic interest' in Northern Ireland and was prepared to accept a united Ireland by consent.

I was in Murphy's bar in Rostrevor when he came on the television news.

'It's all over,' said Brian Madigan, an SDLP man. 'We're going to have a united Ireland.'

'You mean, whenever the unionists say so,' said Red Johnny, a Sinn Féiner. 'The meek shall inherit the earth, if that's all right with the rest of you. They still have a veto.'

'Then we must charm and persuade them that they are better off in a united Ireland,' said Brian, 'for they will never be bombed into one. They are as stubborn as you are, you know, and will never accept being forced into a united Ireland any more than you accepted being pushed into a Northern Ireland.'

'I have no choice but to accept it,' said Red Johnny.

'You could have fooled me,' said David Crothers, a moderate unionist, who picked his words carefully. He was in a Catholic pub. 'And since you don't accept my position today, Johnny, why should I accept your position tomorrow?'

'Because it is the will of the majority on this island, that's why,' said Johnny.

'But it is the will of the majority in this province that we remain with Britain,' said David quietly.

We had heard these arguments before and it was time for another round, so we had another drink and another until we arrived back where we started and began it all again. That's what the politicians were doing too, except they hadn't a drink to ease the pain. ·

In 1992 I received a letter from Robin Wilson, the editor of the progressive magazine *Fortnight*, controversial enough to have a car bomb placed outside its office in 1973. Some people said it could just as easily have been the work of the British Special Branch as the IRA. Wilson had hatched an idea with Simon Lee, a law professor at Queen's, and *Irish Times* journalist Andy Pollak. Initiative '92 was chaired by the Norwegian professor Torkel Opsahl, founder member of Amnesty International and authority on constitutional and international human rights law. It was felt that the Opsahl inquiry, as it came to be known, with no limitation on ideas submitted to it, would help answer 'a widespread desire among all kinds of people for a new means of expressing their views and hopes about the future'. In the space of six weeks it received 500 submissions on behalf of 3000 people. Amongst the findings in *A Citizens' Inquiry: The Opsahl Report on Northern Ireland* was a proposed method of decision-making, consociationalism, a term used by the Dutch political scientist Arend Lijphart to describe the sharing of power between segments of society joined together by a common citizenship but divided by ethnicity, language, religion, or other factors.

It wasn't a new idea. Among the countries governed by its principles were Cyprus and South Africa, as well as Belgium and his native Holland. In a land of divided communities, consociationalism guaranteed a sharing of power among representatives of all significant groups. Another key element was a mutual veto on vital issues. It had its drawbacks, but it was something to think about.

In the meantime, as politicians were searching for gaps in the thorny hedges of the North, artists, singers and poets were painting their own pictures. Seamus Heaney said more through his half-closed eyes than most people said through their mouths. His poems prised open the minds of many. For me his work rescued the noble art from dusty shelves and chalky classrooms and transferred the reality of a Grecian urn to the magic of a rusty bucket in the back garden. We did concerts together. Once he rang me up beforehand.

'I suppose we better talk about what we're going to do,' he said.

At Catherine Hammond's wedding party in Belfast: Arty McGlynn, Seamus Heaney, Frankie McBride, Terry Flanagan, Paul Brady, Tommy and Nollaig Casey (photo Bobbie Hanvey)

'What do you think?' I answered.

'I think we'll know what to do when we get there. What do you think?' he asked.

'I think we will,' I said.

It would be hard not to know what to do. I had long admired Seamus and his work. He came from a family I identified with fondly. They were not unlike my own. They grew up on a farm in south Derry, which had a lore quite similar to south Down. There was digging going on there, not just for the potatoes of today but for the wit and wisdom of the past, the vision and wonders of tomorrow.

'I suppose you could start with a song,' he suggested.

We had already been introduced. The audience was waiting.

'I suppose so,' I whispered back. I brushed a B flat on the guitar.

> Let the circle be wide round the fireside
> And we'll soon make room for you,
> Let your heart have no fear for there's no stranger here
> Just friends that you never knew.
>
> So let the circle …

Heaney was fingering through his collection now and talking about friendship and hopefulness. He opened *The Haw Lantern* and picked a poem. Yes, I had hoped it would be that one, a beautiful sonnet about his mother.

It brought me back to a night in Bellaghy, the night of her funeral. I couldn't make it in time for the wake. They were all back at the house. His sisters Anne and Sheena were making tea and sandwiches, the tears barely dry in their eyes. Dan, Hugh, Colum, Charlie and Pat were there too. Their father, Patrick, was recalling the last hours of her life, every single second it seemed. 'The sadness has become a story,' Seamus whispered. 'A living story.' It was being repeated over and over like a rosary, a bridge between hurt and healing, a call between earth and heaven.

> When all the others were away at Mass
> I was all hers as we peeled potatoes ...

I had no words to follow such beauty. I played a lament on the whistle instead, a *caoineadh*, not to induce sadness but to remove it and to make space again for the dance of life. And a song in praise of what was given but still unseen.

> They wouldn't hear your music and they pulled your paintings down,
> They wouldn't read your writing and they banned you from the town,
> But they couldn't stop you dreaming and a victory you have won,
> For you sowed the seeds of Freedom in your daughters and your sons.

Seamus celebrated with another and so we moved from poem to song and song to poem as I followed him over drills and alleys and hills and valleys, till safely we arrived back exactly where we started, except now perhaps the landscape had changed.

Heaney was turning pages again back to pre-Christian Troy, divining a cure for a Christian conflict in our own time. His words brought a knowing quietness. Hope and history in Northern Ireland had yet to rhyme but perhaps they were moving closer.

29

The Music of Healing and the Citizens' Assembly

Pete Seeger and his wife, Toshi, live in a physically modest but inspirationally palatial log cabin in a forest overlooking the Hudson River. The father of American folk
music is over eighty years of age now, but you couldn't say he is old. In many ways,
he is one of the youngest people I know. He never stops listening and he never stops
learning. With habits like that, it is very difficult to grow old no matter how hard
you try.

Pete sings at breakfast, sings when chopping logs, sings when washing dishes,
sings at his supper, and you can't help but sing along. Often when we are singing old
songs, we are thinking about new ones.

'Do you know a song about eating toast?' said Pete one morning as he placed a
slice of bread in the toaster.

'No,' I said, 'I never heard one about that.'

'Well, let's compose one then,' he said.

We made up silly verses and laughed our way through breakfast with Pete's
grandson Tao tickling a five-string banjo in accompaniment.

Toshi looked up from time to time and shook her head as if to say, Crazy as ever,
you folksingers, but deep down she was enjoying it all. Toshi is a wonderful woman,
an inspiration to Pete and a kind of mother to us all.

'Why don't you write a song about healing those wounds in your country?' she
said, placing a jar of home-made maple syrup on the table.

'Yes,' said Pete, 'it's amazing how music can help to heal wounds between people and within people.'

'Somebody should write a song about *that*,' I said, looking at Pete.

'You write it,' he scolded gently.

Some months later I was back in the US again. I had written 'The music of healing' and I sang it to Pete, who listened intently. Then he stood up and declared quietly as he viewed the Hudson below, 'It needs another verse.'

'You write it,' I said with a smile.

'My father told me once, many years ago, that truth is like a rabbit in a briar patch, you know that it's there, but you can't catch it. I have always wanted to put that in a song.' (Charles Seeger, the founder of ethnomusicology, said many wise things in his lifetime.)

'And my father used to say, "The more you learn, the more you know, the less you knew",' I laughed.

'But isn't it wonderful to learn,' said Pete, 'even if, and especially if, learning makes you realize you were wrong?'

I knew there were two songs being written in his musings, but it was only one verse we needed and we had it already.

> Sometimes the truth's like a hare in the cornfield,
> You know that it's there but you can't put your arms round it.
> All we can hope for is to follow its footsteps,
> Sing me the music of healing.
>
> Who would have thought I could feel so contented
> To learn I was wrong after all of my rambles?
> I've learned to be hard and I've learned how to tremble,
> Sing me the music of healing.

When I got back home, I went into the studio with Arty McGlynn and began to record the song. Pete would sing his verse in Greenwich Village, supported by his talented grandson Tao, Lisa Gutkin and Greg Anderson, and the tape would be 'flown' into the studio mix in the village of Rostrevor.

> Ah the heart's a wonder,
> Stronger than the guns of thunder,
> Even when we're torn asunder,
> Love will come again.

The world was badly in need of healing. Television was bringing the tragedies of Sarajevo into our homes. Vedran Smailovic, a lone cellist appeared dramatically in the midst of the horrors, and Colum had written a song about him. I wanted to have the cellist on our recording, but I had no idea how to track him down. Then Peter Emerson telephoned. He had met Smailovic in Sarajevo on one of his bicycle journeys. Peter was launching *Consensus Politics* in the Mansion House in Dublin. He had written the book when he returned from Moscow and he wanted me to sing 'The music of healing' at the function. He asked if I knew a cellist who could play Smailovic's music.

'Could we find the man himself?' I said.

'We could try,' said Peter.

Several days later, after many phone calls, I drove to Belfast International Airport to await the arrival of a flight from London.

Launching The Music of Healing: Wendy Newton, Roy Garland, John Hume, Bosnian Cultural Attaché, Tommy and Vedran Smailovic

The only son of Yugoslav composer Avdo Smailovic, Vedran had been regarded as something of a young musical messiah, receiving a special award as a child from President Tito. He became the principal cellist in the Sarajevo Opera orchestra and when the war began, his theatre was destroyed by a bomb. On 27 May 1992 twenty-two of his neighbours were killed as they stood queuing for bread.

For twenty-two days, marking each neighbour who had died, Smailovic went out onto the street, dressed in evening suit and bow tie, and sat down to play the Albinoni's Adagio. A CNN reporter ran to him, complete with camera and flak jacket, and shouted, 'Mr Smailovic, are you not crazy for playing your cello while they're shelling Sarajevo?'

Smailovic looked at him, more in sadness than in anger. 'You ask me if I am crazy for playing my cello while they shell Sarajevo,' he said, 'but you don't ask if they are not crazy for shelling Sarajevo while I play my cello.'

Vedran arrived at Belfast airport without his cello. It had disappeared in the rubble of war. We quickly set about the task of borrowing an instrument for him.

'The music of healing', with Pete's voice and Vedran's cello, became the opening track on a *The Heart's a Wonder*. John Hume launched the CD at an event organized by Kevin McCaul in Derry's Calgach Centre, and declared 'The music of healing' a new anthem for our times.

One day in January 1995 the phone rang. 'What are you doing on Sunday?' Smailovic said.

'What have you in mind?' I asked.

'We must go to New York,' he said. 'Sarajevo is one thousand days under siege and no one is doing anything about it. We must go and tell the American media. They must do something. My people are dying day after day and no one cares. Do you know any musicians in New York?'

I knew Pete Seeger and Odetta for a start.

'Please telephone them,' he said. 'I will phone Vanessa Redgrave, Bianca Jagger and Joan Baez. They came to see me in Sarajevo; they will come to New York too.'

I considered our plan of action. This won't work, I thought, the media can't be gathered just like that and these people, generous and all as they may be, might not be able to come.

The following morning Smailovic was on the phone again. 'Did you call Pete and Odetta?' he asked.

'No,' I said lamely. 'I don't think it will work.'

'Sometimes it is better not to think,' said Smailovic. 'It is better to do.'

He was right. Vanessa Redgrave, Joan Baez and Bianca Jagger were all set to come. I rang Pete and Odetta. And yes, they would come too. Chris Hugo from the London-based Living Bosnia organization helped arrange the flights and we were on our way to America.

Violetta Smailovic, Vedran's sister and first violinist in the Dallas Philharmonic, joined us at the Statue of Liberty, along with several Bosnian musicians. We also played in the church of St John the Divine, a large, inspiring building on the edge of Harlem. It seemed that every religion under the sun found a welcome to worship in that wonderful place. Pete arrived with Rande Harris, guitar man with the Platters, and they had the whole church singing almost immediately. Next it was Odetta – I have never seen a woman who can move an audience like she can. Bianca Jagger had composed a poem to honour Vedran's work, and the MC was Vanessa Redgrave, who had taken time off from rehearsing a Broadway production.

'When I was visiting Sarajevo,' she said, 'a shot rang out. There was panic. I was frightened. Suddenly, I felt myself being pushed to the ground and a large figure fell on top of me …' She smiled, pointing to the side of the stage, as she introduced Smailovic.

Vedran walked out, in full evening dress and with a borrowed cello, and began to play 'Bembasa', a haunting and moving melody from the Sephardic tradition, which was known and loved by every child in the multicultural Bosnia of his youth.

Many people signed our petition and many newspapers carried the story. We hoped that it would bring attention to the agony of Sarajevo.

I wrote 'Ode to Sarajevo' for that day, the thousandth day of the siege, and we all sang it together.

> A thousand days of sorrow, I can hear your mournful cry,
> It echoes o'er the ocean, it rises in the sky,
> Oh city where the Muslim call and church bells intertwine
> Come sing with us a chorus, a song for better times,
> Sarajevo, Sarajevo, the whole world sings your song,

With Joan Baez and Robin Cook

On 29 February 1996 the Bosnian government declared that the siege of Sarajevo was over.

When Vedran and I were recording the song for the CD *Sarajevo-Belfast* for Jim Musselman's Appleseed record label, Joan Baez arrived in Rostrevor to join us. She had been unable to come to the event, but she'd promised she'd make up for it. To sit in Colum's studio and listen to that legendary voice sing the words I had written is a moment I will always cherish.

> On May the twenty-seventh day they were waiting there for bread
> Then a blinding flash of agony and twenty-two lay dead
> And as the streets lay bleeding a pain no words can say
> Suddenly a cello, it slowly starts to play
> Sarajevo, Sarajevo, the whole world sings your song,

Joan had travelled from the States with her mother, also called Joan Baez. She listened gracefully and proudly applauded when her daughter had finished singing. Later young Joan and I went for a jog in the oak forest behind my house. When Fionán came home from school that day, there was no one in the house except an unfamiliar elderly lady sleeping on the sofa.

She opened one eye. 'Hi kid,' she said. 'I'm Joan Baez.'

Fionán had heard of the great singer, of course, and loved her voice, but he had never actually seen her. He didn't know what to say. Finally he managed to stammer,

'You've a great voice … for your age.'

She threw back her head and laughed. 'I don't have a voice,' she said, 'but God gave me a beautiful angel for a daughter and she's out running in those hills with your father.'

Swift as a deer she was, and me panting by her shoulder. At last she stopped and looked around. The Mournes were never more radiant as they swept down to the sea below. She looked across the lough to the hills of Cooley in the Republic, where the great Ulster Cycle had been played out between the legendary Cú Chulainn of Ulster and Queen Medb of Connacht. To our left was the village of Carlingford, founded by the Vikings; to our right was Narrow Water Fort, built by the Anglo-Normans. Further west we could see the hills of south Armagh rising defiantly through the mist.

'It's glorious,' she said. 'Is it really as peaceful as it looks?'

'Things are getting better,' I said.

In late August 1994 the Republican movement, becoming more confident that their aims could be forwarded by political means, called a long-awaited, much-prayed-for Ceasefire. There was a new glimmer of hope spreading throughout the land.

Catherine, being French, decided we should celebrate with a dinner party. Friends and family were invited and in-between the many courses from the Gallic tradition were toasts aplenty from the Irish tradition. We had new poems from Peter Makem, special compositions from musicians Siobhán Ó Dubháin and Eibhlis Farrell, and visions for the future toasted in prose, verse, song and story. Senator John Robb was there too. He was founder of the New Ireland Movement and the surgeon who had attended the very first bullet-ridden victim of the Troubles. He hoped there would be no more victims. Mirsad Popara, a wounded Bosnian, sat beside him and despite his arm injuries obliged the gathering with a song on the guitar.

We parted that night with great hope in our hearts. More good news came when the Combined Loyalist Military Command, led by Gusty Spence, followed suit in October, declaring unreserved remorse for past deeds. Unionist politicians, however, refused to accept Sinn Féin into talks until the IRA had given up their weapons. The IRA said it was a cessation, not a surrender. Why should they give up their weapons? Some said there should be no guns, loud or silent, on the table or under the table. Others said there was as much chance of the IRA in Ireland giving up their guns as there was of the NRA in America giving up theirs. The stand-off and stalemate continued week after week and people feared that violence might return to fill the vacuum. Various cross-community groups around the North in their own way were making efforts to get the opposite sides around a table, the same table, any table. We felt that deep down they both wanted it.

At the Fiddlers Green Festival in Rostrevor in 1995 we decided to let 'The music of healing' flow into a seminar. We invited a few musicians to create an atmosphere of humanity and neighbourliness and two politicians from opposing sides to talk about the common ground we all shared. They were Francie Molloy from Sinn Féin and Belfast Unionist Roy Garland, who had links with loyalist paramilitary groups. Their talk was forthright and straight, what was on their mind and on their party line, but, they talked. We met in Harmony Hall in Rostrevor and I asked my good friend and neighbour Mary McAleese to chair the discussion.

Mary was a brilliant lecturer in law at Queen's University. She knew the issues at stake in Northern Ireland politics and was very supportive of community events in Rostrevor. Local playwright Siubhán Ó Dubháin cast Mary and myself as long-lost lovers in a play she was putting on in the local hall. I played the rat catcher and Mary was the sanitary inspector. Before the final act was consummated, however, Mary was auditioning for another role in real life. When she was elected president of Ireland in 1997 and she took up residence in Áras an Uachtarán in Dublin's Phoenix Park, she would make 'bridge-building' her presidential theme. She invited me to present a number of Music of Healing events, featuring Irish uilleann pipes and Orange Lambeg drums.

When the Provisional IRA ended its Ceasefire in February 1996 with a bomb at Canary Wharf, London, killing two men and injuring over a hundred people, I got a call from Smailovic.

'We must go to London and play,' he said. I called my friend Roy Arbuckle in Derry. Roy was from the Protestant persuasion; he would come too and bring a Lambeg drum, a symbol of unionism. We were under no illusions about changing the world but we were tired of cursing the dark. We went to Westminister and played a lament for the people who died and a song of protest to the politicians who still refused to talk. Séamus McKee on BBC's *Good Morning Ulster* rang us up. 'Do you think a Lambeg drum can help to heal divisions?'

'It is what I have,' answered Roy.

Each year we continued the Music of Healing event in Rostrevor, with poets, musicians and politicians from opposing camps taking part. In a way, the Citizens' Assembly was an extension of this event. But instead of a few politicians, we decided to invite representatives from every party and grouping.

Heaney and Sophocles were right. They knew 'no poem or play or song can fully right a wrong' but 'a fire on the mountain' can start with the smallest spark and be kindled by the softest breeze. We all had a part to play, no matter how small. There were many who thought that the deadlock was driving hope into the ground. Politics was boxed in a corner of its own making.

I was in the drawing room of Narrow Water Castle, a building that had been standing since the sixteenth century. The Hall family were benign landlords. That's why the castle was still standing and they were still there. The gatehouse had been blown away in 1979 on the day the IRA detonated two massive bombs, killing eighteen British soldiers, sixteen of them from the Parachute Regiment. Maeve Hall wanted her house to be a healing place, and she opened her door to our thoughts and our music.

The politicians were not talking, yet we knew that the people who voted for them on both sides wanted the talking to begin. There were many points of difference – social, religious, cultural, political and economic – but the most fundamental question when elections came around, it seemed, was on the border issue. There were multitudes of bread-and-butter issues left a-begging while Old Mother Hubbard checked the colour of her cupboard before attempting to open the door. 'Are you British or are you Irish?' That was the problem. We were both. Could the question be rephrased?

Peter Emerson was nearby with a pencil in his mouth. His *Consensus Politics* mapped decision-making and voting procedures and the phrasing of referenda. 'It's not the vote that counts,' said Emerson with a smile, 'but who counts the votes.'

I sat down with pen and paper and began to compose a letter.

Dear All,
For a long time now, ordinary people have been more and more concerned about the rate of political progress here. It's like sitting in never-ending traffic jams, watching bus drivers shake their fists at each other while we in the bus wait and wonder what's going on. It's all too easy to blame the politician, raging behind the wheel, yet it was we who sent him up this narrow road. Perhaps there's another road, maybe it's time to get out and walk, since we have stopped anyway, and ask directions.

Politics, which is supposed to be the art of compromise, is the one profession which seems to be incapable of it. In all other walks of life we compromise daily ... We have tried it before and we know it works. We have experienced the advantages in accommodating each other.

Perhaps the reason why unionists and nationalists fear the first move towards compromise is because it has never seriously been tried before. 'Not an inch' or 'All or nothing' are expressions which seem like a good idea to catch a vote but disastrous for anything else. Answers to questions regarding union with Britain or union with the rest of Ireland have never been expected to venture beyond yes or no. Such answers will ensure everlasting conflict. Perhaps it's time to change the question. Perhaps it's time to ask new questions to new people, that is, ordinary people, who have long ago mastered the art of compromise and the advantages of accommodation in everyday life, citizens unchained to party whips and political dogmas.

Perhaps it's time for some sort of Citizens' Assembly that could sit down in a setting of neighbourliness and understanding and offer some suggested solutions to the politicians, who ironically feel restrained by us, the voters. Traditionally, leaders look over their shoulders to see where their followers are leading them. Perhaps it's time for us to lead in another way.

We sent the letter to every political party and paramilitary grouping. We sent it to every newspaper and broadcasting company. We invited the participation of everyone, whether or not they were aligned to a party; whether or not they exercised their vote. Perhaps they didn't vote because they felt it made no difference. Every voice would be heard in the weekend event, which was planned to last 'a night and a day'. The night would come first with music, song, poetry and dance, followed by a day when we would gather in a circle and seek to find another way of asking the awkward question. We would use Peter's ideas to search for a consensus.

As the word got out, the idea was met with a predictable cynicism, which was soon swept aside as more and more people came on board, their energy gaining momentum as ideas and encouragement flowed in from everywhere. From New York came a letter of support from Pete Seeger, encouraging us with a song and a reminder that if Northern Ireland could find a solution, then many other troubled lands with similar problems could benefit. The title of his song, 'All mixed up', seemed apt.

> There were no red-headed Irish men
> Before the Vikings landed in Ireland,
> How many Romans had dark curly hair
> Before they brought slaves from Africa,
> No race on earth is completely pure
> Nor is anyone's mind and that's for sure,
> The winds mix the dust of every land
> And so will woman and man.

A knock on my door one evening heralded the arrival of Sister Majella McCarron, who had been a colleague of my Uncle Ben's in Nigeria. She was accompanied by Diana Barikor-Wiwa, sister-in-law of the Ogoni patriot poet Ken Saro-Wiwa. His fearless stand against Western oil companies, whose profits seemed more important than the survival of a tribe or the health of an environment, had led to his execution in Nigeria a few months earlier.

Majella and Diana brought great energy and inspiration to our plans. They explained the importance of consensus in traditional African tribal thinking, how a bus driver on country routes needs permission from his passengers before he takes a turn. And each passenger realizes that in order to get to his or her destination there may be other roads to take first to accommodate everyone.

Support came from Christians, Muslims, Buddhists, and from an Earth group with members throughout the world who would begin a ritual to attempt to exorcize the curse of Macha, which had been put on the men of Ulster in ancient times. And even Toby Hall informed us that his contacts in the world of astrology suggested that the appointed time was astrologically sound.

We had planned to hold the event in Rostrevor but as the idea blossomed we realized there wouldn't be enough room in any of our village venues. The Mandela Hall in Queen's University Students' Union seemed the right name and the right place.

I looked through the list of artists who had promised their participation. From the world of theatre there were Marie Jones, Martin Lynch and Roma Tumelty. Musicians included Janet Harbison with the Belfast Harps, Susanne McAlinden,

Julie McNeill, Barbara Hall, Different Drums with Roy Arbuckle, Steve Mateer, Charlene McFee, Elaine McCoy and the piper Brendan Monaghan. Also pledging their support were Rosemary Woods, Briege Murphy, Martin McAllister, Fred Connery, Lily Fitzsimmons, Tracy McRory, the Dr Wright Pipe Band, the Fermanagh Community Band, Lisa Gutkin from New York, Vedran Smailovic and ourselves, The Sands Family. Amongst the poets and storytellers were James Simmons, Sam McAughtry, John Campbell and Crawford Howard. And Pamela Mussen came with canvas and brush to paint the proceedings. I felt privileged to have such a wonderful group of friends. They had the power to cool the hottest head and warm the coldest heart. It would be in this company, we hoped, that opposing parties could find the space and intimacy to trust and discuss difficult issues – that's if the all parties turned up. Many regarded this as a futile endeavour.

Out of the mouths of babes comes wisdom, they say, and my son Fionán came up with the idea to invite a man and a woman from each party. It was so obvious that only a child could see it. A man and woman conversing together had more chance of progressing than two men locked in traditional ram-like conflict.

We gathered up phone numbers and addresses of every political and militant grouping. Not one group refused our invitation. To make matters more interesting, we soon discovered that many of the delegates were musicians also. Sinn Féin sent its Downpatrick representative Gearóid O'Faithna; from the loyalist Ballybeen estate, Dundonald, on the outskirts of Belfast came a wonderful song-and-drama act, all staunch Democratic Unionist Party supporters. Among the speakers was Mirsad Popara, the wounded Bosnian soldier who could still manage a few chords on the guitar.

The evening event was revealing. Softened by song, enchanted by word and moved by music, strangers became friends for long enough to return to talk the next morning. Two well-known journalists, Éamonn Maillie and Anne Cadwallader, agreed to referee the proceedings, and two ex-prisoners, republican Liam Maskey and loyalist Billy Mitchell, undertook the role of judges. They knew their communities well and in turn they were well respected.

Some political leaders were dubious at lower ranks taking the initiative. Some journalists were sceptical, but many were supportive, noting that it was the first time all parties and groupings had been under the same roof. In the crowded Citizens' Assembly, packed with every kind of deeply held view under an Ulster sky, everyone had a say and no one held back. Someone shouted, 'It's only a talking shop, this,' and someone answered back, 'Isn't that what democracy is about, talking?' Some academic complained that, 'The people on the street should be here, not academics.' 'Get yourself out then!' said two Ballybeen women. 'We *are* the people on the street.'

All sat in a circle and each delegation put forward their constitutional viewpoint within a strict time frame. In the centre were traffic lights operated by a timekeeper. Green meant talk, orange meant wind up and red meant stop. If a speaker insisted on continuing after 'red', the rest of the room bowed their heads and ignored the extra comments. If a speaker became abusive or disrespectful, the same procedure occurred. All constitutional options were put up on a large computer screen, and debated upon. Eventually votes were fed into the computer to find out which option had the highest average preference.

As we waited for the result more songs were sung and tunes were played and I felt a strange relaxed feeling amongst the gathering that I could never have imagined. Regardless of the outcome, people felt that there would be no losers in this exercise. The option with the highest average preference suggested that we maintain the UK link as long as the majority desire Britishness, but that a meaningful relationship be established with the Republic of Ireland to cater for the minority's legitimate aspirations for Irishness. Although further voting would be necessary to tease out finer details we already knew there was no outright victory for either side but rather a fair result for all sides.

This specific result, although interesting, was much less important than the actual method of reaching it. We had gradually reached an obvious yet rather revolutionary conclusion that the more palatable your view is made for your opponent, the more likely to succeed that view will be. It is not by bowing to the greed of your own side that preference votes will be won, but rather by respecting the reasonable needs of the other. The voting system of first past the post encouraged hardline extremism; consensus voting, on the other hand, seemed capable of calming people towards confluence and agreement.

Later in Paris I spoke about the Citizens' Assembly project to a special Unesco study group researching a paper on 'The culture of peace', headed by David Adams, a radical American. Adams claimed that our education systems taught the culture of war. History was a collection of dates and doings centred around battles and generals. He wanted the UN to put funding into the study of peace.

Adams discovered, however, that in order to forward his point, it was necessary to prove scientifically that mankind did not need war. We all knew cigarettes were bad for our health but it was only when it was proven scientifically that it was possible to take legal action against the tobacco manufacturers. It seemed that modern evolutionist theories like the survival of the fittest, which suggested the inevitability of conflict, was helping to legitimize war. Adams had gathered a group of leading psychologists, anthropologists and genealogists from all over the world to give their opinion. In a historic report, later published as the *Manifesto of Seville*, it was concluded that instead of the 'fittest' surviving, the opposite, in fact, was the case. The tribes who had survived in the long term were those with a tendency to compromise with each other, rather than kill each other.

From Paris I continued to Brittany with more hope for the future but prepared for sadder times in-between.

30

Goodbye Love, There's No One Leaving

Early on 22 August 1996, long before the narrow beams of Brittany's sun had begun to shine through the window shutters of our *gîte*, I was already awake. I had felt a presence in the room and I mentioned it to Catherine even before the knock came to the door. It was like some strange waking dream but I knew at once that I had heard the voice of my mother.

She had been in my mind a lot recently. Each time I left home I would bid her goodbye and tell her when I would be coming back again. Just a few days earlier the parting had been more difficult than usual. She was sitting in her chair in Kennedy's Nursing Home in Rostrevor. She couldn't talk or walk now with the advancement of Alzheimer's disease but she seemed to manage a vague little smile. She was looking at something far away. We all knew she hadn't long left in this world.

In the big room of the nursing home a CD was quietly playing 'Goodbye love, there's no one leaving'. Frank Patterson was singing the song, which I'd written about having to take my mother away from her home on the Ryan Road. His cover of the song had been beamed across the States from the White House on the previous St Patrick's Day. I had wanted to tell her about the song's success and how so many had found her words inspirational, but she was drifting, like the old people of Alaska who traditionally stole away on ice floats, not wanting to be a burden any longer.

'She's a saint, you know,' whispered one of the young nurses who had become her good friend.

I recalled Sister Josephine of the Glenvale Carmelites saying the same thing about Ma, when she urged those in need of help to go to my mother for prayers rather than to the monastery.

Lying in bed in the *gîte* that morning, I remembered how we had walked out through the door of our family home on Ryan Road for the last time. I was holding her hand and could sense her fear in the same way, I imagined, as she had sensed mine when she left me to the end of the lane on my first day of school. Even though I knew we weren't able to look after her any more, as she needed special care and attention twenty-four hours a day, I still couldn't help feeling I was betraying her: she had given me round-the-clock care when I needed it. As we moved through the doorway she was suddenly aware again of everything around her. She looked at my children and smiled. I looked after my children, she seemed to say; now you must look after yours.

John and Stella Kennedy met her at the door of Glenbeigh and gave her a big hug. She was their child now and I knew she would be given all the loving care she so rightly deserved to her dying breath.

> Now is the moment of leaving, I can feel all the fear in your hand.
> Leaving a home full of memories on the verge of a strange new land.
> It doesn't seem so long since the last time, the first day you took me to school.
> Searching for words that are gentle, being brave so the tears won't come though.
> Goodbye love there's no one leaving
> Goodbye love there's no one leaving
> How swiftly the years seemed to follow but I never could see you grow old
> We both turned the hay in the summer and we sang when the winter was cold
> And the stories I tell to my children are the ones that you told me before
> But the story now slowly unfolding is the saddest story of all
>
> Goodbye love there's no one leaving
> Goodbye love there's no one leaving
>
> I don't know how much you can hear me but you seem quite content on your own
> Are you drifting away like the summer to the days of your childhood at home
> And just when I feel I've betrayed you, I am lost and I don't know what to do,
> You smile and you whisper, 'My darling, you must go and take your little one to school'
> Goodbye love there's no one leaving
> Goodbye love there's no one leaving

Now here in France, I was hearing her voice again. 'People call me a saint and an angel,' she whispered, 'but what can I do for my children or anyone, trapped as I am in a body like this? Do you mind if I ask to be set free?'

Later that day I stood in the telephone box in Langoat.

'Mother passed away,' Hugh said.

She was free at last.

Some years later I got a call from Judith Thurley in Belfast. She is a sensitive soul known to be blessed with a special awareness.

'I was at your concert recently in the Bangor Heritage Centre and you sang that song about your mother,' she said. 'Tell me, were you using a backing track or a tape?'

'No,' I replied, 'it was only myself and the guitar.'

'Were you aware,' she asked tentatively, 'that there was a woman singing the song with you that night?'

'I was not,' I said.

'It may have been your mother who was singing with you,' Judith said. She paused a moment. 'I am sorry,' she said. 'I hope this has not upset you.'

'No,' I answered truthfully, 'it has not upset me. On the contrary, it is reassuring.'

Slowly the older generation were leaving us and yet we knew in a way they would always be with us. Even Auntie Maggie, though as children we had told her many times that she was not allowed to die. Catherine and I had called up to see her before heading for Amsterdam. 'When are you going?' she asked. She was in bed and looking old.

'Tomorrow,' I said.

'And when are you coming back?'

'Next Wednesday,' I replied, 'all being well.'

'Well, you'll miss my funeral then,' she announced.

'You're not going to die. You're not allowed,' I teased.

'I'll be dying on Sunday,' she insisted, 'and I'll be buried on Tuesday, for that's St Anthony's Day, and I was hoping Catherine would carry my coffin, for I would like six women to do that.'

I had loved Auntie Maggie all my life. She was my godmother and favourite aunt. St Anthony was her favourite saint.

'What about Amsterdam?' said Catherine when we got home.

'We can't go,' I said. Auntie Maggie had never spoken like this before and I didn't want to take any chances.

We gave the tickets to my god-daughter Kellie and waited, hoping Auntie Maggie's prediction would not come true.

We went to see her on Saturday and she was rambling a little, talking to us like we were children again. On Sunday she died, as she had said she would.

It was one of the biggest funerals I have ever attended and strong men wept silently as they remembered being little boys taken by the hand on walks to Warrenpoint and to St Brigid's Well in Faughart. Six women carried her coffin from her home at Hall View to Betty's graveyard.

I sometimes look around Sheeptown graveyard and other ones too and think of all those people. My father would often say, coming near the end of his days, 'I know more people under the ground than I know on the top of it.' Now they were part of the otherworld and knew much more than us mere mortals. I thought of all the musicians who had left us and all the tunes they had passed on to us. They had no opportunity to travel the world in their lifetime. They rarely moved more than a few miles from home yet the music they played knew no borders. Without them we would have been nothing. I thought of how much they had given to make the world a better place for their daughters and sons. Life had not been easy, yet they tried in the best way they knew to pass on those seeds of hope and freedom. Now it was our turn.

And now your music's playing and the writing's on the wall
And all the dreams you painted can be seen by one and all
And now you've got them thinking and the future's just begun,
For you sowed the seeds of freedom in your daughters and your sons
In your daughters and your sons
In your daughters and your sons
You sowed the seeds of freedom in your daughters and your sons.

31

Good Friday

At midday, Sunday, 20 July 1997, the IRA declared an 'unequivocal restoration' of their Ceasefire. Six weeks later they were in cross-party talks, the outcome of which would be put to the people North and South in a referendum. The talks were scheduled to finish, regardless, on Holy Thursday 1998. Today was that day and things at Stormont were not looking good. The policeman, however, whose granny had been almost uncoffined by my father had wished me well on my journey and I felt the better for it.

As I moved away from the RUC roadblock, I checked my rear-view mirror. There was a snarl of traffic stretching backwards, further than the eye could see, like the Troubles themselves, everyone wondering what was causing the hold-up at the front. And how far back do the Troubles go? How often had I been asked that question on my travels abroad? How far back do you want to go? I would always feel my face slackening into a smile. Back with the geologists, 500 million years to the time when Ireland was divided by the Iapetus Ocean, or 400 million years to the time of its rock-bending unification?

Or back with the mythologists to the arrival of the first human in Ireland? Her name was Cessair, the granddaughter of Noah, who in search of a God who didn't want to drown people, arrived with fifty women and three men on the shores of Ireland. They didn't last too long. Ladra, the pilot, according to the holy monks who recorded the oral tradition, died of women or with an oar up his posterior and achieved the doubtful distinction of being the first dead man of Ireland. Bith, the son of Noah and the father of Cessair, died soon after, leaving the celebrated Fionntan to singlehandedly cater for Cessair and her companions. Weighed down with such responsibility, however, he took flight in the form of an eagle, a hawk, a salmon and other creatures, and it was he who passed on the story of Ireland to future poets and seers.

Or back with the historians to 1170 and the Breakspear-blessed Anglo-Norman invasion of Henry II, or 1650 and the wedding-inspired marchings of Henry VIII? Or perhaps the better-known date of 1690 when James II and his son-in-law, Prince William of Orange, escaped the bloody Battle of the Boyne without a scratch but marked the country with blood for the 300 years that would follow? Or back to 1798 or 1916 or 1969? Or back again to early Ulster problems in the fourth and fifth century when the north's most powerful tribe, the Ulaidh, who held Ulaidh's tir (Ulster) had differences of opinion with the Dal Fiatach (the true Ulaidh)? That's when land was fought for cruelly but honestly, hungrily or greedily, without the pretence of religion or patriotism as the excuse.

Or back further still to the time when truth was hidden from mankind? According to my father, when the Almighty and All Humorous One brought the world into being, he decided to hide truth. At first he thought a good place would be at the bottom of the deepest ocean – no one would think of looking there. Then he thought that, perhaps, beyond the furthest star would be more elusive. Eventually, however, he decided to hide truth in one place where we would never think to look – within the human heart. While the world searched vainly with submarines, satellites, reason and war for ultimate power and pleasure, the All Humorous One was chuckling quietly to himself. Maybe now, as the politicians were gathered at Stormont, he was wondering, Are they searching in the right place at last?

I turned in through the gates of the Parliament Buildings at Stormont. There were more security checks to pass and passes to be secured, but they seemed to know me by now and as the gates swung open, my front-seat passenger, Vedran Smailovic, smiled through his well-known moustache. He was instantly recognized by a television cameraman who had filmed him in Sarajevo.

'Will you go back?' the cameraman asked.

'I don't go back,' answered Smailovic; 'I go forward.'

We walked with guitar and cello towards the police cordon that shielded a roomful of politicians from a worldful of press. We were joined by Roy Arbuckle and Steve Mateer on Lambeg drums, Brendan Monaghan on uilleann pipes, and Robbie Dinsmore, Loretta Phillips, David Hammond and about thirty children from Catholic and Protestant schools. Suddenly the press were everywhere. Cameramen were standing on boxes and ladders. We were afraid the children might get hurt. These were war photographers who would stop at nothing to get a shot.

We aimed our voices at the room in Castle Buildings, where the negotiators were wrestling with the truth. They were tired now, we were told; hungry too. The makeshift canteen tent was running out of food. They would be more tired and hungrier still before they would finish their work the following morning. It was like a Lough Derg pilgrimage, where people deprived of food and sleep stretch beyond the physical to find the spiritual. Some say that when truth is presented in such circumstances, it can't be rejected.

Occasional press briefings when political groupings came out to the gate suggested that the Talks were in serious trouble. There were a few key issues that seemed irresolvable. Unless one side or the other brought fresh ideas to the table, the summit would collapse.

We began to sing in the chosen key of D, to ensure that our voices would rise above the wind and the anxious hum of humanity:

> We are standing by your castle
> In the hopeful Belfast breeze
> With a new song for your table
> To try again for peace,
> Carry on, carry on,
> You can hear the people singing,
> Carry on, carry on,
> Till peace will come again …

Suddenly the door swung open and the lone figure of a woman could be seen making her way towards us. As she got closer, I could see her lips moving to the words of the chorus. It was Secretary of State Mo Mowlam. She had given much and suffered much in her efforts to bring about a new agreement. Her impromptu press conference had recently been interrupted by the Reverend Ian Paisley. He didn't approve of her leanings and dealings with 'terrorists'. According to unofficial but reliable sources, their brief conversation went something like this:

'Dr Mowlam,' began Dr Paisley in a loud voice, 'I'm a straight-talking man …'

'Dr Paisley,' finished Dr Mowlam, 'I'm a straight-talking woman. Piss off!'

She had been under a lot of stress, politically and personally. She had made no attempt to conceal the wig she wore, nor the cancer she was suffering. Now she wasn't hiding her joy either, as she sang along with tears running down her cheeks.

> Carry on, carry on,
> You can hear the people singing,
> Carry on, carry on,
> Till peace will come again.
>
> Don't betray your children's birthright,
> That's the right to stay alive,
> For there is no greater treachery
> Than to let your children die …

The politicians were now leaving the table to join the singing. It was heart-warming. Loyalist negotiator Gusty Spence arrived with PUP man Billy Hutchinson and shook my hand. 'Do you remember the man from God knows where?' he said. I saw David Ervine, too, who came into politics from paramilitarism with progressive words more powerful and penetrating than any gun. And my neighbour Mick Murphy, who had served time in prison for Republican activities. He had suffered much but now looked upbeat and positive. I recognized several 'soldiers' from both sides of the struggle. Would gentleness move, more than force could move us to gentleness?

At the 'Talks' with Gusty Spence. In the background are Steve Mateer, Vedran Smailovic and the children from Dundrum (photo *Down Democrat*)

Some would have the ways and means to turn swords into words, others were standing around as though on watch or waiting for something.

Traditionally when wars end soldiers get pensions or land-grabs, but what happens to illegal soldiers? Would they get a job? Or somehow make ends meet by continuing to do what they do best? I saw another neighbour, Jeffrey Donaldson from Kilkeel. When he was seven his cousin Samuel had been blown up by the IRA in South Armagh. When he was twenty-two his other cousin Alex had suffered the same fate in Newry. Now he was thirty-five and negotiating on behalf of the Ulster Unionist Party. Peace was far from an absence of war. No one had a monopoly on suffering, for the Troubles had left their scars on everyone. Perhaps the winners would be those who could forgive first.

And there was my old teacher too, Frank Feely. He had lost his job while striving for the SDLP. He had stopped teaching history to take part in the power-sharing Executive back in 1974. Then it had stopped. Many were singing along now. Bairbre de Brún, from Sinn Féin, who I hadn't met for twenty years, came over with Gerry Adams. He asked the children if they would like a drink. He had found cola and biscuits somewhere and soon another party was beginning to take shape. John Alderdice, leader of the Alliance Party, stood quietly to our right. He would later be elevated to the peerage and become Speaker in the new Northern Ireland Assembly.

David Trimble was under more pressure than most. His party colleague John Taylor, whose jaw had been shattered by Official IRA bullets in an assassination attempt in 1972, had declared that he wouldn't touch the current deal with a 'forty-foot pole'. Trimble stood behind us, trying to read the song title on Vedran's music stand. That wasn't easy either. It was written in Serbo-Croat.

Celebrating hope in the great hall of Stormont after performances from (standing) Jane Morrice, Deputy Speaker, with a poem; Bairbre de Brún, Minister for Health; Bríd Rodgers, Minister for Agriculture and Fisheries; and Progressive Unionist Party leader David Ervine; all with songs. (sitting) Tommy and special guest Mary Black

> All the lonely years of sorrow,
> Let the tears be not in vain,
> We can build a new tomorrow
> And everyone will gain …

Jane Morrice, Anne Carr and Monica McWilliams from the Women's Coalition were singing loudest of all. I had known Monica for many years. We were all neighbours' children after all, like everyone else in a small place such as Northern Ireland.

> In the Bogside and the Waterside,
> In the Shankill and the Falls,
> All around the hills of Ulster
> You can hear them sing this song.
> Carry on, carry on,
> You can hear the people singing,
> Carry on, carry on,
> Till peace will come again …

John Hume was wandering about alone. 'What's the chances?' I asked.

He looked worried. 'Fifty-fifty,' he replied. 'It's all up to Trimble. We've still a long way to go.'

Some months later both men would receive the Nobel Peace Prize, fifty-fifty. But now they would have to go back in there. President Clinton was on the phone.

Blair had his sleeves rolled up on the third floor and had been living on Mars Bars and coffee for the past three days. Taoiseach Bertie Ahern had just returned from his mother's funeral with renewed vigour.

In-between a reporter/cameraman with an English accent asked me whether I was a Roman Catholic singer or an Ulster Protestant singer. 'Both and neither,' I said. His free eye blinked. I had long concluded that I would never sing a song to a Catholic audience that I wouldn't sing to a Protestant one.

'What church do you go to on a Sunday then?' he asked, tightening the focus on his camera.

'Sometimes none and sometimes all,' I answered truthfully. I regularly attended Methodist, Anglican and Presbyterian Sunday services as well as the Catholic one and felt equally welcome in them all.

'What's your favourite one?' he asked, changing weight from right foot to left.

'The present one,' I said, pointing at the sky, admiring this dome with no walls, only horizons. We'd no need to travel there for we were already here, gazing through the clouds for some shape of Truth.

He took a shot of a passing crow for a possible cutaway in the unlikely event of the piece being aired. 'You're a bit complicated,' he said, 'for the six o'clock news. Give us that song again.'

He was right. I went back to the singing.

> Carry on, carry on,
> You can hear the people singing
> Carry on, carry on, till peace will come again

Slowly the politicians began to leave the midday party and head towards the dark rooms of Castle Buildings once again. Perhaps they were stronger. We did not know. The children reluctantly headed for home. Perhaps we hadn't much to give, but we felt we had given what we had – a small voice of encouragement, a cry for the future, and a song for the six o'clock news.

Later in the new Assembly, Deputy First Minister Séamus Mallon would declare that the sound of the children singing was a defining moment for those around the table. 'We knew we must leave no stone unturned to find a way forward,' he said. 'We had no right to hold back the future from those young voices.'

The *Guardian* quoted 'an acerbic American scribe, who noted, "In Dayton, the Serbs, Croats and Muslims made peace in Bosnia because the threat of American B-52 bombers loomed over their heads. In Belfast they've got to get agreement because they don't want to look like they've let these little kiddies down."'

At the end of a long, dark, Good Friday night a new dawn would emerge. No amount of darkness can dim a single candle. It would herald the birth of a child called Peace. That little creature, we knew, would slip and stumble many times before it would learn to walk, but somehow we all believed that there would come a day when the child would dance.

Index

Pages where photos appear are indicated in italics.

Fegan family, 30
Felix, Judy, 78
Fermanagh Community
  Band, 246
Fianna Éireann, 68–70
Fidel Michel, 127
Fides, Mother, 33, 36
Fifteenth of August, 72–5
Filí, Na, 126
Finnegan, Big Patsy, 78
Finnegan family, 30
Fisher Family, The, 137
Fitt, Gerry, 86, 87, 156, 160
Fitzpatrick, Big Barney, 73
Fitzpatrick, Gene, 67
Fitzpatrick, Jim, 191
Fitzsimmons, Lily, 246
Flagell, Claude, 141
Flanagan, Mike, 118, *119*
Flanagan, Terry, *235*
Flanagan, Wee Tarry, 78
Flanagan Brothers, The, 118,
  119, 172, 181
Flatley, Michael, 181, 196
Folk from the Mournes
  (album), 82
franchise, 71–2, 209–10
Freiri, Paulo, 94
Friel, Brian, 214–15
Friers, Rowell, 160
Fuller, Bill, 98, 99, 108–9
Furey Brothers, 78, 126, 137

Gadaka, Archbishop Gabrial
  Gonsum, 35
Gael Linn, 49
Gaelic Athletic Association
  (GAA), 7, 41–2, 158; All-
  Ireland final, 57–8; Down
  camogie, 100
Gaelic League, 40
Gallowglass Céilí Band, 62–3
Gamble, Pearl, 67
Gandhi, Mahatma, 175
Garda Síochána, 96, 186

Garland, Roy, *239*, 243
Garland, Seán, 80
Gaughan, Dick, 129, 137
gerrymandering, 71
ghosts, 13–14, 64–6, 112
Gilmore, Christy, 74
Glen Folk Four, 188
Glencree Reconciliation
  Centre, 106–7
Glenny, Jem, 36
Goering, Hermann, 202
Golden, Donny, 196
Good Friday Agreement, 161,
  252–7
Gorman's, 21, 57
Goss, Kieran, 186, 204
Goulding, Cathal, 80
Graham, Billy, 192
Graham, Bobby, 21
Graham, Ginger, 83
Granada, 182–3
Grant, Jack, 57
Grant, John, 59
Grant, Paul, 196
Green Fields of America,
  The, 181, 196
Gribben, Baldy, 74
Gribben, Paddy, 30
Gribbin, Barney, *150*
Griffin, Shaun, 223, 227
Griffith, Colleen, 95
Griffith, Tom, 108
Groome, Tommy, 94–5
Guthrie, Arlo, 198
Guthrie, Woody, 62, 197, 199
Gutkin, Lisa, 200–1, 238, 246

Hale's pub, Newry, 42, 56
Hall, Barbara, 246
Hall, Maeve, 244
Hall, Toby, 245
Hammond, Catherine, 235
Hammond, David, 204, 253
Hand, Rowan, 127
Hanna, Vincent, 188

Hanvey, Bobbie, 165–6, 168,
  169, 190
Hanvey, Hilda, 165–6
Harbison, Janet, 245
Harden, Geoff, 186, 204
Harp and Bard, Boston,
  112–18
Harris, Rande, 240
Harte, Nick, 176
Hawkins, Maurice, 172
Healy, Shay, 112
Heaney, Patrick, 236
Heaney, Seamus, 160, 234–6,
  235, 243
Hein, Piet, 175
Henry II, King, 91, 253
Henry VIII, King, 91, 253
Heritage, 186
Hermitage, Newry, 161
Hewitt, John, 230–1
Hiroshima, 200
Hitchcock, Alfred, 48
Hobson, Bulmer, 68
Hollywood, Sean, 86, 103, 151
Howard, Crawford, 186, 204,
  246
Hugo, Chris, 240
Hume, John, 4, 86, 87, 184,
  192, *239*, 256
hunger strikes, 174–6, 233
Hutchinson, Billy, 254

Illimani, Inti, 129, 182, 216
Imlach, Hamish, 112–13, 115,
  124, 137
Initiative, 92, 234
internment, 86, 100–1
Irish Republican Army (IRA),
  35, 53–4, 67–70, 72, 96,
  98, 102, 108, 116–18, 192–3,
  232, 233, 234; ceasefire,
  252; hunger strikes, 174–6;
  and Sands, 104–6: see also
  Official IRA; Provisional
  IRA